A BROKEN LINE
DENIS DEVLIN AND IRISH POETIC MODERNISM

Alex Davis lectures in English at University College, Cork. He is the author of numerous articles on modern Irish and British poetry, and is co-editor of two collections of essays, *Modernism and Ireland: The Poetry of the 1930s* (Cork University Press, 1995) and *Locations of Literary Modernism: Region and Nation in British and American Modernist Poetry* (Cambridge University Press, 2000). He is currently editing Devlin's uncollected and unpublished poems for Dedalus Press.

A BROKEN LINE

DENIS DEVLIN AND
IRISH POETIC MODERNISM

Alex Davis

University College Dublin Press
Preas Cholóiste Ollscoile Bhaile Átha Cliath

First published 2000 by University College Dublin Press,
Newman House, 86 St Stephen's Green, Dublin 2, Ireland

Cataloguing in Publication data available from the British Library

Typeset in Ireland in 10/12 Sabon and Palatino
by Elaine Shiels, Bantry, Co. Cork
Index by John Loftus
Printed in Ireland by Colour Books, Dublin

For Lee

CONTENTS

ABBREVIATIONS

The following abbreviations for Devlin's works have been adopted, and follow quotations in the text:

CP   *Collected Poems of Denis Devlin*, ed. J. C. C. Mays (Dublin: Dedalus, 1989)

CP (Coffey)   *Collected Poems*, ed. Brian Coffey (Dublin: Dolmen, 1964)

HF   *The Heavenly Foreigner*, ed. Brian Coffey (Dublin: Dolmen, 1967)

TE   *Translations Into English, from French, German and Italian Poetry*, ed. Roger Little (Dublin: Dedalus, 1991)

PREFACE

Among his contemporaries, Devlin was generally fortunate in his critics
and editors. How many other poets of his day could have claimed the
approbation of readers as different as, on the one hand, Samuel Beckett
and Brian Coffey and, on the other, Allen Tate and Robert Penn Warren?
More recently, Devlin has found admirers in Roger Little, J. C. C. Mays,
John Montague, Michael Smith, Stan Smith, and Robert Welch, to name
a few. However, while the critical literature on Devlin is in the main
impressive, it is scanty. One reason for this, I suspect, is that a proper
understanding of Devlin's poetry requires reading his work in the context
of European and Anglo-American modernism, and not solely within the
parameters of Irish poetry after Yeats. In contrast to his two most notable
contemporaries, Austin Clarke and Patrick Kavanagh, Devlin was not
unduly anxious about Yeats's influence, although he had a qualified
admiration for the older poet's work. Rather, Devlin's poetry takes its
cue more from the verbal pyrotechnics of Hart Crane and the Surrealist
eroticism of Paul Éluard, to take just two of its intertexts, than the poetry
of the Irish literary revival.

This is not to say that Devlin's poetry has no relation to Irish poetry of
this century. Our comprehension of the literary revival, I argue, is greatly
enlarged by recognising it as a movement within European modernism.
From this perspective, the poetry of the 'Thirties generation', which would
include that of Thomas MacGreevy, Coffey, Beckett and Sheila Wingfield,
as well as Devlin, can be read as a reactive, second-generation mod-
ernism. Subsequent to the 1930s poets, there is a rich vein of modernist
and postmodernist poetry in Ireland, a lode which includes Eugene
Watters's *The Week-End of Dermot and Grace*; Thomas Kinsella's poetry
from *Nightwalker* and *Notes from the Land of the Dead* through his
Peppercanister series; Hugh Maxton's *The Puzzle-Tree Ascendant* and
other works; the preponderance of the poetry published by Michael
Smith's New Writers' Press, that of Trevor Joyce, Geoffrey Squires, and

Augustus Young; and the writing of a number of younger poets, including Randolph Healy, David Lloyd, Billy Mills, Maurice Scully and Catherine Walsh, whose formally innovative work bears points of comparison with that of North American Language poetry. In chapter 5 and the coda to this study I have concentrated on a handful of poets for whom the procedures of poetic modernism have been enabling. To those I discuss could be added several others, most notably Medbh McGuckian and Paul Muldoon, whose linguistically innovative work is not wholly unrelated to the story this book tells. That said, there is, it seems to me, some sense of continuity – not a continuum, but a 'broken line' – between Devlin and the poets I have chosen to discuss in the latter part of this book, a connection which does not exist between Devlin and other Irish postmodernist poets. It is not the case that those poets I label neo-modernists and neo-avant-gardists take their formal bearings from Devlin; but that, like Devlin before them, they self-consciously position their work within the matrix of modernism.

My aim in what follows has been both to provide an introduction to the poetry of Denis Devlin and to read his work in the literary historical context of Irish poetic modernism from the literary revival to the present day. To that end, this book sandwiches its reading of Devlin between a modest reappraisal of the literary revival and, more ambitiously, an account of modernist and postmodernist poetry produced after Devlin's death in 1959. My intention is not to argue for the existence of an experimental counter-tradition pitted against a 'mainstream' poetry given over to ruralist-cum-nationalist preoccupations and stilted poetic forms. Such polemics have been made by others, most memorably by Beckett in the 1930s and Michael Smith in the 1970s. The narrative told in the following pages is doubtless less enjoyable than the polemics, but it may be of more help in contextualising Devlin's work for the reader.

With a few exceptions, the poems by Devlin discussed in the following pages are all included in *Collected Poems of Denis Devlin*, ed. J. C. C. Mays (Dublin: Dedalus/Winston-Salem, NC: Wake Forest UP, 1989). A number of other poems were published posthumously in *Selected Poems*, eds Allen Tate and Robert Penn Warren (New York: Holt, Rinehart & Winston, 1963) and *Collected Poems*, ed. Brian Coffey (Dublin: Dolmen, 1964), both of which are long out of print, and in various journals. I have reserved extended discussion of this material, and other unpublished poems, for the introduction to my edition of Devlin's uncollected and unpublished poetry, in the ongoing Dedalus complete poems.

For assistance of various kinds in the writing of this book I would like to acknowledge Graham Allen, Ron Callan, Mark Chu, John Coffey, Dick Collins, Patricia Coughlan, Mary FitzGerald, Anne Fogarty, John

Goodby, Colbert Kearney, Michael Kennedy, Carmel McCallum-Barry, Mari McKay, J. C. C. Mays, and Susan Schreibman. I am grateful to the staff at the National Library of Ireland, Dublin, and the Manuscripts Room of Trinity College, Dublin, for facilitating access to Devlin's mansucript materials; and to Rebecca Johnson Melvin, at the Special Collections, University of Delaware Library, for invaluable help with Brian Coffey's papers and for providing the frontispiece photograph of Devlin. Many of the poets discussed towards the end of this book courteously responded to numerous enquiries: my thanks in this regard to Randolph Healy, Trevor Joyce, Billy Mills, John Montague, Maurice Scully, Michael Smith, Geoffrey Squires and Catherine Walsh. At University College Dublin Press, Barbara Mennell has been a model editor; my thanks to her, and to the two anonymous readers for the press for their comments on an earlier version of this book. Stephen Devlin very kindly gave permission to quote from unpublished materials by his father. The publication of this book was made possible, in part, by grants from The National University of Ireland and the Faculty of Arts, University College, Cork.

Donal and Vivienne provided necessary distractions from writing this book, which is for Lee Jenkins.

Portions of this book have appeared, often in very different forms, in *Angel Exhaust, Angelaki, Critical Survey, The Colby Quarterly, Éire-Ireland, The Irish Review, Symbiosis,* and *For the Birds: Proceedings of the First Conference on New and Experimental Irish Poetry,* ed. Harry Gilonis (Sutton: Mainstream Poetry/Dublin: hardPressed Poetry, 1998). I am grateful to the editors of these publications for permission to reprint material.

Alex Davis
Cork
19 October 1999

Denis Devlin (Brian Coffey Papers, University of Delaware Library, Newark, Del.)

1

'A BROKEN LINE': IRISH
POETIC MODERNISMS

YEATS, THE LITERARY REVIVAL
AND EARLY MODERNISM

Irish poetic modernism dates from the literary revival of the 1880s and
1890s, and continues, albeit as 'a broken line',[1] with a fairly closely
affiliated group of poets, Thomas MacGreevy, Brian Coffey, Samuel
Beckett and Denis Devlin, and more isolated figures such as Sheila
Wingfield and, at least in some of her work, Mary Devenport O'Neill.
With the exception of the older figure of O'Neill, these poets published
their first collections (in MacGreevy's case, his only collection) in the
1930s. Despite the obvious differences between the work of the younger
poets and that of the literary revival their work does not register a rupture
with high modernism comparable to that announced by the continental
avant-garde, as in Dada's and Surrealism's explosive reconfigurations of
the category of the aesthetic. It is reductive to see Irish modernist poets of
the 1930s as simply rejecting Yeats as an example, in favour of Joyce and
avant-garde European modernism, even when their own critical writings
on occasion encourage such a view. Of MacGreevy, Coffey, Beckett and
Devlin, Robert F. Garratt claims that 'they regarded both Yeats and
revivalism as false trails', adopting 'modernist techniques, which they
derived from *Ulysses*'.[2] While these statements are not untrue, their over-
simplified nature renders them misleading. The younger poets' break
with revivalism stems from the different inflections of their modernist
poetics from the modernism of Yeats. To state that these writers derived
their 'techniques' from *Ulysses* is implicitly to claim a monologic and
monolithic (in this case, a Joycean) understanding of modernism, to
which Yeats, as a 'last romantic', somehow stands opposed.

Garratt constructs the kind of 'straw-man modernism' critics such as
Marjorie Perloff and Peter Nicholls have done much to discredit.[3] His

crude binarism, revivalism/modernism, would be better replaced by an
approach which takes account of the plural nature of modernism –
indeed, the kaleidoscopic array of modernisms – in which movements and
writers often stand in antagonistic relations to one another. The
questioning of New Criticism's narrow conception of the modernist text
as a 'well-wrought urn' or manifestation of 'spatial form', and the recog-
nition that modernism embraces a wide, and often conflicting, diversity of
practitioners, theorists and propagandists, allows us, in turn, to reappraise
the literature produced in Ireland from the 1880s to the 1930s, and beyond.[4]

   John Wilson Foster's important 1981 essay, 'Irish Modernism',
contributed to this process by drawing attention to the close connections
between the Irish literary revival and certain strains or tendencies within
early modernism, the shared preoccupation with 'mysticism, symbolism,
millenarianism and anti-modernization'. Foster's conception of modernism,
however, is still somewhat narrowly conceived. In particular, his belief
that 'it would be difficult to regard as Modernist' the 'obstinate nativism'
of the literary revival can be called into question by observing the
centrality of nationalism to much modernism prior to the First World
War.[5] As Terry Eagleton argues, the literary revival's modernism is
inextricably entwined with its nationalism:

> modernism, like nationalism, is out to translate [its] abstract forms [its
> deep structures and universal archetypes] into the aesthetic experience of
> difference, uniqueness, of the ineffably particular and stubbornly specific,
> of all that escapes the levelling commonness of modernity. Like nationalism,
> then, it is dependent on that modernity for its universal forms, while resisting
> them in its idiosyncratic content. . . . Both pit image and intuition against
> what they see as the reified rationality of the modern world, a rationality
> which for nationalism reaches its grim apotheosis in the bureaucracy of the
> colonial state.[6]

The reactionary cast to the revival's modernism, according to Eagleton,
offered a number of Anglo-Irish writers 'an ersatz kind of identity and
belonging, a community of sorts which was painfully lacking in historical
fact'.[7] In other words, the Celticism and romantic nationalism of the
literary revival can be seen as related to, and as preceding that of, other
modernist appeals to 'tradition' in the face of the 'levelling commonness',
the 'reified rationality', of modernity. In the later terminology of T. S.
Eliot, the individual talents of the revival appeal to the 'monuments' of an
Irish cultural tradition which their texts consequently recover for a
culturally denuded present.[8] In Terence Brown's words: 'Literary production
conducted in the context of nationalist feeling accordingly revives and
translates texts from the dim past not for antiquarian reasons but to
allow them to exist again in the timeless spirituality of the nation's

continuous being'; thus, Brown adds, the centrality of translation, in both a broad and narrow sense, to the revival and other movements in European modernism.[9] Such a recuperative backward look allows the artist to perceive in his or her work a social and political relevance to what might otherwise seem a disinterested concern with the nation's cultural past. George Russell ('AE') gradually came to see, over the early to mid-1890s, correlations between his mysticism and aspects of Celticism. From around 1895 he deployed the latter as a central device in his poetry's spiritualism, the values of which henceforth become associated with an Ireland free from the materialist encroachments of modernity. In 'A Call of the Sidhe', for instance, 'earth's faery children' summon the reader to 'the Land of Youth':

> the trees grown heavy there
> Drop on the purple wave the starry fruit they bear.
> Drink: the immortal waters quench the spirit's longing.[10]

Russell views the relationship between the Celtic past and the present moment in a synchronic fashion, as will Eliot in his depiction of the modern poem's place within the literary tradition. To this extent, his poetry's overtly mystical preoccupations have a nationalist subtext: the Sidhe signify the colonised's spiritual superiority over the colonisers, functioning as a yardstick by means of which late Victorian Britain can be measured and found wanting. In Yeats's case, as W. J. McCormack argues, Celticism is equally 'a strategic rather than an intrinsic aspect of his [early] aesthetic project': 'Metropolitan cultural values, and exotic themes culled from Indian literatures, theosophy, and Buddhism, were gradually discounted in favour of the west of Ireland, or village Ireland, or vestigial Ireland.'[11] Allied to the heady formal innovativeness of *fin de siècle* poetry, such Celticism reaches an apotheosis of sorts in the *symboliste* experiments of *The Wind Among the Reeds*, the opening poem of which, 'The Hosting of the Sidhe', bears comparison with Russell's 'A Call of the Sidhe'. Yeats's 1899 collection is an important document in the history of the literary revival because it foregrounds the extent to which the revival, in line with high modernism in general, does not radically rethink the autonomous artwork of late nineteenth-century aestheticism: a residue of the notion of *l'art pour l'art* percolates into the revival's literary practice, coming into tension with its nationalist concerns.

It is important to realise the considerable overlap between the poetry of the revival and English aestheticism and Decadence. Yeats stands at the heart of both movements, of course, and one of his co-founders of the London-Based Rhymers' Club was another Irishman, T. W. Rolleston (the third co-founder, Ernest Rhys, was also a Celt of sorts, being a

Londoner of Welsh extraction). Linda Dowling has observed the extent to which 'Victorian literary Decadence presented itself to Yeats as a useful weapon in the struggle to establish the Irish movement, providing him as it did with a dramatic principle of contrast between English and Irish writing, a contrast that worked for once in Ireland's favor'.[12] It is a contrast Yeats explicitly draws in his reflections on the poetry of fellow Rhymer and Irishman, John Todhunter, in 'The Rhymers' Club', published in the Boston *Pilot* in 1892. Yeats says of Todhunter's Celticism that it is a 'road' that 'leads where there is no lack of subjects, for the literature of Ireland is still young, and on all sides of this road is Celtic tradition and Celtic passion crying for singers to give them voice. England is old and her poets must scrape up the crumbs of an almost finished banquet, but Ireland has still full tables.'[13] Making reference to Yeats's 1901 essay, 'What is Popular Poetry?', Dowling further suggests that Decadent and Symbolist literature shared, in Yeats's mind, the esoteric knowledge embodied in the folklore of the Irish peasantry: 'Yeats intuitively sensed that in the 1890s once again the art of the coteries and the art of the people were drawing together, because he could trace a deep likeness in the imaginative world of the Symbolists and Decadents on one hand and the unlettered Irish country-people on the other.'[14] Though the Rhymers' club had dispersed and English Decadence effectively come to an end by the time of 'What is Popular Poetry?', the specious reasoning of Yeats's essay reveals an anxiety that the aestheticism of his 1890s poetry and prose had little bearing on a world outside the upstairs' room at the Cheshire Cheese, where the Rhymers had convened. It is an anxiety Yeats would, in his 1922 autobiography, *The Trembling of the Veil*, and related poems, project onto those of his contemporaries, several associated with the Rhymers' Club, whom he memorably dubbed 'The Tragic Generation'. It has become commonplace to debunk Yeats's treatment of his past as characteristic shapechanging, yet his 'myth', as Ian Fletcher points out, actually corresponds in its main outlines to the facts as we know them.[15] Moreover, the significance of Yeats's account lies more in its consideration of aestheticism than its historical veracity.

The Yeatsian version of his generation's fate centres on a number of writers, including Ernest Dowson, Arthur Symons and Oscar Wilde, whose lives were wrecked through dissipation, mental breakdown or Victorian homophobia. One of the principal characters in Yeats's narrative of his early manhood and beginnings as a writer is Lionel Johnson, whose turn to the cause of Irish nationalism is valuably read alongside Yeats's more full-blooded commitment. Yeats's account of Johnson is best remembered for its moving account of the young English poet's collapse into ruinous alcoholism, which Yeats allows Johnson himself to link to Wilde's liking for rough trade. Of the possible destitution to which his habit might lead, Yeats says that Johnson 'seemed to contemplate a vision that gave him pleasure, and now that I look back, I remember that he once said to me that Wilde's pleasure and excitement were perhaps increased by the degradation of that group of beggars and blackmailers where he sought his pathics, and I remember, too, his smile at my surprise, as though he spoke of psychological depths I could never enter'.[16] The parallel between Johnson's dipsomania and Wilde's homosexuality centres on their shared pursuit, as Yeats here depicts it, of self-degradation through inebriation or carnality. (One should note at this juncture that Yeats, for all his lack of political correctness by our own *fin-de-siècle*'s standards, was not homophobic – as his depiction of Wilde's treatment by late Victorian society in the *Autobiographies* clearly illustrates.) Johnson and Wilde, in Yeats's account, seek out their opposite, the 'anti-self' of their being, in their self-destructive behaviour. Johnson, a convert to Roman Catholicism, a sexually abstemious man (in part owing, one presumes, to the suppression of his own homosexual inclinations), deeply read in theology as much as the classics, finds himself in Yeats's speculations on his fascination for 'the Vision of Evil' drawn to the dark contrary of this side of his personality, as was Wilde in taking lovers lacking his wit and panache and alien to his social position.

Yet Johnson was drawn not only to a Vision of Evil in the shape of the whiskey decanter, but to Irish nationalism, at least in its Celticist form, and the effects of the latter could be as disastrous for his poetry as drink was to his person. Seamus Deane rightly sees 'The Celtic Twilight [as] a regional variation on aestheticism and impressionism', and neatly remarks how, for the 'honorary Irishman' Johnson, 'Whistler's London was not sufficiently twilit; Yeats's Ireland had more of the tremulous glimmer so beloved of the decadent school'.[17] The ill-starred conjunction of aestheticism and Celticism in Johnson is most evident in the execrable title poem to *Ireland, with Other Poems* (1897); while the placing in *Poems* (1895) of a celebration of the idyllic charms of rural England immediately after an elegy for Parnell is indicative of the shallowness of the poet's identification with Ireland.[18] In this respect, Johnson's poetry is representative of the political paucity of much aestheticist poetry (a vacuity which the counter-Decadent W. E. Henley's realist *In Hospital* does little to fill), with, it needs be said, the significant exception of certain poets' engagement with the sexual politics of the period (as in the feminism of Constance Naden's and 'Michael Field's poetry and A. E. Housman's subtle exploration of homosexual desire in *A Shropshire Lad*).[19] Johnson's Celticism has little foundation in Ireland (or the Wales he also rhapsodises): it signifies instead an elemental, ancient authority and, as

Dowling comments, is 'identified with the powers of aesthetic and spiritual order'.[20] Johnson's strength as a poet is apparent in those poems in which this authority seems on the point of collapse, where his poetry's usually muted Decadence comes into conflict with its reiterated appeal to the supports of theology and the literary tradition. These texts reveal an aestheticist awareness of their own social purposelessness, a knowledge that in the hands of Wilde becomes the occasion for a jubilant assertion of art's uselessness. In Johnson's 'Mystic and Cavalier', for example, the persona's exhortation, 'Go from me: I am one of those, who fall',[21] is more than just an admission of his unworthiness as a man. It illustrates the aesthete's alienation from the bourgeois society embodied in the poem's addressee: 'Yours are the victories of light: your feet / Rest from good toil, where rest is brave and sweet.' The speaker's uncertain condition, unable to inhabit the clarity of the 'common light' inhabited by his auditor, is imaged as a murky 'crystal sphere', one in which his future cannot be discerned: 'Canst read a fate there, prosperous and clear? / Only the mists, only the weeping clouds'. As a metaphor for the plight of aestheticist poetry, this 'crystal ball' will find a distant echo in Ezra Pound's final *Cantos*, as in Canto CXVI's despairing cry: 'I have brought the great ball of crystal; / who can lift it?'[22] Pound's Preface to Johnson's 1915 *Poetical Works* had identified in certain poems proto-Imagist elements and a classical 'hardness'.[23] The deeper connection between Johnson's aestheticism and Pound's high modernism is their shared functionlessness, to which the fragmentary close to *The Cantos* pays eloquent witness.

Wilde's closing aphorism to the Preface to *The Picture of Dorian Gray*, '*All art is quite useless*',[24] is a possibility that preoccupies Yeats from his earliest poetry, written prior to his contact with English aestheticism, and can be sensed in the poem Yeats chose to open *Crossways*, his grouping of early poems in his 1895 *Poems*: 'The Song of the Happy Shepherd'. *Crossways* and the song are preceded by a quotation, or rather a *mis*quotation, from Blake's *The Four Zoas*: 'The stars are threshed, and the souls are threshed from their husks.' Blake's words from 'Night the Ninth' of his epic poem are rendered in Yeats's and Edwin John Ellis's 1893 edition of *The Works of William Blake* thus: 'And all the Nations were threshed out, and the stars threshed from their husks.' Yeats's alteration of Blake's line denudes it of its social and political dimension, and emphasises, by way of contrast, the individual 'soul' at the expense of collectivity. In miniature, the discrepancy between Blake's original line and Yeats's version encapsulates Yeats's divergence from the tradition of British romanticism. The shepherd's isolated predicament certainly looks back to the romantic solitary: there is more than an echo of Blake in the persona inveighing against the soullessness of empiricism, the 'Grey Truth' that has supplanted poetic truth. However, romanticism's intense concentration on solitariness does not preclude a concomitant concern with the interaction between the poet and the public sphere. The poet is a privileged figure, yet his or her aspiration is to be representative; he or she aims, to paraphrase Wordsworth's Preface to *Lyrical Ballads*, to communicate to others in a recognisable because shared language of experience. For all the hermeticism of the symbolism in *The Four Zoas*, Blake's prophetic book, and indeed his work as a whole, works towards a regeneration of intersubjective experience – towards the 'state', in both an individual and political sense, envisaged in the magnificent final plates of *Jerusalem*: 'And from the thirty-two nations of the earth among the living creatures: / All human forms identified, even tree, metal, earth & stone.'[25] In contrast, the theme developed in Yeats's 'The Song of the Happy Shepherd' is the absence of intersubjectivity. An earlier title for the poem was 'Song of the Last Arcadian', which is, perhaps, more in keeping with the poem's intense concentration on the isolation and belatedness of the persona than the *Crossways* title. He is the *last* Arcadian, deprived of a community which has vanished into an indefinite past: 'The woods of Arcady are dead, / And over is their antique joy'.[26] The poem's romantic emphasis on the individual's specificity – the claim that 'there is no truth / Saving in thine own heart' – strikes an aestheticist note to the extent that the speaker's isolation is a consequence of his awareness of the problematic relationship between poet (or singer) and the public sphere. The Arcadian's advice to the reader is premised on the belief that the cultural and the social no longer possess any meaningful contact with one another:

> Go gather by the humming sea
> Some twisted, echo-harbouring shell,
> And to its lips thy story tell,
> And they thy comforters will be,
> Rewording in melodious guile
> Thy fretful words a little while,
> Till they shall singing fade in ruth
> And die a pearly brotherhood;
> For words alone are certain good:
> Sing, then, for this is also sooth.

The penultimate line of this passage marks a retreat into poetic language, a withdrawal which derives from the speaker's despair over the role of poetry after Arcady has gone. It is a linguistic turn that marks a break with romanticism's moving aspirations for poetry to have a social purpose. To put this another way, for all Yeats's explicit admiration for Shelley,

'The Song of the Happy Shepherd' articulates an antithetical claim to that of *A Defense of Poetry*: Yeats's last Arcadian does not believe that the poet acts as an 'unacknowledged legislator' for his or her society – the poet is simply unacknowledged.

This dimension to Yeats's early lyric looks foward to his more developed symbolism in *The Rose* and *The Wind Among the Reeds*. Prior to the poetry he wrote under the partial influence of French Symbolism (through the mediation of Arthur Symons), Yeats's work evinces the Symbolist abstention from the social as developed from Baudelaire to Mallarmé and Verlaine.[27] Baudelaire's own version of Symbolism, in which the material, historically embedded word grants an apprehension of a spiritual realm, is deeply imbued with a rejection of any correspondence of the poetic and the political. As Peter Nicholls argues, the Symbolists' rejection of 'nature' marks more than just a break with 'a poetic taste for trees and rivers': 'more fundamentally, they were denying the connection between poetic vision and social transformation which had underpinned the political optimism of an earlier Romanticism.'[28] The Baudelairean correspondence links the poetic symbol to a realm that transcends society's corruptions and venality, any hope in political change having ended at the Parisian barricades of 1848. In Raymond Williams's words, 'this form of poetic revelation involved a fusion of present synaesthetic experience with the recovery of a nameable, tangible past which was yet "beyond" or "outside" time'.[29] For the young Yeats, that 'nameable' past 'outside' temporality is called Arcady, and his last Arcadian confronts a dismal modernity which is backdated, as it were, to a point at which it embraces historical time. The only solace lies in words divorced from communicative action with other inhabitants of this landscape: in symbols alone are certain good.

Yeats, of course, is not to be equated with the happy shepherd. The symbolism he more self-consciously developed during the course of the 1890s is, in Edward Larrissy's felicitous phrase, a '*fin-de-siècle* Fenianism' to the extent that it constitutes an ambivalent engagement with various currents within Irish nationalism.[30] But from its inception Yeats's poetic is conscious that an autotelic poetry courts accusations of historical irrelevance. Decades later, the posturingly arrogant claims made on behalf of the imagination in the third part of 'The Tower' –

> Death and life were not
> Till man made up the whole,
> Made lock, stock and barrel
> Out of his bitter soul – [31]

will constitute an attempt to turn the tables on such accusations; but as such they are simply the flip side of Yeats's self-doubts, those expressed in the poet's moving recognition of the gulf that separates his literary activity from the lives of the combatants in 'The Road at my Door', one of the 'Meditations in Time of Civil War': trying to 'silence the envy in my thought', the poet 'turn[s] towards my chamber, caught / In the cold snows of a dream'.[32] Such doubts gnaw at the vitals of Yeats's work, long outlasting his Decadent and *symboliste* phase, and inform the self-interrogative mood of his late poem 'Man and the Echo'. In the course of that poem, Yeats famously asks, 'Did that play of mine send out / Certain men the English shot?',[33] and it is hard to determine whether an answer in the negative would not disturb the speaker more than a positive reply. The play in question, the nationalist allegory *Cathleen ni Houlihan* (as much Lady Gregory's play as Yeats's, it needs be said), exemplifies an important element of the revival's modernism, that which Eagleton terms its *'non-realist* representation, art faithful to an action which is itself realistically improbable, or one which represents it in a non-realist way'.[34] *Cathleen ni Houlihan* undermines realist theatrical conventions, not, as in Yeats's later Noh-inspired drama, by rejecting them, but by means of the introduction of the symbolic figure of Cathleen into a representational drama set in Mayo, 1798, on the eve of rebellion. 'Man and the Echo' questions the political efficacy of the play's modernist form and, by extension, the entire literary revival's contribution to the nationalist cause in the run-up to the 1916 rising and the War of Independence.

Yeats's late poem thus casts a quizzical eye on a view of the revival that Yeats himself had helped to foster. With the fall of Parnell in 1891, it is often assumed, the supposed change thereafter from hopes of constitutional reform to a revolutionary mindset went hand in glove with the emergence of a cultural renaissance which informed and channelled the Irish populace's increasingly militant attitude towards Westminster. As one of the chief architects of this retrospective view of the interface between Irish nationalism and Irish literature, Yeats argued, in his 1923 lecture to the Royal Academy of Sweden, 'The Irish Dramatic Movement', that 'The modern literature of Ireland, and indeed all that stir of thought which prepared for the Anglo-Irish War, began when Parnell fell from power in 1891. A disillusioned and embittered Ireland turned from parliamentary politics; an event was conceived [i.e. the Easter Rising]; and the race began, as I think, to be troubled by that event's long gestation.'[35] Yeats's claim has been questioned by, among others, R. F. Foster, who contends that, 'Looking ahead even as far as 1910, one should still be cautious about assuming that cultural revivalism had produced an implicit revolution in politics. Not many Dubliners were reading the new literature.' In Foster's revisionist account, the 'event' of 1916 was not gestated by the cultural and literary revivals of the 1880s and 1890s, but owed more to the Volunteer movements of 1913 and perhaps more still to the First World War, and the Irish population's antipathy towards being drawn into a European war on the coat-tails of the British Empire. Yeats's ingenuousness in conflating cultural and political nationalism (or seeing in the former the powerhouse driving the latter) reveals a conscious desire on his part of being seen, in Foster's words, 'at the centre of Irish history'.[36]

Foster's remarks on the revival's place within the political climate of this period are strikingly prefigured in Austin Clarke's 1939 article on 'Verse-Speaking and Verse Drama'. His remarks on verse drama in the following passage, as the essay as a whole makes clear, can also be applied to the poetry of the revival:

> The deliberate removal of poetry from the political and moral sphere during the Parnell split undoubtedly improved our art, but it carried with it implications that poetry is not strong enough to express or analyse the passions of real life. Separated from the vital human drama of good and evil and the exciting historic complications in our life here, our verse drama had a bad start. In destroying the tradition of popular political poetry, a tradition which carried on, however inadequately, the Gaelic practice of the eighteenth century, we narrowed the function of poetry and banished the great ugly emotions which have shaped our national life.[37]

The echo in this passage of the title of Yeats's 1903 collection of essays, *Ideas of Good and Evil* (in which 'What is Popular Poetry' was collected), coincidental or not, is telling: at the time of writing these essays and his early poems and plays, Yeats and the literary revival as a whole were adrift, in Clarke's opinion, from the socio-political forces that were shaping this era. The revivalists' work stands in stark contrast in this respect to the closeness to 'national life' expressed in the ballads of the Young Irelanders of the 1840s (which Yeats distances himself from in 'What is Popular Poetry') and the previous century's Irish-language poetry, for example that of Art Mac Cumhaigh and Eoghan Rua Ó Súilleabháin.

Clarke does not see in this separation of the aesthetic sphere from the 'political and moral sphere' a modernist dimension to the revival, though elsewhere he lambastes several modernist poets – Pound chief among them – for precisely this 'removal' of art from the praxis of life. Eliot and Pound, for example, are viewed as 'Escapists' from 'contemporary life', while the language of Joyce's *Finnegans Wake* is as remote from Hiberno-English as the nineteenth-century stage-Irish diction of Samuel Lover and Charles Lever, and 'as monstrous and ugly as the later-day Abbey brogue'.[38] Yet the 'removal' of which Clarke speaks is valuably considered in the light of Peter Bürger's analysis of the origins of late nineteenth-century aestheticism and the movement's influence on high modernism. That which Clarke saw as the revival's abrogation of a concern with 'the passions of real life' can be viewed in the broader context of the 'apartness from life' which for Bürger characterises European art in bourgeois society. Art's disengagement emerges at the end of eighteenth century as it becomes autonomous as an institution, and culminates in its purposeless-ness in the aestheticism of the late nineteenth century. As an institution, art in a bourgeois social formation is separate from life praxis: even if its content is political, art is still removed from life through its status *as* an institution. With aestheticism, argues Bürger, even 'the contents . . . lose their political character, and art wants to be nothing other than art. . . . The apartness from the praxis of life that had always constituted the institutional status of art in bourgeois society now becomes the content of works . . . [owing to] the ever-increasing concentration the makers of art bring to the medium itself.'[39] Bürger's account isolates the beginnings of the intense self-reflexivity characteristic of that strain of high modernism stemming from the aestheticism of the *fin de siècle*, which, in English-language modernism, is exemplified by the poetry of Pound, Eliot and Wallace Stevens, among others.[40] It is also that of the literary revival to the extent that Yeats's 1890s combination of Celticism and Symbolism, Synge's synthetic Hiberno-English and Augusta Gregory's Kiltartanese (as spoken by the peasantry in *Cathleen ni Houlihan*) can be all viewed as high modernist attentions to the 'medium' of art rather than as imbricated in life praxis. This is not to downplay the importance of the revivalists' nationalist intentions and respective political agendas: *pace* Foster and Clarke, *Cathleen ni Houlihan*, and the cultural nationalism of the revival as a whole, may well have been formative in the politicising of some of its audience. After all, one of the casualties of the Easter Rising was Seán Connolly, an actor at the Abbey Theatre from 1913, whom Yeats memorialises in another late poem, 'Three Songs to the One Burden': 'Who was the first man shot that day? / The player Connolly'.[41] Perhaps the player's actions owed something to the Abbey's plays. My point is rather that the revival's modernism is apparent in Yeats's highly self-conscious anxiety with regard to the *relationship* between his literary output and the social and political context in which it is produced. While the cultural nationalism of the revival is informed by a desire to *re-present* Ireland to itself in literary form, the 'Ireland' constructed to this end took on its own autonomous existence. Hence the antipathy it generated in later writers, several of whom tended to conflate the revival's representation of Ireland with the more obviously ideological national self-images promoted by Irish Ireland and de Valera.[42] The older Yeats admits to the free-floating nature of the revival's Ireland in several contexts. In 'The Municipal Gallery Re-visited' the portraits among which the speaker stands, 'the images of thirty years', have precisely that property of '*non-realist* representation' Eagleton identifies in the revival's modernism. 'This is not', the persona declares, 'The dead Ireland of my youth, but an Ireland / The poets have imagined, terrible and gay'.[43] Likewise, in 'The Circus Animals' Desertion' Yeats confesses that 'Players and painted stage took all my love, / And not those things that they were emblems of'.[44] Partially unhinged from its referent, Yeats's Ireland – 'terrible and gay' – is an *emblematic* Ireland, that is, it relates to its horizon of production in the manner of an 'emblem' or moral fable. The autonomy of these images is that of the high modernist artwork, which can never attain the closeness to lived experience once enjoyed by the medieval artefact.

Paul de Man argues that as early as *The Countess Cathleen and Various Legends and Lyrics* (1892) the emblem figures in Yeats's work as the contrary to the natural image. Emblems, as opposed to images, 'have no mimetic referent whatever. . . . They are taken from the literary tradition and receive their meaning from traditional or personal, but not from natural associations'. For de Man the appearance of the emblem in Yeats signals the difference between his poetry and that of European romanticism in general (within which he overhastily places French Symbolism), which still insists on 'the ontological priority of natural things'. The 'unresolved conflict between image and emblem' de Man reads out of Yeats's career has been recast by David Lloyd in terms of Yeats's earlier cultural nationalism, and its symbolist poetic, and his later, allegorical or 'emblematic' work, the non-mimetic quality of which reflects Yeats's increasingly tangential relationship to Ireland after independence.[45] Both de Man's and Lloyd's approaches to Yeats can be seen, in the present context, as germane to the problematic interface between nationalist politics and modernism in the literary revival, and its consequences for the later poetry of Yeats. Lloyd draws attention to Yeats's complex allusion to 'the Homeric epic tradition' at the end of 'Coole and Ballylee, 1931', and to the poet's tacit admission that he, and the other revivalists, failed to create 'what poets name / The book of the people':

> Where fashion or mere fantasy decrees
> We shift about – all that great glory spent –
> Like some poor Arab tribesman with his tent . . .
>
> all is changed, that high horse riderless,
> Though mounted in that saddle Homer rode
> Where the swan drifts upon a darkening flood.[46]

Lloyd contends that the poem's emblem-making ('Another emblem there!' cries the persona on observing a 'mounting swan' by the lakeside at Coole) signifies a resistance to a mimetic poetics, which would entail an organic connection between the poet and his environment, and that this foregrounds the 'radical dislocation' of the poet, not only from the poem's Galway setting, but from independent Ireland. The signature of Yeats's poetry at this date is that, paradoxically, it is in and through his alienated condition that the poet 'finds the sources of his power' in the autonomous reaches of his poetic language.[47] To this I would add the mild caveat that the 'dislocation' Lloyd analyses in *The Winding Stair and Other Poems* can be sensed, albeit in a restrained vein, in the symbolism of Yeats's early poetry. As the example of French Symbolism suggests, Yeats's early poetic is not fully reducible to the symbolism that informs cultural nationalism, in which, Lloyd avers, there is an 'organic continuity between the symbol and what it represents'.[48] Yeats's symbolism is modernist, rather than late romantic, to the degree that it is conscious of its aestheticist 'apartness from life'. Rainer Emig has pointed out the 'suspicion' in several of Yeats's early poems, such as 'The Man who dreamed of Faeryland', that 'the escapism of a hermetic symbolism is eventually unsatisfactory', an unease Emig links to 'the closed internalising nature of modernist techniques' which produces 'texts [that] can only imagine their outside to be like their own texture'.[49] Emig's understanding of modernism, for all its sophistication, is a definition of the high modernism suffused by the aestheticism of the 1890s. His argument would find little purchase on the writings of, say, Gertrude Stein or Louis Zukofsky (neither of whom he mentions in the course of his argument). For precisely this reason, his thesis usefully brings into focus Yeats's particular form of modernism: that 'twisted, echo-harbouring shell', into which the happy shepherd urges us to pour our 'fretful words', is the same shell as that into which 'The Sad Shepherd' tells his '*heavy story*', and which 'Changed all he sang to inarticulate moan / Among her wildering whirls, forgetting him'.[50]

'THE BREAKDOWN OF THE OBJECT': IRISH MODERNIST POETRY AFTER THE REVIVAL

Yeats's Ireland becomes the target for a number of poets writing in the wake of the literary revival, many of whom were equally uncomfortable with the pastoralism of such post-revivalists as Padraic Colum and F. R. Higgins. Writers as diverse as Clarke, Patrick Kavanagh and Beckett confronted, and sought to evade, Yeats and the revival through a variety of strategies. Kavanagh's dismissal of Yeats as a Victorian, whose idealised evocations of an imaginary Ireland should be read as the target of Kavanagh's mature realism in *The Great Hunger* and elsewhere, constitutes a powerful riposte to the literary revival as a whole, at least as Kavanagh understood it. In Kavanagh's words:

Yes, Yeats, it was damn easy for you protected
By the middle classes and the Big Houses
To talk about the sixty-year old public protected
Man sheltered by the dim Victorian Muses.[51]

Clarke's lifelong attempts to be free from the shadow the older poet's work
cast over his poetic and dramatic endeavours are, arguably, more com-
plex and more interesting than Kavanagh's overt rejection of revivalism.
From his experiments with Celto-Romanesque material in *Pilgrimage* as
a possible alternative to Yeats's early Celticism, through the intense
dialogues with Yeats in *The Echo at Coole and Other Poems*, to the sexual
exuberance of his late poem, *Tiresias*, Clarke's texts inscribe themselves
within the margins of Yeats's, paradoxically remaining parasitical in their
very defence of their own autonomy.

Kavanagh and Clarke illustrate the extent to which the attempt to
overcome the revival's 'removal of poetry from the political and moral
sphere', as Clarke put it, was made not by an avant-garde, as in the
Dadaist and Surrealist assaults on institutional art in continental Europe,
but by a *mélange* of writers relatively unmoved by the technical innovations
of modernism. The dominant modes of Irish writing in the 1930s and
1940s are realist: the fiction of Seán Ó Faolain and Frank O'Connor, the
mature poetry of Clarke and Kavanagh, to which one can add the
cultural probings in *The Bell* for the real 'hidden Ireland' behind the
political rhetoric of the day.[52] Clarke, late in life, said of his generation
that 'The influence of T. S. Eliot came belatedly to us', an influence
Clarke believed had no empowering effect on those Irish writers – 'all in
revolt against the Irish Literary Revival' – enthused by Eliot's work,
among whom he numbers Lyle Donaghy, Valentin Iremonger, Donagh
MacDonagh, and Denis Devlin.[53]

Dillon Johnston sees in Clarke's disparaging response to modernism
the stultifying effects of the Censorship of Publications Act (1929), the
result of which was 'that writers suffered nearly as much from the sup-
pression of European "modernist" books and journals as from the
banning of Irish books, against which Clarke, for one, took his stand'.[54]
The implementation of censorship must be seen in the context of the
cultural exclusiveness promoted by a number of writers and journals
during the first three decades of the twentieth century: that of the 'Irish
Ireland' ideology promulgated by D. P. Moran in editorials to *The Leader*
and in the essays collected in *The Philosophy of Irish Ireland* (1905), and
the related attempt to define bona fide Irish literature in Daniel Corkery's
The Hidden Ireland (1924), and, published after the passing of the censor-
ship act, *Synge and Anglo-Irish Literature* (1931). Such ideas, in Terence
Brown's opinion, 'did nothing to encourage an openness to foreign

literary and cultural influences . . . [and] must be associated with the conservative climate of opinion in which the Censorship Bill of 1929 was enacted and put to work'. As a consequence, Brown continues, those poets, including MacGreevy, Beckett, Coffey and Devlin, drawn towards continental European and Anglo-American modernism could expect little hope of a readership within 'the very small Irish bourgeoisie that in its urban tastes and values had been overtaken by the populist rural values of the new state'.[55] Though less hampered by censorship, modernism in the visual arts initially confronted the same crushing problem of audience, and this may be one reason why, as S. B. Kennedy observes, 'Irish artists merely reacted to Modernism, they did not help to shape its development'.[56] In the field of music, the literary revival was wedded, as Harry White argues, to 'the idea of music, the "supreme theme of Art and Song" in Yeats's phrase', but the symbolic importance of music 'proved itself so expressively fertile that the inherent cultivation of an art music was silently neglected'. In the aftermath of the revival, though interest in traditional music remained strong, the discoveries of the Second Viennese School made little impact in Ireland.[57] For Irish writers attuned to modernism, Joyce's self-exile had obvious attractions: MacGreevy, Beckett, Coffey and Devlin all chose to pursue careers which took them outside Ireland, though MacGreevy would return in 1941, his poetic energies largely spent. In conversation with Michael Smith, the novelist Mervyn Wall points out the 'urban origin' of himself and his peer-group: 'I, and I suppose most of my acquaintances, only learnt about small town and rural Irish life through visits to the Abbey Theatre and subsequent reading.' Wall recalls the conservative outlook of Ireland in the 1930s, viewing censorship as 'not imposed from above, but the will of the entire people', and points out the attractiveness of Paris for writers who 'did not wish to remain in, or be influenced by the already thoroughly-ploughed four fields of Ireland'.[58]

Beckett, shuttling between Dublin, Paris and London during the early to mid-1930s, provides a contemporary response to Irish literary culture in his coruscating 'Censorship in the Saorstat', commissioned by *The Bookman* in 1935 but not published until 1983. Beckett views the Register of Prohibited Publications 'a most happy idea, constituting as it does, after the manner of Boston's Black Book, a free and permanent advertisement of those books and periodicals in which, be their strictly literary status never so humble, inheres the a priori excellence that they have annoyed the specialist in common sense'.[59] A year before, in his 1934 appraisal of 'Recent Irish Poetry', Beckett can be seen atomising the consequences for those poets who have failed to avail themselves of the register. Dividing the field into 'antiquarians and others', Beckett presents the former camp as poets satisfied with reusing revivalist themes, 'delivering with the altitudinous complacency of the Victorian Gael the Ossianic goods', among whose number Beckett places Yeats and those whom he, somewhat simplistically, identifies as his progeny (Clarke, Monk Gibbon, Higgins, James Stephens, et al.). The 'others', in Beckett's eyes, are linked through their 'awareness of the new thing that has happened . . . namely the breakdown of the object, whether current, historical, mythical or spook'. This arresting phrase is an umbrella under which huddle a rather mixed crowd, all united solely in refusing to find shelter in an outmoded revivalism. Pre-eminent in this group, concludes Beckett, are Coffey and Devlin; poets who have allowed their work to be influenced not by revivalism but by the work of 'Corbière, Rimbaud, Laforgue, the *surréalistes* and Mr Eliot, perhaps also . . . Mr Pound'. [60]

Beckett's reference to the French and American poets whose work colours the poetry he distinguishes from the antiquarianism of the revival is important in considering the precise nature of Coffey's and Devlin's, as well as Beckett's, position within literary modernism. I consider the impact of the *surréalistes* on Devlin's poetry in the next chapter; Eliot's influence on his work, we can note here, is profound and enabling. On Coffey, however, the latter proved a mixed blessing. His early poetry, as Edna Longley rightly says, reads at times as little more than 'pastiche Eliot'.[61] Pound would appear to have made far less impression on both poets. Indeed, it can be argued that Beckett's tentativeness with regard to Pound's relevance to Coffey's and Devlin's poetry stems from the fact that it is Beckett's poetry that is informed, in part, by that of the older American writer. Patricia Coughlan has observed that the modernism of Beckett's poetry does not accord with that of Eliot or Yeats. His texts are characterised by '*de*composition and radical disjunction from a totalizing aesthetic. . . . He is quite outside the kinship of Eliot and Yeats in shoring fragments against their ruins or seeking Unity of Being.'[62] Pound's aesthetic, of course, is as totalising as that of Eliot or Yeats, if not more so, yet his poetic practice is marked by precisely that disjunctive quality which Coughlan finds in the poetry of Beckett. Futhermore, there are similarities between the argument of 'Recent Irish Poetry' and Pound's literary criticism of this and the preceding decade. In a 1928 article on William Carlos Williams, for instance, Pound likens literary creation to the act of 'a man hurling himself at an indomitable chaos, and yanking and hauling as much of it as possible into some sort of order (or beauty), aware of it both as chaos and as potential'.[63] Such yanking and hauling does not conclude with an order made true by the world but with a Stevensian 'supreme fiction' – an artistic structure in which the seeming poverty of reality can be rendered bearable, even beautiful, yet in which the underlying chaos is still apparent. Pound's formulation is echoed six years later in Beckett's account of the 'rupture of the lines of communication': 'The artist who is aware of this may state the space that intervenes between him and the world of objects; he may state it as a no-man's-land, Hellespont or vacuum, according as he happens to be feeling resentful, nostalgic or merely depressed.'[64] In its essentials, Beckett's notion of stating the space is simply a more resigned version of Pound's strenuous yanking and hauling. Likewise, the alternative artistic responses Beckett wittily outlines – no-man's-land, Hellespont and vacuum – broadly correspond to Pound's 'some sort of order'. Present in both passages is the belief that the subject matter of literature in the post-war world is a contestable, problematic category. As a result, shared literary forms are no longer appropriate vehicles to organise such 'chaos and potential'. In the light of these similarities, Beckett's heavily ironised appropriation of elements of the troubadour tradition in a large number of the poems collected in *Echo's Bones and Other Precipitates* (1935), to which I return below, bears more than a passing resemblance to Pound's use of the same materials.[65]

Beckett's chief contention in 'Recent Irish Poetry' is that the poetic modernism of Coffey and Devlin (and, by implication, his own) constitutes a reaction against the conventionality of Irish poetry in the late 1920s and early 1930s. With characteristic *brio*, the young Beckett asserts that their poetry 'does not proceed from the *Gossoons Wunderhorn* of that Irish Romantic Arnim-Brenanto combination, Sir Samuel Ferguson and Standish O'Grady'.[66] Still, we must be careful not to see Coffey and Devlin, along with Beckett and the slightly older figure of MacGreevy, as forming a coherent avant-garde movement of any kind. In his agon with the revival, Beckett deploys his contemporaries as, at least in part, vehicles for his own animosity, a strategy which would be replayed by Michael Smith and *The Lace Curtain* during the 1970s.[67] That said, during the 1930s Devlin clearly agreed with the thrust of Beckett's 'Recent Irish Poetry'. In a 1934 letter to MacGreevy, Devlin records that Beckett's essay 'raised a storm' in Dublin: 'It appears Yeats was furious; it appears that Clarke is vindictive by nature and will pursue Sam to his grave; it appears Seamus O'Sullivan thought he might have been mentioned at least; and my domestic bull Higgins voyez-moi ce type amazed me by being glad he got off lightly.'[68] That Devlin relished these reactions is apparent from the same letter, in which he writes that the current Irish 'atmosphere, political, economic and therefore . . . literary is pre 1870'. Confessing that he has 'no sympathy with the attempt to build up an Irish literature in English', Devlin dismisses Higgins's 'experiments in assonance' as 'experiments in decking out a carcase', while Yeats is contemptuously referred to as the 'bullocky bulwark of contented undereducation'.

Coffey maintained precisely this kind of animosity to revivalism throughout his writing life, and his sporadic ventures into literary criticism on occasion turn a jaundiced eye on Yeats as an example for the Irish poet:

> One remembers that Yeats expressed himself as wishing to 'preserve that which is living and help our two Irelands, Gaelic Ireland and Anglo-Ireland, so to unite that neither shall lose its pride'. But then *we* should have to go well back behind the seventh century, back as far as maybe never to find our aboriginals and their instinctively habitual modes of action and being. All the while, too, we should be forgetting how fruitless paired categories (Gaelic with Anglo-Irish, Protestant with Catholic, insular with missionary, etc.) are for thinking social and political reality with, not to mention poetic reality.[69]

Coffey sees Yeats's overriding ambition as the rooting of his poetry in a sense of national identity, so that, in the words of 'The Municipal Gallery Re-visited', 'All that we [that is, Yeats, Synge and Lady Gregory] did, all that we said or sang / Must come from contact with the soil'.[70] Understandably, in Coffey's eyes, Yeats's vision of a 'living' Ireland as Gaelic and Anglo-Irish, in which noble and beggarman function as privileged figures, is a wholly inadequate prism through which to view the 'social and political reality' of modern Ireland. Coffey's most sustained meditation on 'poetic reality', his 1962 sequence, *Missouri Sequence*, can be read on one level as an extended rejoinder to Yeats. In the course of the poem, Coffey says of his children, 'They know nothing of Ireland, / they grow American'.[71] The comment's immediate context is the poet's relatively unhappy time as an Assistant Professor of Philosophy at Saint Louis University, from 1947 to 1952.[72] More generally, the remark pertains to his relationship to Ireland, and to modern Irish poetry, and is tellingly made in a section of *Missouri Sequence* dedicated to MacGreevy. As the author of the first critical monograph on Saint Louis's most famous literary son, MacGreevy functions as a node around which cluster Coffey's reflections on the baleful influence, as Coffey sees it, of Yeats on Irish poetry, and the consequent failure of an indigenous modernist poetry to emerge. MacGreevy's most extensive work, *Crón Tráth na nDéithe*, is strongly influenced not by Yeats but by the subject of his 1931 book, *T. S. Eliot: A Study*, and specifically by *The Waste Land*, as evinced in its fragmented, collage-like juxtapositions, mix of registers and allusiveness, the similarities between the two texts extending to their shared use of Wagner.[73] Hence the appropriateness of MacGreevy as dedicatee of Coffey's poem, a draft of which states that Yeats, though a 'great poet', 'failed when he advised our Irish poets'.[74] However, it would be overhasty to conclude that the unspoken subtext to Coffey's rejection of Yeats is an unqualified valorisation of Eliot, that Coffey too has 'grow[n] American'. Coffey had been seriously studying Eliot's poetry, as well as Pound's, from at least the early 1930s. His ambivalent reaction to the American's poetry is apparent in a 1936 letter to MacGreevy in which he makes the intriguing claim that Eliot's 'poetry shows him not to understand anything about grace v. the choice of a Becket in Murder in the Cathedral'.[75] In *Missouri Sequence* Coffey's musings on the issues of grace and choice lead him to invoke another American poet, Laura (Riding) Jackson:

> One poet I admire has written:
> *wherever the soul gives in to flesh*
> *without a struggle is home.*
> Would one want home like that,
> rest, supine surrender
> to oneself alone,
> flight from where one is?[76]

The italicised lines are a quotation from (Riding) Jackson's 'Laura and Francisca', a poem in which the 'home' inhabited by her and Robert Graves in Deyá, on the island of Mallorca, becomes the starting point for a series of reflections on, in her words, 'the manifold totality' in which the human exists, the 'truth' of which her poetry, she came to believe, failed to deliver. In the course of the poem the island of Ireland comes to be associated with a refusal of this 'truth'. Maturity, she writes, is where 'continents gives way to islands',

> And keeping house is play –
> A small circle of meaning
> Within a larger, the larger being
> Truth, by which man knows of man.
> And so a refuge-island is only
> A grinning hollow of sarcasm and despite:
> Such is the goatish propaganda
> Of uninhabitable Ireland.[77]

On several occasions *Missouri Sequence* associates poetry with truth ('No servant, the muse / abides in truth'),[78] its concern with quite literally 'keeping house' in the face of 'family cares and crises' an extended metaphor for the relevance of the poetic vocation to the human condition. While (Riding) Jackson's concern with 'the self-sameness in being' that unifies humanity led her to conclude that poetry occluded such truth through its basis in a unique mode of perception, Coffey's sequence makes the contrary claim that 'Poetry becomes humankind' precisely because 'without [it] nothing exact is said'.[79] From the 'small circle of meaning' identified in the sequence with his particular experience as an emigrant, the poem extrapolates the truth of humanity's existential plight,

in which 'We face a testing / based on other grounds than nature's'.[80]
With the composition of *Missouri Sequence*, it is worth noting, Coffey
broke a lengthy spell of poetic inactivity, having ceased to write at around
the same time in the late 1930s as his American contemporary renounced
poetry ('Laura and Francisca' is placed at the end of [Riding] Jackson's
1938 *Collected Poems*). Coffey's primary reason for giving up, it would
appear, had been the increasing incompatibility he felt existed between his
religious beliefs and poetic vocation, a divide *Missouri Sequence* seeks to
bridge. To this extent, the poem can be read as an extended reply to (Riding)
Jackson, a rebuttal, though it predates it by a decade, of her *The Telling*,
which details her reasons for ceasing to write poetry. Nevertheless, in
implicitly juxtaposing MacGreevy's failure to produce a follow-up volume
to his *Poems* with (Riding) Jackson's poetic renunciation, Coffey also passes
oblique judgement on the 'uninhabitable' nature of the Irish literary land-
scape for his own experimental poetry in the decade prior to the Second
World War, a period in which Coffey published only a handful of poems:

> Dear Tom, in Ireland,
> you have known
> the pain between
> its fruiting and the early dream
> and you will hear me out.[81]

The existential 'truth' Coffey identifies with his 'muse' is thus a challenge
to the nationalist 'goatish propaganda', as Coffey views it, of Yeats and
the revival. Ostensibly addressing MacGreevy 'in Ireland', Coffey is also
placing a transatlantic trunk call to 'Our William Butler Yeats', accusing
him of having fallen short of such poetic 'truth': 'He struggled towards
the exact muse / through a sunless day.'[82] In this fashion, the poem
returns us to the same inhospitable terrain sketched out in 'Recent Irish
Poetry', in which Beckett also finds in MacGreevy's poetry a quality of
existential authenticity.

MacGreevy, writes Beckett, is concerned with 'the act and not the
object of perception': 'Mr MacGreevy is an existentialist in verse, the
Titchener of the modern lyric.'[83] In support of this claim, Beckett adduces
the four line poem 'Nocturne':

> I labour in a barren place,
> Alone, self-conscious, frightened, blundering;
> Far away, stars wheeling in space,
> About my feet, earth voices whispering.[84]

Beckett's reflections on MacGreevy seem justified by his choice of text to
the extent that the reactions of the poem's speaker to his predicament
certainly evince the existential angst of being 'thrown' into the world.

However, the being-in-the-world that this short lyric examines is rooted in a specific historical moment, as well as suggesting a given of human existence. MacGreevy served in the British Army during the First World War, and was twice wounded at the Somme. The poem's epigraph, which Beckett does not quote, refers to the fate of a fellow officer in the Royal Field Artillery: 'To Geoffrey England Taylor, 2nd Lieutenant, RFA "Died of wounds"'; and the lyric is placed in a section of MacGreevy's Poems headed '1917–1918' (which denotes MacGreevy's time at the front, not that of the section's two poems' dates of composition). These framing elements to the quatrain turn the 'barren place' of the opening line into a warscape; the bewildered actions suggest the fear of the front-line soldier, while the 'earth voices whispering', with which the poem closes, possess intimations of possible death. The poem lacks the mimeticism that charac-terises the more famous war poetry of Wilfred Owen in that its reference to the Great War is oblique. But reference it makes, and in this respect the poem is indicative of MacGreevy's poetry. As Lee Jenkins has observed: 'his poetry is highly experimental, reflecting the emergent technical innovations of European modernism, and at the same time his poems very often have an urgent and specific subject matter',[85] including conflict in France or Ireland. The obliquity of MacGreevy's allusions to contem-porary events combined with the urgency and intensity of their presence is the signature of his poetry. Its origins lie in his experience of war, which, in his 1931 monograph on Richard Aldington, he claimed prevented combatants from writing poetry too abstract, 'too Mallarmean':

> No poet who went through the war can go back to that. . . . The effect of the war on Aldington and [Jean] Lurçat has been to bring their work closer to objective reality, but I do not think there is any immediate danger of their returning to the undiscriminating realism of the nineteenth century, because in the first place their technical point of departure is not realistic, and in the second place the principal reality that has been impelling them to expression is so vast and so terrible to look back on, that, grasping its full tragic significance as they slowly and sensitively and thoughtfully have done, they cannot, in the nature of things, fall into the mere pathetic of, say, Monet or Zola.[86]

In this passage MacGreevy rejects the ideal of Mallarmé's Symbolism, the desire to wrest language free from its referential function, yet simul-taneously resists naturalism's fidelity to empirical reality. In this respect, MacGreevy prefigures Coffey's complex negotiations with Mallarmé from a position influenced by the aesthetic theories of Jacques Maritain. Coffey also viewed the 'Mallarmean ivory tower'[87] with suspicion, arguing that it marked a total disengagement of art from the social sphere, and an abrogation of the 'humanity' of the artist in its hope for a language divorced from its necessarily human context. As Coffey bluntly states in *Missouri Sequence*: 'This much is certain: / . . . / he [i.e. the poet] must not attempt escape / from here and now.'[88] However, in line with Beckett's pronouncements in 'Recent Irish Poetry', MacGreevy is clearly aware that a 'rupture of the lines of communication' has also rendered unworkable both realist and naturalist conceptions of a transparent relationship between sign and referent. MacGreevy's modernism, fully cognisant of the psychological and social effects of the Great War, seeks to avoid the shortcomings of both 'realism' and aestheticism. Without belittling the horror of MacGreevy's experiences during the war, the impossibility of adequately representing it in its totality is at one with the general predicament of modernist writers (including Yeats) disabused of realist aspirations. Modernist writers find themselves, in Fredric Jameson's words, in 'a historical situation in which the truth of [their] social life as a whole . . . is increasingly irreconcilable with the aesthetic quality of language or of individual expression'.[89] The war is a 'terrible' revelation of art's inability to map an 'objective reality' through the recourses of a shared literary language; yet the omnipresence of that alienated object world presses all the more acutely on the artist. The war, in other words, is an event that throws into relief a more diffuse sense of a crisis in the representational capacity of art, of which Beckett's emphasis on 'breakdown' and 'rupture' is to be seen as a late example.

Crón Tráth na nDéithe, first published in *transition* in 1929, is MacGreevy's most sustained attempt to render an 'objective reality' – in this case, Dublin in the aftermath of civil war – in a non-realist fashion. On first reading, the poem seems overly derivative of Eliot's *The Waste Land* (which MacGreevy greatly admired) in its citations from popular and 'high' culture, montage effects and fragmentation of form. However, the poem can equally be read as a *reply* to a quality of Eliot's work which, in *Richard Aldington*, MacGreevy later formulated as its occasional lapse into a 'remote manner' of expression.[90] MacGreevy's poem seeks to impress upon its reader the immediacy or 'closeness' of its speaker's experiences of the cab-drive through the shattered Dublin streets, as is well illustrated by the opening section of the poem:

Ter-ot. Stumble. Clock-clock, clock-clock!
Quadrupedante, etcetera,
And heavy turning wheels of lurching cab
On midnight streets of Dublin shiny in the rain!

No trams squirt wide the liquid mud at this hour.

The dark-and-light-engulfing box
Wheels through the wetness
Bringing me
From empty healthy air in
Mayo
To Dublin's stale voluptuousness.

Trot
Trot
Clock-clock
Lurch

Such rutty, muddy streets to clock, clock-clock on, horse![91]

The first line's onomatopoeic quality is followed, as Susan Schreibman
has noted, by a reference in the second to the eighth book of the *Aeneid*:
'quadrupedante putrem sonitu quatit ungula campum', a line 'in which
the harsh consonants and dactyls convey the sound of galloping'.[92]
MacGreevy's allusion to Virgil's epic is, in part, a literary joke, but it also
bears upon the relationship of language to 'objective reality' in his work.
Onomatopoeia is, of course, an instance of language in which some
quality of the object or event referred to is said to be evoked by the
sound of the signs themselves. As such, it is a figure that grants the
powerful illusion of being 'closer' to that which it denotes than other
sign-structures.[93] MacGreevy's truncated allusion to Virgil's great example
of this literary effect – '*Quadrupedante, etcetera*' – foregrounds the extent
to which his poem deploys onomatopoeia in the service of a non-realist
poetic which is difficult to construe in New Critical terms (or that of
'spatial form'). Rather, MacGreevy holds what Charles Altieri calls a
'presentational theory' of poetry; that is, his poetry embodies a desire
to articulate his emotions in an artwork that is not a straightforward
'copy' of the non-linguistic world, but a 'purposive structuring of exper-
ience'.[94] This accounts for the centrality to *Crón Tráth na nDéithe* (and
to MacGreevy's work as a whole) of the speaker, whose reactions hold
the poem together as a single narrative in a manner clearly distinct
from Eliot's use of disjointed personae and settings in *The Waste Land*.
MacGreevy's method of 'structuring' experience is apparent in a passage
such as the following:

Wrecks wetly mouldering under rain,
Everywhere.
Remember Belgium!
You cannot pick up the
Pieces

But, oh, Phoenicians, who on blood-red seas
Come sailing to the Galerie des Glaces
And you, gombeenmen
On blue hills of office

No man hath greater lunacy than this.[95]

The damaged buildings in the speaker's immediate range of vision give
way to a recollection of the propaganda used to encourage Irish Catholics
to enlist in the British Army in the Great War. This is succeeded by a
juxtaposition of the Hall of Mirrors at Versailles with the doubtful
practices of government officials, and concludes with a bitter rewriting of
John. These are all fragments or 'Pieces' of a totality, a socio-political
context, which cannot be grasped directly – it is too 'vast and terrible' –
but can be structured only according to an individual's specific experience
and systems of belief. This manner of registering history, as wholly
subjectivised, is comparable to the despair articulated by Yeats's expro-
priated Arcadian, despite the gulf separating the two texts in terms of
formal influences. Where MacGreevy's poem differs from Yeats's is in its
implicit refusal to entertain the consolations of a privatised poetic
language ('In words alone are certain good').

There is thus something faintly incongruous about finding MacGreevy's
name appended to the 1932 *transition* manifesto, 'Poetry is Vertical',
with its call for 'The final disintegration of the "I" in the creative act' in
the search for 'The synthesis of a true collectivism'.[96] Such a polemical
dismissal of the lyric subject is a characteristic avant-garde reflex, but one
which consorts oddly with the centrality of the 'I' to MacGreevy's
minimalist verse. MacGreevy, like Coffey, remained largely undrawn by
the cultural radicalism of the continental avant-garde, despite the
Surrealist inflections of a number of his poems (most notably, 'Homage to
Hieronymus Bosch'). Beckett's reading of his work presciently identified
the older poet's anomalous poetic. MacGreevy, writes Beckett, 'neither
excludes self-perception from his work nor postulates the object as
inaccessible',[97] a phase which we can interpret as registering, if rather too
positively, the ambiguous dialectic in MacGreevy's verse between poetic
subject and an estranged objective environment.

Beckett also signed 'Poetry is Vertical', and his reflections in 'Recent
Irish Poetry' on the 'breakdown' of poetic subject and literary object, and

their realisation in the poems collected in *Echo's Bones and Other Precipitates*, are closer in substance to the 'revolution of the word' advocated by *transition* than MacGreevy's practice in *Poems*. Yet Beckett's work, in poetry, fiction and drama, clearly resists the avant-garde's assault on the institution of art. On the contrary, his texts interrogate their own aestheticism immanently, through the negation, rather than the rejection, of the traditional categories of poetic, novelistic and dramatic form. The gradual attenuation of form in Beckett constitutes an ever-increasing attention to form, not its destruction.[98] This is most apparent in the prose and plays, but it is also at work in the poetry of the 1930s. The troubadour forms that I mentioned above in relation to Pound are subjected, in *Echo's Bones*, to parody, reversal, and conflation, yet they are still essential to an understanding of the texts. Traditional conventions crumble in these poems, but their ruined fragments are still visible. In 'Serena I', for example, Beckett manipulates the Occitan evening song, in which the speaker longs for the night and its amorous delights, in an image which manages to be both redolent of the idea of love's pursuit as a hunt and evocative of a solipsistic withdrawal from a threatening environment:

> I find me taking the Crystal Palace
> for the Blessed Isles from Primrose Hill
> alas I must be that kind of person
> hence in Ken Wood who shall find me
> my breath held in the midst of thickets
> none but the most quarried lovers[99]

The speaker is himself a 'quarry', cowering in the 'thickets' of Ken Wood; but the hunt of which he is the intended prey has none of the erotic connotations it has in the conventions of courtly love. Rather, his alienated condition is one in which the 'Blessed Isles' can be invoked only ironically, trapped as he is within the grimly urban landscape of modernity, a London setting for which the original is Eliot's *The Waste Land*.

The negation of hackneyed convention ('the breakdown of the object') in *Echo's Bones* is also present in two early poems by Devlin, 'O Paltry Melancholy' and 'Now', both of which were collected in his first volume of poetry, *Poems* (1930), which also contains poems by Coffey. The apostrophic title of 'O Paltry Melancholy' is a cliché which the text's first four stanzas proceed to undermine. The melancholy experienced by the speaker is 'Not of the Magdalen . . . her sorrow was her salvation'; it is 'Not of Orpheus . . . His sorrow was the silver sorrow of the poets'; 'Not of Deirdre . . . Fierce was her sorrow'; 'Not even the sorrow / of the lioness . . . questing her stolen cubs' (*CP* 96). Proceeding in this fashion, the 'paltry' nature of the persona's melancholy comes into view through

denying it a religious, mythological-cum-literary (classical and Celtic) or
natural analogue. In the words of Beckett's 'Dortmunder': 'Schopenhauer
is dead, the bawd / puts her lute away';[100] that is, the release from the will,
which Schopenhauer associated with the disinterested aesthetic experience,
is as unattainable as the 'Blessed Isles' of 'Serena I'. Devlin's persona is
left, much like the aimlessly wandering poet of *Echo's Bones*, 'dragging a
songless boredom through sunless and stormless days':

> images firing his brain of never accomplished tasks
> disarming smile of humility hiding coward delays
> on tiptoe in dreams beside action, sophister strutting in masks
> of laughter, of childlike pagan of curled-lipped polished doubt,
> a timid traveller trailing slow steps about and about
> considering which route he shall take at the crossing of ways.
> (*CP* 97)

The repudiation of conventional contexts in which to place melancholia
is not their destruction: cancelled, their denuded forms are still naggingly
present, like the stumps of broken teeth. It is their negation, after all, that
is the subject of the poem. The same effect is achieved, though more humor-
ously, in 'Now'. The title is a pointer to the fraught relationship between
modernity and tradition, a tension encapsulated in the poem's debunking
of revivalist and Georgian topoi, among other poetic conventionalities:

> Eternally emerald pastures of Ireland; English lanes winding
> > *One-ery, two-ery.*
> Through smothering blossom; old book shops in Paris;
> > *Ziccary zan*
> Larks singing in Sussex and Deirdre's now bloodless lips.
> > *Hollow-bone, crack-a-bone.*
> (*CP* 103)

But the poem is equally mocking of the avant-garde's utopian hope that
the abolition of bourgeois aesthetics marches hand in hand with political
liberation: 'Let us be Anarchists by all means / *How many miles is it* /
Dethrone the Verb and the Substantive / *To Babylon*' (*CP* 104).

Devlin's poetry, as we shall shortly see, has little truck with Tristan
Tzara's and others' anarchic toppling of literary conventions, neither, *à la*
his admired Surrealists, does his work view the dethroning of a rational
language of verbs and substantives a prerequisite for an emancipated art.
'Now' is a playfully ludic counterpart to 'O Paltry Melancholy', the latter
poem striking a keynote in Devlin's work which becomes more insistent
in his poetry of the 1940s and 1950s: the problematic but inescapable
relationship of the poem (and poet) to literary and religious tradition.
Beckett's work splits apart the protective carapace of literary forms with
growing surgical precision. Devlin, following his flirtations with the

avant-garde in the 1930s, pursues a different course. His career resembles that of Stevens more than Beckett: a Francophile (or 'Frenchified') earlier phase is succeeded by a New Critical modernism, the transition, in both Stevens's and Devlin's cases, coming about at least in part through the agency of the American poet-critic, Allen Tate. The comparison between Stevens and Devlin is equally pertinent in that, despite their shared Francophilia, neither belonged to a programmatic avant-garde, though both were clearly intrigued by, and knowledgeable of, the writings produced by such movements. The French connection was established prior to Devlin's contact with the New Critics – the latter occurred with his diplomatic posting to the United States at the beginning of the Second World War – and is central to the poetry collected in *Intercessions* (1937), one of the most extraordinary volumes of Irish poetry to be published between the wars.

2

COMMUNICATIONS FROM THE EIFFEL TOWER: *INTERCESSIONS*

The majority of the poems collected in *Intercessions* have their origins in Devlin's sojourn in Paris, from 1931 to 1933, and the volume – as published in 1937 – shows the clear influence of the French avant-garde, particularly Surrealism. The collection's publisher was the experimental poet, George Reavey, whose Europa Press had published in the preceding year a volume of translations of Paul Éluard's poetry, *Thorns of Thunder*, to which Devlin contributed five poems.[1] In the same year as *Thorns of Thunder* appeared, Devlin published translations of four poems by André Breton in *Contemporary Poetry and Prose*.[2] The novelist and friend of Devlin, Mervyn Wall, has remarked upon the interest shown by Devlin and Coffey during the early 1930s in the Surrealists and other French poetry of this period, to which he adds that they also 'read and examined Eliot and Pound'.[3] Devlin's study of Surrealism and the avant-garde in general leaves its mark on many of the poems collected in *Intercessions*, though in a manner deeply modulated by Anglo-American high modernism. For Coffey one difference between Devlin's poetry and that of his admired Surrealists can be seen in Devlin's 'habit' of making 'skeletal plans' for his poems, constructing an 'Intelligible structure' to his poems at odds with Surrealist theories of poetic composition.[4] Coffey argues that Devlin's practice as a writer prior to his reading of Éluard led him to doubt the poetic efficacy of *écriture automatique*:

> He was a *maker of verses* from the start. When he encountered surrealism he was already protected against seduction by his past experience of versemaking. He felt the attraction of Eluard strongly. But he did not find it possible to accept surrealism and its pronouncements as explicative of Eluard's verse. He felt sure, and subsequent revelations have proved him right, that Eluard's style was the result of deliberate choices; it could never have been the uncorrected resultant of spontaneous regurgitations (or would it be gurgitations?) from the vasty depths within the person.[5]

This comment arguably says as much about Coffey's poetic as it illuminates Devlin's. Coffey's views on poetry are deeply coloured by his neo-Thomist beliefs, which entail a poetic in which, after Aquinas's interpretation of Aristotle, the artist is conceived as an artisan, a 'maker' of poems in a rational and pre-determined fashion.[6] In the terminology of Breton's 1924 *Manifesto of Surrealism*, such a poetic partakes of 'the realistic attitude', which, argues Breton, 'inspired by positivism, from Saint Thomas Aquinas to Anatole France, clearly seems to me to be hostile to any intellectual or moral advancement', and has spawned, among other horrors, 'the generous supply of novels'.[7] Despite Coffey's obvious antipathy towards Surrealism, however, his friendship with Devlin and close familiarity with the latter's poetry grant his words a measure of authority that warrants our serious attention. Coffey's comments point in fact to the productive tension in *Intercessions* between a Surrealist patina to the verse and the poetry's deeper adherence to the aestheticism of the high modernist artwork.

The Surrealist appeal to the 'gurgitations' of automatic writing rests on a paradoxical conception of the liberating effects of language when wielded *against* language. As Raymond Williams has observed: 'language was being simultaneously identified with the blocking of "true consciousness" and, to the extent that it could emancipate itself from its imprisoning everyday forms and, beyond that, from the received forms of "literature", as itself the medium of the idealized "pure consciousness".'[8] A language revivified by the irrational has the potential to free the human subject from the deadening forms of a fossilised language of practical usage; this, in turn, would lead to an interpolation of the world of dreams and desire into that of a henceforth redeemed workaday world. In the view of Breton, art anticipates 'the future resolution of these two states, dream and reality, which are seemingly so contradictory, into a kind of absolute reality, a *surreality*, if one may so speak'.[9] While the revolutionary dimension to Surrealism's aesthetic led its advocates to perceive their ideas as compatible with those of historical materialism, the politics of Surrealism can be more carefully defined as the urge to reintegrate art and life by overcoming the autonomous nature of art within bourgeois society.[10] For Peter Bürger this is the definitive gesture of the avant-garde: to turn art against the institution of art. In contrast to the avant-garde, modernism, for all its apparent rupture with the past, preserves and, indeed, intensifies the primary function of art within modern Western society. In Bürger's words:

> Art allows at least an imagined satisfaction of individual needs that are repressed in daily praxis. Through the enjoyment of art, the atrophied bourgeois individual can experience the self as personality. But because art

is detached from daily life, this experience remains without tangible effect, i.e., it cannot be integrated into that life.[11]

High modernism's self-conscious concern with its own materiality, its self-reflexive attitude to its own formal properties, does not mark a break with preceding conceptions of art. Rather, it is the logical culmination of a process that, Bürger argues, dates from the late eighteenth century:

> The apartness from the praxis of life that had always constituted the insti-tutional status of art in bourgeois society now becomes the content of works. . . . The failure of Mallarmé's principal literary project, Valéry's almost total lack of productivity over two decades, and Hofmannsthal's Lord Chandos letter are symptoms of a crisis of art. At the moment it has shed all that is alien to it, art necessarily becomes problematic for itself. As institution and content coincide, social ineffectuality stands revealed as the essence of art in bourgeois society, and thus provokes the self-criticism of art.[12]

The avant-garde, including the Surrealist movement, mounts such a self-criticism, seeking to dispel the 'apartness' from life that characterises the institution of art through negating the 'aesthetic experience' and reinvesting art in individual and social praxis.

Of the poems collected in *Intercessions*, 'Communication from the Eiffel Tower' and 'Bacchanal' most strikingly register Devlin's interest in Surrealism and avant-gardism in general, and both mark the limits of that interest. Coffey notes that Devlin's attention to the 'doctrine' of Surrealism prompted him to record his dreams, and that 'Many of the poems of *Intercessions* incorporate passages worked up from records of dreams, and one poem: "Communication from the Eiffel Tower" draws everything from one dream'.[13] While the dream-logic of the poem gives it a strongly Surrealist flavour, its chief symbol links the poem to earlier modernist responses to the Eiffel Tower. The tower fascinated early French and other European modernists because it offered, in Robert Hughes's influential argument, 'the great metaphor' for cultural change in the period, 'the one structure that seemed to gather all the meanings of modernity together'.[14] The poets Guillaume Apollinaire and Blaise Cendrars and the painter Robert Delaunay, among others, saw the tower as the veritable symbol of modern technology and therefore a challenge to the representational capacities of modern art. In 'Tower' (1913), one of his *Nineteen Elastic Poems*, Cendrars apostrophises the Eiffel Tower, paying tribute in passing to 'the Simultaneous Delaunay' for whom the tower is 'the brush he dips in light':

Gong tom-tom Zanzibar jungle animal X rays express scalpel symphony
You are everything
Tower
Ancient god
Modern animal
Solar spectrum
Subject of my poem
Tower
World tour tower
Moving Tower[15]

Cendrars's Eiffel Tower is both a quasi-Futurist emblem of technological progress (the tower, at one point, is said to 'shine with all the magnificence of the aurora borealis with your radio waves') and an icon of primitivism. To the poet the tower is the definitive 'Subject of [his] poem' because it encapsulates modernity – from Zanzibar to Paris it is the 'World tour tower'. The contradictory nature of Cendrars's paean of praise for the tower – 'Ancient god / Modern animal' – is indicative of early modernist reactions to the aesthetic challenge posed by the tower. As Cendrars observed: 'No formula of art, known at that time, could make the pretence of resolving plastically the problem of the Eiffel Tower. Realism made it smaller; the old laws of Italian perspective made it look thinner.'[16] Despite Eiffel's arguments for his construction's military and meteorological utility, the tower's growing functional obsolescence in the years immediately prior to the First World War was a further spur to non-representational or anti-realist art. As Marjorie Perloff comments: 'The intrinsic uselessness of the thousand-foot iron structure was already apparent to the poets and painters of the *avant guerre*. Indeed, it was its very emptiness as a signifier that challenged the Futurist imagination to invent extravagant metaphors for it'.[17] The nightmarish figurative language of 'Communication from the Eiffel Tower' is faintly reminiscent of the rhetorical extremity of early modernist depictions of the tower, yet the poem's images lack the optimistic ebullience of Cendrars's and Apollonaire's metaphors (or Delaunay's paintings):

Tower O my subduer Tower my tyrant
Loosen your girders I will become one I will conform
Girders are loveable they are like nubile girls bending
Backwards in arcs asleep when smiles are flush with their lips
Smiles risen goldfish through currents of dreaming, tower girded and pliant
(CP 74)

The hyperbolic quality of Devlin's extended simile clearly recalls the immoderate, excessive poetic generated by the Futurists' seduction at the hands of technological modernity. Nevertheless, Devlin's apostrophe, in depicting the tower as a 'tyrant', simultaneously renders its speaker's subjugation as metonymic of the deleterious effects of technocratic power on the human subject. In a fashion characteristic of Devlin, and of much high modernism *entre les guerres* rather than that of the *avant guerre* avant-garde, the persona dwells on the alienation experienced by the individual under urbanisation and industrialisation:

> Tower, that snowy steel town though postulant
> Of full conscience and its confetti of laughter blown about
> In the main street of the sun, then
> Summoned when the trestle-blether texts of poverty are irrelevant
> What can it offer
> More than the pretty tinkling of snowy steel?
> Anything will dislocate the riveting:
> A boy embittered when summer rain smells fresh on hot limbs and
> Desire trapped in a girl's wet hair breathes
> Or a bored mechanic polishing and he mutters
> Caught by sight of his face in one of a million rollers
> (CP 76–7)

Devlin's 'bored mechanic' stands as a laconic indictment of the Futurist obsession with the machine. His reflected image on the machinery he operates is suggestive of Marx's views on alienated labour, the worker not only alienated from the results of his labour but equally from the productive process itself. The 'embittered' boy and frustrated girl reinforce the poem's oblique critique of a society dominated by exchange-relations, a society represented by the bland yet menacing 'snowy steel' tower in the midst of a 'snowy steel town'. If Italian Futurism's aim, prior to the Great War, of integrating art and life constituted a powerful rejection of *l'art pour l'art* of the end of the nineteenth century, by celebrating technological power, energy and dynamism the movement reprehensibly, if naively, championed the cleansing effects of modern warfare. F. T. Marinetti's 1913 manifesto, 'Destruction of Syntax – Imagination without Strings – Words-in-Freedom', for instance, 'opposes[s] the decorative, precious aesthetic of Mallarmé' to a 'typographical revolution that allows [the Futurist] to impress on the words (already free, dynamic and torpedo-like) every velocity of the stars, the clouds, aeroplanes, trains, waves, explosives, globules of seafoam, molecules, and atoms'.[18] Devlin's ironic disparagement of the aestheticising of such triumphs of engineering as the Eiffel Tower, with its 'pretty tinkling of snowy steel', implicitly rebukes an aesthetic whose valorisation of the 'free, dynamic and torpedo-like' word was tantamount to a poetic endorsement of the military hardware behind the wholesale carnage of 1914–18. By 1932, the year in which 'Communication from the Eiffel Tower' was drafted, Marinetti's version of Futurism had grotesquely mutated from its pre-war leftism and anarchism into an equally heterodox fascism. While Devlin's probing criticisms of the tower, and the forces which it was felt to actualise, have a tangential relationship with the Futurist dimension to early modernism, they are also rewardingly viewed in the context of extreme right-wing politics of the 1930s, of which Devlin had had first-hand experience in a trip to Munich at the start of the decade.[19]

This context is registered, in a dream-like displacement, by the curious presence in Devlin's text of Joseph-Arthur de Gobineau. Gobineau, whose infamous *Essai sur l'inégalité des races humaines* (1853–5) was appropriated by apologists for National Socialism's theory of Aryan supremacy, finds a spokeswoman in the persona's companion, who avers:

> In the major labour nurse the treasury
> Of the minority most virtuous
> So, for that for this misery of the many is necessary
> Avert your countenance while my tribal groups of combat
> In a terse putsch strike elsewhere for your sake
> (CP 70)

The speaker's meditation on Gobineau, by way of contrast, pillories him as one of the 'Defenders of the past in the obstinate ditches of sleep', asking, 'Why mock as weakling the hope of the weak for serene years [?]' (*CP* 71–2). Troubling the speaker is the manner in which the woman transmutes the Frenchman's name, as much as his ideas, by means of a typical German suffix: 'GOBINEAU it is why will you keep on saying GOBETHAU?' (*CP* 71). The Germanic form is literally meaningless, though *tauen*, meaning 'to melt', is suggestive of the noun's metamorphosis from French to German and, indeed, of the Dali-like transformations of the poem as a whole, its 'superb dream *bisticcio*', as Beckett describes it.[20] J. C. C. Mays's suggestion that Gobineau 'mutates into German Gobethau in the same way that his *Essai* . . . was distorted by Nazi programmes for the purity of the Aryan race' (*CP* 335) is probably right, given the poem's genesis shortly after Devlin's return from Munich. Along related lines, the woman's reference to 'a terse putsch' just possibly recalls Hitler's and the Nazis' role in the Munich putsch of November 1923, an event of which Devlin was doubtless aware. If so, the poem's immediate, athough not its final, response can be read out of the speaker's adoption of the identity of François-Noël Babeuf, a French Revolutionary, whose radical egalitarianism informs the text's representation of the inequities, and dangers, of social inequality:

> The desiccated mouths the eyes of reproachful prayers
> Hunger and thirst the anger of blood the distress of the heart
> Attend and I declaim that I BABEUF
> BABEUF and I mixed like the play of mirrors
> Make *table rase* ready for primary needs
> Their mouth's tense bows relieve them, releasing fingers
> Their eyes bulge like gates opening
> Of fortresses at morning full of prisoners
> Insisting on promised deliverance.
> (CP 75)

This confusion of identities or 'play of mirrors' in which the persona and Babeuf articulate the need to make a clean sweep of society and concentrate on 'primary needs' brings Devlin's text into the orbit of the revolutionary changes advocated by Surrealism. (Babeuf, it is worth noting, was viewed as a martyr to the cause by French communists.) As I noted above, the Surrealists, through such strategies as automatic writing, also sought 'deliverance' from the *Ancien régime* of technocratic reason, from a society enslaved by means-end rationality. Devlin's enthusiasm, in this poem and elsewhere in *Intercessions*, for the Surrealists' stylistic dislocations, the 'invitation to widen the distance between the objects related in an image', as Coffey describes it,[21] merges powerfully with the text's ventriloquism of Babeuf's revolutionary *Manifeste des plébéiens* (1795). However, at this juncture we need to recall Coffey's claim that, for all his flirtations with Surrealist techniques, Devlin did not accept Surrealism's belief that language had the ability to 'determine a point in man of absolute liberty'.[22] 'Communication from the Eiffel Tower' is not broadcast on that avant-garde wavelength. Rather, the poem admits the possibility of freedom from 'these purlieus of machine forests' only briefly, humorously indulging in an impossible hankering to 'fly to the Sassanian empire and mould in the margin', to lie 'Like an old train among the gay weeds of a sidetrack / It will probably be in America this time perhaps Buenos Aires' (CP 74). Both the unrealisable craving for the remoteness of the Persian Empire under the rule of the Sasan dynasty and the vague desire for a ruinous self-exile in South America have to be measured against the speaker's acceptance that

> My Tower is far and I have seen it seldom
> I know that it is bound in the steel necessity
> Of its own girders Time to one end willing
> Time which is patience of man and hope of birth.
> (CP 72)

Whereas, prior to the Great War, the Eiffel Tower had appeared to artists as the veritable embodiment of the revolutionary, liberatory powers of modern technology, in Devlin's dream narrative it comes increasingly to represent a 'steel necessity' that does not admit of radical change:

My tower strong swimmer breasts the clouds
Warning me that fruits only follow
Skies anxious with rain and dreary furrows
(CP 75)

'Let BABEUF fade', he says, exhorting the tower's 'Mounting resolution of awry steel' to be his 'exemplar of the hero', 'Who grasps his strength with bolts, obeys and only seems to sway / When the bad weathers drive' (CP 77–8). The poem's intense engagement with social injustice, a lifelong preoccupation of Devlin, thus shrinks from advocating the insurgency with which the poem nevertheless remains fixated: 'The lidded anger of the oppressed / Stutters through chinks; and may it detonate!' (CP 72). The text's appropriation of Surrealist devices and deployment of a Futurist icon are in fruitful tension with its resistance to the appeal of convulsive insurrection that bewitched the avant-garde, both before and after the First World War.

First drafted during Devlin's sojourn in Paris, 'Bacchanal' also engages in a highly mediated fashion with the political climate of the early to mid-1930s, its evocation of extreme exertion, in Thomas Dillon Redshaw's words, 'melt[ing] into militarism':[23]

The blood beats drums in the runners' temples, the news is safe as a yacht in a cove
And hearts, throbbing squadrons of nocturnal seaplanes, moving stars above
Stars fixed in the sea, it will be fine, the ground is cleared, material stored,
With fervid violence Come forerunners release the news at this anxious port.
Red trains lap up the licking rails, east the horizon snarls alarms
Relief from the wheatfields, printing presses toss their tresses with steel arms
Come up! Up up! The thunder at one with your voices in order chants things
Are with you, rolling her rump Earth in bacchantic rumbas grave swings,
Multiple antennae of blind gunnery tremble, invest the fibrous night
And the armies' crystal shock makes laughter of girls in a forest pool out of sight.
(CP 66–7)

Randall Jarrell, reviewing Devlin's 1946 collection, *Lough Derg and Other Poems* (in which 'Bacchanal' was reprinted), rather surprisingly heard in these lines the accents of Louis MacNeice.[24] In reply, Coffey has pointed out that the first version of 'Bacchanal' was written in 1931–3, when 'MacNeice was an unknown name so far as Devlin was concerned'.[25] Be that as it may, the poem was revised and expanded before its final publication in 1937, by which date Devlin could hardly have been unaware of MacNeice's work. To my mind, our understanding of the poem is enriched by recognising the very different approach it takes to events in the years in which it was composed from the stance *vis-à-vis* contemporary history adopted by MacNeice and other *engagé* British and Irish poets of the 1930s, whatever Devlin's knowledge of their work at the beginning of the decade.

unpolitical x Spender

A sense of the difference between Devlin and these poets can be gleaned from Stephen Spender's antipathetic review of *Intercessions*, which he saw as suffering 'from that enormous inflation of purely verbal values which one associates with American writers in the magazine *transition*'.[26] Indeed, although none of the poems collected in this volume had appeared in the pages of Eugene Jolas's journal, Devlin contributed to *transition* the year before the publication of *Intercessions*.[27] Spender's interpretation of *transition* as a platform for literary navel-gazing, however invalid, is inseparable from his reflections in the same review on the problems of writing in an age which 'has created no style'. Devlin's poetry, and the verbal pyrotechnics of *transition*, are indicative of a literary period in which 'Instead of a common style, what we have is a series of experiments, the best of them brilliant and exciting, the worst lazy and unobservant' – the former a poetry of pylons, perhaps, as opposed to a poetry of the Eiffel Tower. Spender goes on from this observation to the hope that 'a vigorous and energetic school of poetry' may develop out of 'the working class writers who, if they are without technical knowledge, at least have the inestimable boon of having something to write about other than their own personalities so lacking in significant experience'.[28] These patronising speculations silently condemn their (socially advantaged) author's own poetry to the status of merely another addition to the lengthening 'series of experiments'. Moreover, Spender's fond hope, like others', for a 'school of poetry' of social and political relevance – whether rooted in the proletariat or not – would shortly come to grief in the crisis for 'committed' literature precipitated by the Munich agreement of 1938. After that event, many of Spender's contemporaries, most memorably W. H. Auden and MacNeice, busied themselves in confessing the *irrelevance* of their poetry to the world outside, in Auden's phrase, 'the valley of its making'.[29] MacNeice's *Autumn Journal* (1939) is the period's most achieved instance of this disclosure, the sequence 'setting the seal', as Peter McDonald argues, 'on a period of literary contact with the "political" which does not just admit failure, but rather *insists* upon its failure in certain respects'.[30] The stormclouds were also gathering over the continental avant-garde: the year before *Intercessions* was published witnessed the opening of the *Entarte Kunst Ausstellung* (Degenerate Art Exhibition) in Munich, an event which publicly demonstrated Goebbels's and the Nazis' antimodernist (and anti-Semitic) cultural programme (simultaneously, 16,000 modernist artworks were removed from the state's galleries).[31]

'Bacchanal' registers the political climate of the 1930s as much as any poem by Auden, MacNeice or Spender, and quietly confirms, in its own distinctive manner, the disparity between the poetic and the revolutionary act. As Redshaw notes, the years during which it was composed and revised 'saw the rise of Nazism, the bombing of Guernica during the Spanish civil war, the appearance of Haile Selassie before the League of Nations, and the Berlin Olympiad of 1936'.[32] Indeed, the poem's 'topicality' prompted MacGreevy – to whom Devlin had sent the poem for his opinion – to advise against publishing the poem, given Devlin's sensitive position within the Department of External Affairs, which he had joined in 1935.[33] Where Devlin's representation of this turbulent period differs most obviously from that of his contemporaries in Britain is in his text's powerful co-option of Futurist and Surrealist devices. There is a singular lack of documentary realism or attention to specific, extra-textual events in the poem:

> Forerunners with knees flashing like scissors raced by the hostile
> telegraph wires,
> Start for the ships with the news, Cut Through, all is against them
> despair inspires:
> The poor made limp by want and cackling brainstopped youth,
> a seaweed crowd . . .
> How the road that smokes through the mountains, whose
> pantherbounding shadows applaud, is loud
> With the confident feet of pursuing criers, their eyes diamond with
> thousands of years
> Of domination and lands held of fictitious papers by right of fears
> Easy on which to maintain the sneering feet of the lovely lords of might,
> They and the courtiers of prudence insured against danger of life
> and number and light.
> (*CP* 64; Devlin's ellipsis)

Notwithstanding the presence of these devices it would be overhasty to see in the stylistic resemblances between 'Bacchanal' and the avant-garde a deeper politicisation of form. True, on a superficial reading 'Bacchanal' seems to echo Walter Benjamin's famous dictum that Surrealism's project is 'To win the energies of intoxication for the revolution'.[34] (Especially in such a disorientating image as 'the sneering feet of the lovely lords of might'.) Yet 'Bacchanal' does not turn language against language by self-critically addressing the autonomous nature of art: its revolution of the word is confined to its (successful) appropriation of avant-garde techniques, rather than being in the service of a programmatic attempt to rethink radically the production and reception of the artwork within society (as was the Surrealists' intention). A fine example of the latter demand is to be found in the collective Language Events of the Surrealists, in which the participants, seated at a table, write 'a clause beginning with "if" or "when", and, on a separate sheet of paper, an independent clause in the conditional or future mood, unrelated to the preceding'. The resulting sentences are arbitrarily conjoined to read, for example:

If tigers should prove grateful to us
sharks would volunteer to be used as canoes.
(*Elsie Péret, Suzanne Muzard*)

Or:

When a statue is erected to the association of ideas
the angel of the bizarre will invent the art of billiards
(*Pierre Unik, Louis Aragon*)[35]

The revolutionary nature of such experiments has, clearly enough, little to do with their individual content – indeed, the above exercises can hardly be said to have a determinate or meaningful content at all. They are 'events', unpredictable and indeterminate in their effects, which attempt to undermine the received notion of the artist as an individual whose praxis stands apart from other areas of life, by throwing into question art as an institution removed from intersubjective experience (hence, in the present examples, the use of collective composition). With such 'events' in mind, Bürger rightly insists that the content of the avant-garde work is largely irrelevant to its political function:

> When the avant-gardistes demand that art become practical once again, they do not mean that the contents of works of art should be socially significant. The demand is not raised at the level of the contents of individual works. Rather, it directs itself to the way art functions in society, a process that does as much to determine the effect that works have as does the particular content.

The avant-garde thus concurs with the high modernist and aestheticist rejection of the means-end rationality of bourgeois society; where it diverges from high modernism is in its aspiration to go beyond this rejection and 'attempt to organize a new life praxis from a basis in art'.[36] In contrast, as Coffey recalls, Devlin deployed 'so-called surrealist techniques for the purpose of enhancing the texture of his poems. He did not attempt, at any time, the *surrealist life*, Tzara's automatic poetry-activity-of-the-psyche.'[37] The divergence between 'Bacchanal' and, for instance, Tzara's Dadaist and later, Surrealist work is apparent in Devlin's depiction of revolution:

The wind thrusts knives in their teeth, harrows the stubble of parched throats
The front line licks its fire, leaderless, can they cut their way to the boats?
They have never eaten nor drunk nor slept their fill, and have no quick-wit means,
Only envy learnt in feeding the shutfist pistoned right machines.
Canaille, canaille, what red horizons of anger for humbled lives lie
Tumbled up in the old times, the long-fermenting now, canaille!
Tradition if wanted, you can taunt with bequeathed pain, unslaked hate,
For neither the slow-travelling signal from the pyramid builders comes too late,
In spite of imposed ignorance, No, nor intelligence from a brave new State.
(*CP* 64–5)

The third-person pronoun of these lines announces the speaker's distance from the events that he narrates, one reinforced by the poem's change of title prior to first publication, through which its 'News of Revolution' assumes an orgiastic quality.[38] Likewise, while the poem's emphasis on the oppressiveness of the past ('Tradition' with its bequest of 'pain' reaches back to 'the pyramid builders') sounds a distinctly Futurist note, any easy optimism in a 'brave new State' is countered by the 'envy', 'unslaked hate' and 'imposed ignorance' propelling the rebels against the old order. As a consequence, the poem's bacchants are distanced in a fashion that stands in marked contrast to the self-absorbed quality of Tzara's reflections, in the *Dada Manifesto 1918*, on the anarchic celebrants of Dada: 'Drunk with energy, we are revenants thrusting the trident into heedless flesh.'[39] Mays gets the curiously measured tone of this seemingly frenetic poem exactly right when he comments that 'It is about those who work for revolution, from the outside, and it contains a dimension of pathos as well as hope' (*CP* 30). Such 'pathos', perhaps, was only available to a poet whose own nation – a 'brave new [Free] State' – had in the recent past emerged out of not only revolution but also civil war.

The problematics of Devlin's poetry, in short, differ from both those of a number of 'committed' poets of the 1930s (including the sceptical MacNeice) and those of the continental avant-garde, regardless of Devlin's obvious delight in the latter's heady mannerisms. His poetic, as Coffey's remarks quoted above suggest, is permeated by the high modernist conception of the artist as an artisan or maker, and is informed by a keen sense of the division between the spheres of art and the praxis of life that the avant-garde dramatically sought to erase. It is possible to see in Devlin's resistance to the avant-garde's noisy hankering for a new totality of life and art an oblique reflection of the economic base to Irish culture between the wars. Terry Eagleton has argued that, 'If there is a high modernism in Ireland, there is little or no avant-garde – little of that iconoclastic experiment which seeks to revolutionize the very conception and institution of art itself, along with its relations to political society'[40] – a fact which Eagleton explains as due to the relative paucity of technology in Ireland's rural-based economy: without the omnipresence of the machine there is no need to react against or to celebrate the technological, and Futurism, for example, can find no purchase on such a social formation.

Devlin's poem 'Daphne Stillorgan' beautifully evokes an industrially stagnant Free State in its hyperbolic account of the disturbance caused by a train's arrival at the 'modest station set in the glen' at Stillorgan, a Dublin suburb which still preserved something of its original village character in the 1930s:

Fuchsias revive and breathe through scarlet mouths
Rumours on wind:
Far-off the humid pounding of a train
Wind-cylinders boom along
Steel wires, the rails drone
Far-off thudding, trampling, thud
Of thousand pink-soled apes, no humorous family god
Southward a storm
Smashes the flimsy sky.
(CP 61–2)

The train's arrival in these lines strongly recalls a key moment in Hawthorne's *American Notebooks* in which, seated in Sleepy Hollow, Hawthorne hears 'the whistle of the locomotive – the long shriek, harsh, above all other harshness, for the space of a mile cannot mollify it into harmony[–] . . . bring[ing] the noisy world into the midst of our slumbrous peace'.[41] In both instances, the rending sound of the approaching train tears asunder a version of pastoral, be that Hawthorne's 'beautiful diversity of green' or Devlin's more obviously eroticised (and mildly Surrealist) 'trees' green bazaar and patches / Of light like muslin girls in forest lost'. Leo Marx's celebrated study of technology and pastoralism in American literature, *The Machine in the Garden*, takes Hawthorne's account as emblematic of the American variant of an archetypal clash 'between two worlds, one identified with rural peace and simplicity, the other with urban power and sophistication':

> Most important is the sense of the machine as a sudden, shocking intruder upon a fantasy of idyllic satisfaction. It invariably is associated with crude, masculine aggressiveness in contrast with the tender, feminine, and submissive attitudes traditionally attached to the landscape.[42]

In conjoining Stillorgan and Daphne (a nymph from the ur-pastoral ideal, Arcadia), Devlin's poem implicitly identifies the train with Apollo, whose amorous pursuit of the nymph was forestalled by her fortunate metamorphosis into a laurel tree. To this extent, Devlin's poem is richly informed by the element of sexual aggression that Marx locates in this recurrent trope. However, the locomotive's ravishing of pastoralism in Hawthorne's notebook has more in common with the symbolic railway's progress in Dickens's *Dombey and Son*, the roaring, shrieking engines of which articulate the text's confused response towards burgeoning industrialism in Britain, than with Devlin's classically allusive commuter-line. While Hawthorne's and Dickens's texts register in their distinct fashions the rapidly increasing centrality of technology to their respective authors' societies in the mid-nineteenth century, Devlin's poem deprives technology in early 1930s Ireland of any genuine feeling of threat – through both the extravagance of his mythic conceit ('Is the menace

bestial or a brusque pleiad / Of gods of fire vagabond?') and the amusingly
Surrealist inflections of many of his images (as in the likening of the train's
rapid approach to the 'thud / Of thousand pink-soled apes'). It is not that
the railway was an insignificant feature of Irish life before and after inde-
pendence, but that, as an image, Devlin's train lacks the freight of historical
meaning – the rapid social changes brought about by technology – it
clearly bears in Hawthorne and Dickens. In this regard, Devlin's poem,
notwithstanding its ludic dimension, refracts the relatively impoverished
technological condition of Ireland at this time. As J. J. Lee observes:

> Irish society remained technologically under-developed in the century after
> 1850, despite the early, extensive and rapid diffusion of the railway, and
> despite the fact that daily life was shaped by technological developments in
> numerous ways. These developments were experienced largely at individual
> consumer level, however, rather than at mass production level. Technology,
> from the coming of electric light to television, was something that happened
> from outside, and to which one contributed little beyond consuming its
> products.[43]

If the high modernism of the literary revival found in Ireland's
technological backwardness a last bastion against the 'filthy modern tide'
of which Yeats, late in his life, speaks in 'The Statues',[44] the European
avant-garde is supervenient, at least in part, on a developed or developing
industrial base. In this regard, it is not without relevance that the myth
informing 'Daphne Stillorgan' has a literary resonance, involving a god
associated with poetry and music and a nymph's transformation into a
traditional emblem of poetic distinction. There is something almost
parabolic in the Futurist dynamism of the poem's Apollonian train, which
thunders inconsequentially, if energetically, through the Irish station.

Of course, it would be over-reductive to take Devlin's qualified avant-
gardism as simply the mediated cultural product of southern Ireland's
relative dearth of industrialism. Devlin's poetic modernism evinces none
of the revival's antiquarian fascination with the peasantry of the West
and appropriation of myth and other Gaelic materials, and appears
untouched by the attractions of a Saturnalian, pre-industrial past. Devlin's
distance from the avant-garde owes less to Yeats and the revival, and more
to the examples of Eliot and Pound, in whom, as Mervyn Wall recollected,
Devlin was equally immersed during his reading of the Surrealists.
Devlin's 'The Statue and the Perturbed Burghers' illustrates the extent to
which his poetry registers, in an aestheticist as opposed to an avant-garde
fashion, a wrenching division between art and the praxis of life. Though
not 'Poundian' in any obvious manner, the poem quietly reiterates Pound's
exasperation with the commodification of art,[45] with the burghers of the
poem's title exemplifying a bourgeois understanding of art as constituting
a sphere largely separate from their lived experience as a whole:

> They have stayed this fluttering boy in tight marble
> For a fresh similitude
> Of their rare immersion in stillness
> (CP 54)

Art, for the burghers, grants a 'similitude' of satisfaction largely absent from their lives. It functions in an escapist fashion, providing a faint intimation of a life in which – in the words of the later poem 'From Government Buildings' – 'want and have are equal' (CP 137). For the burghers are 'People of worth and wealth / Glancing with care at their modes of life', and art offers them the promise of a 'stillness' of being that, the poem strongly implies, is missing from their daily lives. In the face of such an audience, Devlin's poem quietly reiterates Tzara's dismissive question, 'Do we make art in order to earn money and keep the dear bourgeoisie happy?'[46] Giving an answer in the negative, Devlin's poem nonetheless does not repeat the avant-garde injunction that art reintegrate with the burghers' lives by overcoming its autonomous condition and reinvesting itself in other areas of their existence. (Characteristically, Tzara asks of 'Every page' that it 'explode'.) Rather, the speaker demands that the artwork preserve its autonomy, thus granting an aesthetic experience distinct from 'their modes of life', and in so doing pass judgement on the world of solid respectability represented by the burghers:

> My watch ticks as loud as a sledgehammer in an empty street
> Muffle the panting hours my fountain, disdain them
> Boy with the beaked chin

The statue is invited to 'disdain' a bourgeois conception of art as a temporary, imaginative release from the workaday world's 'panting hours'. Mays adroitly identifies the irony of the poem's title, as 'the burghers, you come to realize, are not perturbed and that is what is cause for perturbation. It is the poet who is perturbed by the coincidence of art with burgherly values' (CP 35). As Mays further notes, the poem's discussion of the relationship between 'art [and] morality' bears comparison with Wallace Stevens's roughly contemporaneous sequence, Owl's Clover (1936). The first section of Stevens's poem, 'The Old Woman and the Statue', opens by sketching a scene remarkably close to that of 'The Statue and the Perturbed Burghers: 'Another evening in another park, / A group of marble horses rose on wings / In the midst of a circle of trees'. Against this symbol of art Stevens juxtaposes the old woman, emblematic of the 'poverty' – in Stevens's extended sense of that term – of reality, be that imaginative deprivation or the social effects of the economic depression of the 1930s: 'She was that tortured one, / So destitute that nothing but herself / Remained'.[47] Art's function in relation to the old woman's destitution, and, by extension, to political justice per se, is developed at length in the poem's second section, 'Mr Burnshaw and the Statue'. In his bracing review of Stevens's *Ideas of Order* for the leftist journal the *New Masses*, Stanley Burnshaw had chastised Stevens for refusing, as Burnshaw saw it, to acknowledge the often distressing historical realities of the 1930s, in America and elsewhere. In response, Stevens chose to depict Burnshaw, not altogether fairly, as advocating a crudely socially committed art, one which will inaugurate 'A time in which the poets' politics / Will rule in a poets' world'. For Stevens, such an aesthetic is a denial of art's necessarily autonomous condition, positing 'A world impossible for poets'. Burnshaw's position, in Stevens's eyes, is inimical to art: it sees the statue as 'this gawky plaster', irrelevant to and abstracted from the exigencies of history:

> The stones
> That will replace it shall be carved, '*The Mass*
> *Appoints These Marbles Of Itself To Be*
> *Itself*'. No more than that, no subterfuge,
> No memorable muffing, bare and blunt.[48]

Stevens's agon with communism in *Owl's Clover* elicits from the poet a 'disdain' for committed literature compatible with Devlin's rejection of the consumerist sensibility of the bourgeoisie in 'The Statue and the Perturbed Burghers'. For both poets, art's 'memorable muffing' is perceived as irreducible to a purpose, whether that be radical or simply ameliorative. Theirs is a high modernism given its most eloquent critical formulation by Adorno, as in the famous dialectical formulations of his essay 'Commitment':

> Literature that exists for the human being, like committed literature but also like the kind of literature the moral philistine wants, betrays the human being by betraying what could help him only if it did not act as though it were doing so. But anything that made itself absolute in response, existing only for its own sake, would degenerate into ideology. Art cannot jump over the shadow of irrationality: the fact that art, which is a moment in society even in opposing it, must close its eyes and ears to society. But when art itself appeals to this and arbitrarily restricts thought in accordance with art's contingent nature, making this its raison d'être, it fraudulently turns the curse it labors under into its theodicy.[49]

Stevens's poetry, more so than Devlin's one feels, runs the risk of transforming art's 'curse' into the 'theodicy' of the supreme fiction. Indeed, Burnshaw's objections to *Ideas of Order* clearly touched a raw nerve in Stevens, as the defensive quality of 'Mr Burnshaw and the Statue' confirms. Be that as it may, Devlin's poem's repudiation of its burghers' values is a far cry from an espousal of the committed art promoted by certain of his contemporaries in Britain and the United States.

Devlin's interest in the experimental poetry of André Spire, whose work had been introduced to American readers in Burnshaw's 1933 study, *André Spire and His Poetry*, is worth adducing in this context. Alan Filreis has drawn attention to the manner in which Spire's poetry's occasional similarity to the 'so-called proletarian portraits' of William Carlos Williams and other Objectivists left it open to the charge, from a section of the American left, of superficial attentiveness to the 'externalities' of quotidian existence. Such 'portraits', it was charged, constituted little more than a gauche and sentimental depiction of the vicissitudes of contemporary life, when what was needed from literature was an *exposé* of the political and social causes for such misery.[50] For Devlin and Burnshaw, albeit for different reasons, such a reproach misses the mark. In Burnshaw's case, there is simply no disjunction between radical politics and formal innovation, as Spires's poetry demonstrates;[51] in Devlin's, as the poems in *Intercessions* suggest, the being of art is not readily harnessed to political ends. The decidedly *non*-committed close to 'The Statue and the Perturbed Burghers' equally avoids the assault on the institutional view of art advocated by the continental avant-garde. Instead, the poem concludes with a commitment *to* art in its institutional sense, yet an art both arrogantly and uneasily indifferent to the values of a degraded bourgeois sensibility. A 'silk music' is heard 'From the hollow of scented shutters':

> Crimson and blind
> As though it were my sister
> Fireflies on the rosewood
> Spinet playing
> With barely escaping voice
> With arched fastidious wrists to be so gentle.

That final line's mannered syntax beautifully matches its 'arched' imagery, both reinforcing the text's aesthetic implications. This, we feel, is no Suzanne Muzard at the keyboard, no avant-gardist seeking to wrest art away from its bourgeois consumers and return it to a basis in daily life. Devlin's spinet-player – who, as his imagined 'sister', embodies an aesthetic presumably 'related' to that of the speaker himself – is rather a striking image of the high modernist artist and her predicament within a world of burgherly mores. The poem thus self-reflexively considers its own social purposeless, but, unlike the avant-garde work, this does not lead to a self-criticism of its own isolated ineffectuality. The solitary spinet-player's plight, fingering behind her shutters, is simply the artistic condition.

That said, Devlin's poetry does not accept its autonomous condition by, in Adorno's words, 'making this its raison d'être'. On the contrary, it is a poetry fully aware of its inconsequentiality in the face of the all too apparent injustices of the 1930s. Devlin's ambivalence towards the kind

of modernist poetics with which *Intercessions* nevertheless aligns itself
is evident from an unpublished poem of the period, 'Statement of an
Irishman', which makes clear the attractions of committed art in this
decade for Devlin as for many of his contemporaries. The poem's initial
theme is the Irish poet's relationship to his divided linguistic and literary
inheritance, that problematic bequest Thomas Kinsella has labelled 'the
dual tradition':

> The language of my race does not excite me
> Like others to archaic cries of pride.
> I don't care about it.
>
> As for the language of those that did evil
> For centuries to my people:
> It was made by one poet and is not free
> But is imprisoned and he and all that speak it
> In circles of contented or querulous feeling.
> I don't care about it.[52]

The coolness of Devlin's attitude towards an issue that has vexed many
Irish poets who write in English is, on the face of it, surprising. If
the speaker's rejection of Irish consorts ill with Devlin's and Niall
Montgomery's joint project of translating a number of modern French
poems into Irish, some of the results of which appeared in *Ireland Today*
in 1937, then his equally dismissive judgement on the English language
seems to fly in the face of the very medium in which the statement, in
line with the majority of Devlin's poems, is made.[53] The poem's
continuation reveals, however, that it is the reification of a particular
language, as in, say, some of the more extreme pronouncements of the
Irish Ireland movement, that is its chief target:

> I don't care for any language,
> Except with any and every language armed
> To strike them down, the company of the evil heart.
>
> Afterwards, complaint stilled, gesture
> Will suffice for the little necessary pure expression.

The argument of these lines, perhaps responsible in part for the poem
not reaching a version Devlin felt fit for publication, advocates an admir-
able, albeit woolly, commitment to justice that is indifferent to aesthetic
ends. The purpose of language is to have a purpose. What this leaves out
of consideration, however, is the 'apartness from life' of art, which, in the
poem's last two lines, is portrayed as a 'gesture' secondary to the imperative
demand to strike down the 'the company of the evil heart'. The centrality
of this 'gesture' to Devlin's sensibility is quietly registered in the counter-
pressure exerted by the word 'necessary' in the deprecations of the

phrase, 'little necessary pure expression'. Such a necessary gesture is made by the spinet-player's 'arched fastidious wrists' in 'The Statue and the Perturbed Burghers', and by the poem and collection in which she figures.

Nevertheless, the finally unresolved deliberations, if not the unachieved quality, of 'Statement of an Irishman' are present throughout *Intercessions*, as is attested to by the volume's 'Argument with Justice':

> Beautiful named because from time abstract and therefore sacrosanct?
>   Ah, what good if the
> Cunning have bandaged thee thus with eternity, turned thee lodestar
>   blandishing them and the
> Innocent in the ignorant ruin of
> Kingdoms and fevered republics babbling dry-lipped
> Beneath thy blind silence?
> (*CP* 89)

Devlin's appeal on behalf of those who inhabit 'the ignorant ruin' silently indicts the very poem in which it is expressed: the modernist artwork, after all, is small beer to those 'babbling dry-lipped' for justice. Devlin's poetry is preoccupied with this quintessentially 1930s dilemma in a way that Beckett, in his writings of this period, is seemingly not. Reviewing *Intercessions* in *transition* in 1938, Beckett took umbrage at the dismissive notice of the collection in the *Times Literary Supplement*, which found only 'lines here and there which rise above the gulf of tangid [*sic*] incoherence, but not enough of them to form a bridge between the poet and the reader'.[54] For Beckett the notion of a 'bridge' between poet and audience is of secondary importance beside the fundamental 'need' that drives poetic expression. In line with his earlier reflections on a 'rupture of the lines of communication' in 'Recent Irish Poetry', Beckett argues that art is 'pure interrogation, rhetorical question less the rhetoric – whatever else it may have been obliged by the "social reality" to appear, but never more freely so than now, when social reality . . . has severed the connexion'. *Intercessions*, according to Beckett, is of 'the art that condenses as inverted spiral of need', as opposed to that in which a 'solution [is] clapped on problem like a snuffer on a candle, the great crossword public on all its planes'.[55] Interestingly, Beckett's review perceives no such 'inverted spiral' in 'Argument with Justice', a poem which Devlin himself considered significant enough to reprint in *Lough Derg and Other Poems*. On an epistemological level, Devlin shares with Beckett the sense of a 'rupture' between subject and object, one consequence of which, for both writers, is a problematising of the 'connexion' between art and 'social reality'. Nevertheless, as Mays comments, if for Beckett 'the acutely problematic relation between self and non-self was cause for despair', for Devlin 'it was a relation to be worked through' (*CP* 43). Part of that working through is the poetry's recurrent preoccupation with social injustice, towards which its autonomous condition deprives it of any snuffer-like solutions. Indeed, the very title of Devlin's 1937 volume suggests the extent to which the poems are attempts to intercede, to mediate, in some unspecified form on behalf of the self and others.

MacGreevy's review of *Intercessions* and *Echo's Bones and Other Precipitates* for *Ireland Today* also draws a sharp distinction between Devlin and Beckett, though MacGreevy's interest in the relationship between self and non-self in their respective collections is informed more by existential and metaphysical preoccupations than by the issue of the social dimension to art:

> Where Mr Beckett gathers all his forces into single precise statements . . . Mr Devlin is all evocation. . . . The one eliminates, the other accumulates. Mr Beckett is cloistered within himself. He is a poet of the cloistered self on whom experience is an intrusion. Sometimes his poetry has the temper of *The Imitation*. . . . If there be a work of religious literature that Mr Devlin's work recalls, it is surely the *Fioretti*. He has something of the riotous poetry-making quality of Francis. He sees poetry everywhere and identifies himself poetically with all the phenomena about him.[56]

MacGreevy's Franciscan Devlin is a poet of *jouissance*, that near-sexual bliss afforded by literary language which Barthes, praising Severo Sarduy's *Cobra*, calls 'a kind of Franciscanism', which 'invites all words to perch, to flock, to fly off again', the plethora of playful signifiers shaping 'a marbled, iridescent text'.[57] A comparison of Beckett's 'The Vulture', the opening poem in *Echo's Bones*, and Devlin's 'Death and Her Beasts, Ignoble Beasts' simultaneously supports and qualifies MacGreevy's interpretation of Devlin. Beckett's scavenger is portrayed

> dragging his hunger through the sky
> of my skull shell of sky and earth
>
> stooping to the prone who must
> soon take up their life and walk
>
> mocked by a tissue that may not serve
> till hunger earth and sky be offal[58]

Both the precision and tendency towards elimination that MacGreevy sees as characteristic of Beckett's poetic procedure inform this poem's dense, mordant conceit: the poet's relationship with his *materia poetica* rendered comparable to that between a vulture and the carcass it worries.[59] The speaker's solipsism, a parodic Cartesianism in which the self is imprisoned in the 'skull', splits consciousness from the world in which it exists, producing a persona, 'a poet of the cloistered self', whom MacGreevy finds representative of *Echo's Bones* as a whole.

In Devlin's 'Death and Her Beasts, Ignoble Beasts', by way of contrast, the same imagery of feeding vultures betokens not the alienated or 'cloistered self', but the non-self. They are 'death's vultures', tempting the speaker to self-dissolution:

> The dried pus of vultures drags the horizon
> The noble beasts retired, their turn now, dried
> Mouths of my fears are death's vultures craving saliva:
> They would feed sick life on the smashed mouths of the weak
> Whose nostrils death has plugged with stale love-smells
> And suicide charms with racked face in a wall of marble,
> Their eyes decharged have numbness that looks like peace.
>
> Smeller-out of strangers! curious Death
> Your noble beasts were not fearful for they
> The emerald bergs of doom, Cybele and the drums,
> Startled my stupor into spite at least
> (CP 49)

While Devlin's imagery is as repellent as Beckett's, it works in different ways and to different ends. As MacGreevy points out, Devlin's poetry 'accumulates' rather than 'eliminates', the vultures' accruing significance over a stanza and a half through extravagant imagery and the speaker's increasingly ejaculatory tone. Consider, for instance, the Surrealist quality of the poem's first line, which defamiliarises the actions of the vultures by its bold suggestion that it is their 'dried pus', rather than the birds themselves, that 'drags the horizon'. The text's proliferation of signifiers, its Barthesian iridescence, constitutes precisely that Franciscanism of which MacGreevy speaks, regardless of the inappropriateness of vultures to the bird-loving saint. It is a cumulative as opposed to a minimalist poetic procedure that will yield its finest fruits in *The Heavenly Foreigner*, the baroque opulence of which stands in marked antithesis to the increasingly spartan style of Beckett's post-war work.

MacGreevy is wrong, I feel, to see in this aspect of Devlin's poetry a near-Keatsian capacity to identify 'himself poetically with all the phenomena about him'. The relationship between self and non-self is more troubled in Devlin than this remark suggests. The subject in Devlin is phenomenologically imbricated in the object-world in which it finds itself pitched, and in this respect differs from Beckett's attenuated Cartesian self. On one level, it seeks to merge with the natural world, as evinced by the glancing reference in 'Death and Her Beasts, Ignoble Beats' to Cybele, in which the speaker casts himself as a perverted Attis figure, initially enraptured by Death and her 'ignoble' vultures much as Attis emasculated himself in his worship of the great goddess of fertility, attended upon by her 'noble beasts' or lions.[60] On another level, however, the persona fears non-existence, vehemently suppressing his death-wish – 'There is none so much as you, none you, I think of. / / But I turn to Move' – by launching into violent, fruitless activity:

> Attack me in the dark, I'll extreme fear
> With the first of all landscapes given its eyes
> In the frantic group of naked man and horse;
> With the cheering of shredded men in lost forts
> And to go on with, the length of to-day and to-morrow,
> The evidence that lifting needles make the cloth.
> (*CP* 50)

Anne Fogarty has drawn attention to the 'precarious balance' of this conclusion. The poem abruptly yaws from its abject worship of death to what is little short of an adolescent fantasy of masculine prowess coupled to a now safely domesticated vision of femininity: 'The merging of feminine powers of creativity with masculine bravado permits a momentary laying of the feelings of terror which haunted the poem.'[61] But the existentially 'thrown' subject of the poem can counter only partially the dreadful allure of death: if the association of femininity with needlework represents an attempt to allay, even master, a femininity previously conjoined to death, the poem leaves open the possibility that what is being sewn is his winding-sheet. Fogarty maintains that 'Victory of Samothrace', which immediately follows 'Death and Her Beasts, Ignoble Beasts' in *Intercessions*, is unable to sustain even this fragile equipoise:

> Our Lady of Victory!
>
> And your voice, which has the opulent contentment of a June stream, babbles
> And I feel with relief:
> Better in danger with a goddess than float safe like a barge on the sea:
> Fingers again at my throat
>
> Baptism by immersion in the numerous sea
>
> As the water closes over me, I look up while life keeps interest
> To see the impersonal gleam in your eyes
> And the soft ebb and flow of your breasts.
> (*CP* 52–3)

Fogarty writes: 'The tidal imagery in the final line, while it suggests the fusion of the heroic, creative artist with the natural rhythms of the world around him, also indicates that such balance and unity are impossible. The goddess remains other; her aloofness and distance highlight and give dimension to the male subject's needs and desires.'[62] In other words, and *contra* MacGreevy, poetic subjectivity in Devlin is defined by its alienation from the object-world, though, cruelly, it is in the desire to unite the self with the non-self that the poetic impulse has its origins, that unappeasable craving to write Beckett terms 'the need to need'. In this respect, the phenomenological dimension to Devlin's poetry shades into an agitated form of idealism:

> I will make another prayer
> Give me an object of art, a statuette of Diana: I will caress
>   her limbs closely with my fingers
>
> For these graces, spirit of movement, I will build you an altar,
>   to be destroyed immediately,
> And make offering of promise
> Of heroes once again
> Of women's eyes before love has drowned their sweetness.

The subject's fetishisation of the art-object derives from its status as a substitute for the goddess, the full possession of whom can come only with death: his Prufrockian vision of a 'Baptism by immersion' is, in the end, indistinguishable from a Death by Water. Yet, as a stand-in, the artwork is inevitably lacking, and hence the speaker's urgent assertion that he will destroy the very altar he intends to raise to Nike. Such is the conundrum confronting Devlin's personae. Driven by the need to restore the, in Beckett's words, 'lines of communication' between self and non-self, his poetry is posited on the very 'rupture' it seeks to overcome. The Franciscan exuberance of *Intercessions* is ultimately less an exhibition of Barthesian *jouissance* than an expression of desire, an anxious, because foredoomed, attempt to pin the sign to a referent that wriggles free from the poet's conceptual grasp. To this extent Devlin and Beckett share the belief memorably stated in the latter's 'German Letter of 1937', written to Axel Kaun: 'As we cannot eliminate language all at once, we should at least leave nothing undone that might contribute to its falling into disrepute. To bore one hole after another in it, until what lurks behind it – be it something or nothing – begins to seep through'.[63]

'Est Prodest', a poem which Beckett praised in 'Recent Irish Poetry', constitutes Devlin's most sustained attempt during this period to work on language as with an awl. The poem, central to the religious side to Devlin's poetry, works towards an awareness of a divine 'something or nothing' that, as a prose plan of the poem indicates, lies beyond the compass of rational thought:

Affected by the Oneness of the Sun we believe him Personal, Causative, Unique. But experience shows him as broken among us his mirrors, waves. Since he is broken how can he be? Hence reasoning, whence Reason, trying to prove what thought (example) invented and thought destroys.
(*HF* 39)

The poem's elaboration on these reflections posits a 'One' 'darkly . . . broken among us / In frosty slopes at hazard', like 'Sunlight on the frangent / Mirrors of the sea':

> Phrases twisted through other,
> Reasons reasons disproofs
> Phrases lying low
> Proving invalid that reason
> With which I prove its truth
> Identity obscured
> Like the reflections of
> One mirror in another,
> Reasons reasons disproofs.
> (CP 82–3)

Like 'Victory of Samothrace', 'Est Prodest' is on one level a meditation on representation. The manuscript plan makes clear that to conceive of God as 'One', that is 'Personal, Causative, Unique', is to be beguiled by a convenient image for God, the 'Oneness of the Sun'. The reality of the deity, as a consequence, is occluded by a metaphor: supplanted by a sign its 'Identity [is] obscured' by the very reflections which provide the only glimpse of the 'One' possible for the human individual. This is a dilemma forced upon Devlin by his conception of language as somehow interposing between subject and object, a view shared by Beckett in his 'German Letter' and by many other modernist writers. Furthermore, as each individual will have a specific experience of God, and the totality of those experiences is our sum knowledge of God, it would seem difficult to prove his independent existence above and beyond that of his devotees. While the poem's (and the prose's) distrust of rationality, which is shown to work remorselessly against a belief in God, is faintly reminiscent of the Surrealists' onslaught on reason, the very existence of a prose *plan* for the poem demonstrates the extent to which the speaker is caught on the rocks of the 'Reasons reasons disproofs' that obviate an adequate comprehension of God.

The prose manuscript suggests and then immediately discounts one possible response to this impasse: 'We try to escape from the anguish of the uncertainty of the mind by plunging into active love. But this is no relief because the image Love is ourselves reflected' (*HF* 39). In the words of the poem:

> Getting away with love
> Drylipped love that takes
> No action but battens
> On misery its guest its prey
> And if the pipes of my nerves
> Steam at high tension
> Is it then satisfaction?
> Alas, that One which loves me
> Is my bribe to imperfection,
> By the muffled brain invented,
> Is self-love in reflection.
> (CP 83)

The strategy advocated yet questioned in these lines will continue to haunt Devlin's work, reaching its apotheosis in the religious eroticism of *The Heavenly Foreigner*. Through the intercession of another, the poem suggests, an intimation of the deity (who, after all, is 'broken among us') may be gleaned. The danger of this form of worship is that once again it substitutes a sign – in this case, a lover – for that to which the sign refers. This, then, runs the risk of becoming a form of narcissism or 'self-love' as the lover's specificity plays second-fiddle to his or her function as a meta-phorical vehicle, 'By the muffled brain invented', for another's religious need. The solution finally adopted is, in the prose's words, '[to] be content with what we learn by looking at one another, reality be made by the connecting line between us, not by our reflection of the sun' (*HF* 39). In the poem this dispassionate pronouncement takes on a terrible urgency:

> Frightened antinomies!
> I have wiped example from mirrors
> My mirror's face and I
> Are like no god and me
> My death is my life's plumed gnomon
> As a bride's embrace cruciform
> Reckless antinomies
> Your asymptotic gasps
> Have no hold on me . . .
>
> O fillers in of gaps!
> Pure winged linking
> To that which reflects me
> The third from the twain distinct not
> Is love of me in action.
> (CP 85–6)

Daniel Murphy would have us believe that Devlin here challenges 'the tenets of transcendental idealism', the poem stressing instead 'the imme-diacy of the mind's perceptions of natural, physical, external forms: to crystallise the momentary contact of the self with a universe of concrete presences'.[64] It is true that, from this point on, the poem identifies the male deity with a 'Lord of delight and absence' who pervades the natural world, borne to the speaker by the 'Favouring wind', the sky 'his breath' (*CP* 86). Yet the notion of 'fillers in of gaps' is a somewhat desperate response to the 'Frightened antinomies' that have, up to this moment, beset the speaker. It is a frantic attempt to side-step the textualist dilemma in which the sign obtrudes between self and non-self, a view of language that inexorably leads to scepticism regarding our knowledge of the extra-linguistic, and which is arguably to be seen as modernism's twist on the epistemological implications of nineteenth-century idealism.[65]

Coffey has said that Devlin drew the title for 'Est Prodest' from Horace's *Ars Poetica*, Devlin paraphrasing Horace's requirement that poetry exists to be beneficial.[66] It is an allusion that adds to the ethical weight of the title of the collection as a whole, and bears upon its nego-tiation of the antinomies of the continental avant-garde and aestheticist modernism. In the last instance, it sides with the latter. But the Surrealist colours are dazzling, and blinded more than one contemporary critic. Reviewing *Intercessions* for *The Criterion*, George Every caustically wrote: 'Mr Devlin evidently wanted to write little poems about windtackers windjamming which might have been at least pleasant, but someone told him that he must be revolutionary and not criticize his unconscious, and so he left them in the raw and listened in to something called a com-munication from the Eiffel Tower which he could not quite make out.' Every's review had earlier praised Allen Tate's recent *Selected Poems*, linking it to the poetics of T. E. Hulme, Pound and Eliot, writers who 'conceived the modern classical poem as a possibility'. [67] It is of some interest that this reviewer saw Devlin's work as incompatible with that of these writers, and consequently as at variance with the kind of modernism advocated by the conservative quarterly, *The Criterion*, founded by Eliot in 1922. Michael H. Levenson sees *The Criterion* as the vehicle by means of which Eliot could achieve his aim of 'a *rapprochement* between modernist literature and traditional authority'. It signalled a definitive break with the 'severe anti-institutional assault' of the avant-garde, as in the Vorticism promoted by *Blast*, sponsoring instead a 'classicism' premised on an 'accommodation between artist and society, art and tradition'.[68] For Every, *Intercessions* is patently flawed by its author's naive adherence to the poetics and their political implications of the Parisian 'revolutionary' avant-garde, and thus at variance with the 'reservation' Hulme declares definitive of the classical poet in his seminal essay 'Romanticism and Classicism': 'The classical poet never forgets this finiteness, this limit of man. He remembers always that he is mixed up with earth.'

In the classical attitude you never seem to swing right along to the infinite
nothing. If you say an extravagant thing which does exceed the limits inside
which you know man to be fastened, yet there is always conveyed in some
way at the end an impression of yourself standing outside it, and not quite
believing it, or consciously putting it forward as a flourish.[69]

Hulme's words, ironically enough, describe well Devlin's 'reserve' with
regard to the avant-garde, though the Englishman's hope for a dry, crisp
verse is not fulfilled by the dizzying verbal high-jinks of *Intercessions*. It is
thus less of a surprise than it might at first appear that Devlin's second
collection, *Lough Derg and Other Poems*, was promoted by Tate and
Robert Penn Warren, and is marked by precisely that 'classicism' which
Every cannot discern in the contents of *Intercessions*. Coffey, in contrast
to Every, claims that, with *Lough Derg and Other Poems* and to a greater
degree with the last, post-1950 poems, 'Devlin shows as what he always
had been, a poet of classical temper'.[70] Yet this too is not wholly accurate.
The Surrealist elements of *Intercessions* continue to pervade Devlin's later
poetry, if in a less *outré* fashion, testifying to their enduring impact on
his poetic.

    In the light of the foregoing, I want to suggest that there is a crucial
continuity between Devlin's mildly Surrealist adventures of the 1930s and
his work from the early 1940s on, in which his poetry, while not
completely abandoning the Surrealist inflections of *Intercessions*, shows
an increasing conformity to some of the poetic principles laid down by
the American New Criticism.

3

'WITH MULLIONED EUROPE SHATTERED': *LOUGH DERG AND OTHER POEMS*

DEVLIN AND THE NEW CRITICISM

Devlin's career within the Department of External Affairs took him to the United States for the duration of the Second World War. In 1939 Devlin was appointed Consul at the Consulate General in New York; from 1940 to 1947 he was First Secretary to the Irish Legation in Washington. During those years Devlin met the influential poet-critics Allen Tate and Robert Penn Warren, both of whom responded warmly to his work. Warren, by the time he and Devlin met through the offices of Katherine Anne Porter, had already published 'Lough Derg', the title poem of Devlin's 1946 collection, in *The Southern Review*,[1] and both Americans were to introduce a *Selected Poems*, published after Devlin's death. The interest shown by Tate and Warren in Devlin's work indicates the extent to which his poetry accords with some of the central tenets of the American New Criticism.

Tate and Warren had developed their ideas on literature out of the work of John Crowe Ransom, who wrote out of a deep concern for the fate of culture within a neocapitalist American that was experiencing structural renewal under Roosevelt in the 1930s. Ransom's aesthetic beliefs were to dominate American literary theory from the mid-1930s through the 1940s, the influence of the New Criticism (the title of a 1941 work by Ransom) continuing in an almost naturalised fashion into the late 1950s. The offspring of the reactionary, aggressively anti-capitalist Agrarian movement, the New Criticism, in line with its forerunner, conceived art to be essential to a developed sensibility and knowledge of the world. Nevertheless, in contrast to Agrarianism's more radical demands, the New Criticism advocated, as John Fekete has noted, 'both knowing and living with the *established* reality through the contributions that the aesthetic sensibility can make'.[2] That is, the element of ideological critique central to the Agrarian movement has drained away in New Critical poetics to reveal a formalism as seemingly disinterested (in the Kantian sense) as that of the Russian Formalists. Gone is the Agrarians' vociferous challenge to science. In its place art is construed as a specific form of knowledge about the environment and the human's place therein: aesthetic experience grants its participant a different form of objective knowledge of the world from science because the epistemological reaches of art and science are discrete. The retreat from the values of Agrarianism is apparent in the extent to which, for the New Criticism, as Fekete cogently argues, 'the structure of alienated reality is accepted even at its surface as being permanently unchangeable. The project of humanising our concrete experience is ruled out; it is argued that we can humanise only our thought, symbolically, by way of "compensation".'[3] In this respect, New Criticism can be viewed as constituting the theoretical (and, eventually, pedagogical) canonisation, in the English-speaking world, of precisely those aspects of high modernism that stand opposed to the aspirations of the avant-garde. The autotelic nature or 'spatial form' of the modernist artefact, as construed by the New Critics, and as read out of and into the work of Eliot and others, is a conceptualisation of poetic form profoundly at odds with the European avant-garde's yoking of poetic to individual and political emancipation.

Tate's and Warren's Preface to their selection of Devlin's poems reveals the extent to which Devlin's poetry was seen to conform to New Critical dogma as developed from Ransom on. Tate and Warren single out for praise 'three great poems': 'The Passion of Christ' (dedicated to Tate), 'From Government Buildings', and 'Lough Derg', 'a poem', they write, 'that may rank with Stevens's "Sunday Morning", Eliot's "Gerontion", and Crane's "The Broken Tower".' These poems, the editors claim, place Devlin, not in the tradition of 'the Celtic Twilight', but as 'one of the pioneers of the international poetic English which now prevails on both sides of the Atlantic'.[4] The confidence of that final statement in the early sixties was not without some justification, though it is important to realise that it was a *critical* hegemony that prevailed, excluding any serious consideration of the divergent practices of many poets in the years succeeding high modernism. J. C. C. Mays has observed that Devlin's relative neglect (in Ireland and also in America after his modest success in later life and immediately following his death) finds a faint parallel in the initially desultory critical reception of writers such as Lorine Neidecker, George Oppen and Louis Zukofsky in the United States, whose work stemmed from the example of Pound's *Cantos* and the poetry of Williams, rather than from that of the canonical New Critical poets, Eliot, Stevens and Hart Crane (see *CP* 22–7). Yet, as the interest of Tate and Warren strongly implies, Devlin's work does not belong in the Pound–Williams modernist tradition as interpreted by a number of younger poets; that is, it is not assimilable to that which Marjorie Perloff has dubbed 'the poetics of indeterminacy'. For Perloff, there are two principal strands to modernist poetry: 'the Symbolist mode that Lowell inherited from Eliot and Baudelaire and, beyond them, from the great Romantic poets, and the "anti-Symbolist" mode of indeterminacy or "undecidability", of literalness and free play, whose first real exemplar was the Rimbaud of the *Illuminations*.'[5] In considering Devlin beside various 'anti-Symbolist' modernists, like Neidecker and Zukofsky (or Basil Bunting and Hugh MacDiarmid in Britain), one runs the risk – as Mays's argument acknowledges – of occluding the fact that Devlin's poetry is based on a poetics distinct from those held by the figures Perloff loosely groups together. After all, Devlin had a low opinion of Williams, portraying the American poet, in a review of *The Wedge*, as a writer 'who threw out all the literary luggage, [and] continues to stand peering, in a mixture of rage and uncertainty, over the threshold of poetry'.[6] Similarly, while Devlin greatly admired Rimbaud, *Intercessions* is only tangentially touched by the kind of 'undecidability' which permeates the Frenchman's work. In this respect, the collection is not as dissimilar to his subsequent poetry as it might appear to be on a cursory reading. (That Devlin chose to reprint several poems from *Intercessions* in *Lough Derg and Other Poems* suggests that he did not consider the latter collection a radical break with the former.) Neither phase of Devlin's poetic career is more than superficially a part of what John Ashbery (and, after him, Perloff) calls the 'The Other Tradition'.[7] As I argued earlier, Devlin's career, in its broad outlines, is not unlike that of Stevens, in that both poets' interest in the European avant-garde is limited to a willingness to experiment with Surrealist and other devices. Neither poet's oeuvre constitutes a radical interrogation of the role poetry plays in modern society.

Warren's acceptance of 'Lough Derg' for publication in the New Critical journal *The Southern Review* may well be due to the manner in which it establishes, in Perloff's words, 'a perfectly coherent symbolic structure'[8] comparable to that of meditative works by Eliot, Stevens and Crane. The setting of the poem, Saint Patrick's Purgatory, anchors the text in a powerfully evocative and symbolically resonant location.[9] Initially the object of the speaker's contempt –

> With mullioned Europe shattered, this Northwest,
> Rude-sainted isle would pray it whole again:
> (Peasant Apollo! Troy is worn to rest.) –
> (*CP* 132)

the empty rounds of the pilgrimage have, by the end of the poem, become an objective correlative, in Eliot's terminology,[10] of the speaker's despair in the face of a world marred by human injustice. The pilgrims, 'doughed in dogma', are

> No better nor worse than I who, in my books,
> Have angered at the stake with Bruno and, by the rope
> Watt Tyler swung from, leagued with shifty looks
> To fuse the next rebellion with the desperate
> Serfs in the sane need to eat and get
> (CP 134)

This transition from ironic disdain of to culpability in the pilgrims' plight is concluded by an ambivalence or tension in meaning that holds together, at the poem's close, both reactions in one simple, twice repeated phrase: 'and so, knelt on her sod, / This woman beside me murmuring *My God! My God!*' (CP 135). The richness of this ending resides in its fore-grounding of the chief, if unresolved, preoccupation of the poem's densely symbolic argument: the discrepancy the observer discerns between a human need to believe in divine justice and the palpable cruelty of a world in which prayer seemingly goes unheard. Having played off the splendours of Jerusalem before Christ – 'Where prayer was praise, O Lord! the Temple trumpets / Cascaded down Thy sunny pavilions of air' (CP 132) – the intellectual grandeur of Athens' Academy – whose 'tolerant wranglers / Could hear the contemplatives of the Tragic Choir / Drain off man's sanguine, pastoral death-desire' (CP 133) – and the religious passion of Celto-Romanesque Ireland – 'when monks in convents of coracles / For the Merovingian centuries left their land, / Belled, fragrant' (CP 134) – against the banal rounds of the contemporary penitents at Lough Derg, the speaker's arrogant despair finds itself tempered by a recognition of the humanity he shares with 'The poor in spirit on their rosary rounds' (CP 132). We are left with precisely the coherent, closed structure Perloff identifies in the poetry of Eliot and others: an autotelic construct of ambivalent, but not indeterminate, meaning that is the hallmark of the New Critical 'verbal icon'.

On a more localised level, it is worth briefly noting tonal resemblances between Devlin's poem and those canonical New Critical texts with which Tate and Warren chose to compare it. The poem's densely patterned conceits and regular form look back to the metaphysical wit and metrical regularity of Eliot's *Poems* (1920) (which includes 'Gerontion'), the source of much New Critical theory about the relation between the form and argument of the successful poem. Eliot's grim portrayal of Donne, in 'Whispers of Immortality' –

> He knew the anguish of the marrow
> The ague of the skeleton;
> No contact possible to flesh
> Allayed the fever of the bone. – [11]

imbues, and is countered by, Devlin's glancing celebration of Florentine art's powerful fusion of spiritual and physical love:

> man took to wearing his death, his own,
> Sapped crisis through cathedral branches (while
> Flesh groped loud round dissenting skeleton)
> In soul, reborn as body's appetite:
> Now languisht back in body's amber light,
>
> Now is consumed.
> (CP 134)

Moreover, the demise of the Renaissance's brief interfusion of soul and body – which 'Now is consumed' – is conveyed in language that has the accent of early Stevens in its combination of lushness and urbane generality: 'O earthly paradise! / Hell is to know our natural empire used / Wrong, by mind's moulting, brute divinities' (CP 134). Lines like these prefigure the later more obviously Stevensian poem, 'The Colours of Love', which includes aphoristic challenges to the reader – 'But is that beauty, is that beauty death? / No, it's the mask by which we're drawn to him' (CP 277) – highly reminiscent of moments in Stevens's 'Sunday Morning': 'Death is the mother of beauty'; 'Is there no change of death in paradise / Does ripe fruit never fall?'[12] Yet the dominant tone of 'Lough Derg', in line with much of Devlin's poetry of this period, recalls most strongly the heightened, exclamatory mode of Crane:

> Water withers from the oars. The pilgrims blacken
> Out of the boats to masticate their sin
> Where Dante smelled among the stones and bracken
> The door to Hell (O harder Hell where pain
> Is earthed, a casuist sanctuary of guilt!).
> (CP 133–4)

Devlin's ejaculatory mode, as Tate and Warren observe, closely resembles the voice of Crane's magnificent late poem, 'The Broken Tower':

> The bells, I say, the bells break down their tower;
> And swing I know not where. Their tongues engrave
> Membrane through marrow, my long-scattered score
> Of broken intervals . . . And I, their sexton slave![13]

More significant than these stylistic correspondences is the fact that 'Lough Derg' shares the same basic structure as the poems of Eliot, Crane and Stevens invoked by Tate and Warren. Each is constructed around an opposition Perloff labels the 'Symbolist dualism' between self and world, the latter removed from the speaker yet into which he 'reads meanings' of symbolic import.[14] In 'Lough Derg', Devlin's preoccupation with issues of faith and justice is prompted by the objective event of the pilgrimage, the pilgrims' spiritual predicament gradually seen as the speaker's own. Devlin's often complex syntactical structures and his method of forwarding his poetry through startling transitions of argument and imagery (as discussed well by Dillon Johnston and Robert Welch)[15] make high demands of his reader; but, ultimately, his symbolism is distinct from the kind of open indeterminacy argued for by Charles Olson in his 1950, anti-New Critical essay 'Projective Verse'. Olson makes a powerful case for a poetry in which syllable and line take precedence over the sentence, in which the stanza, logic, syntax and grammar are rejected in the search for a 'field' of open meaning. Olson's strictures on Crane in this essay can be applied, *mutatis mutandis*, to Devlin: 'What strikes me in him is the singleness of the push to the nominative, his push along that one arc of freshness, the attempt to get back to word as handle. . . . Does not Hart miss the advantages, by such an isolated push, miss the point of the whole front of syllable, line, field, and what happened to all language, and to the poem, as a result?' We do not have to endorse Olson's polemical disparagement of Crane to see the relevance of his comment to the work of Devlin. The 'isolated push' of 'Lough Derg' is, in Olson's terminology, that of 'NON-Projective' verse. That is, the poem constructs a closed system of symbolism derived from its subject's imaginative response to an exterior object world, a symbolist dualism Olson dismisses as '*the private-soul-at-any-public-wall*'.[16]

In this context, there is an intriguing correspondence between Olson's 1949 projective poetic manifesto, 'The Kingfishers', and Devlin's 'Ank'hor Vat' first published in 1943.[17] Devlin's poem pits Western tradition against Eastern, the latter epitomised in the statue of the Buddha in the Cambodian temple:

> No Western god or saint
> Ever smiled with the lissom fury of this god
> Who holds in doubt
> The wooden stare of Apollo
> Our Christian crown of thorns
> (*CP* 159)

The conjoining of Christ and Apollo in these lines brings together the speaker's religious and poetic dilemmas in a manner, as we shall see, not unrelated to that of 'Lough Derg'. That the 'doubt' experienced by the speaker is as much aesthetic as it is spiritual is made clear in the association drawn between the Buddha and writing: 'Buddha has covered the walls of the great temple / With the vegetative speed of his imagery'; 'The prolific divinity of the temple / Is a quiet lettering on vellum' (*CP* 160). The West, in contrast to the abundant, 'vegetative' East, appears to the speaker as a petrified or 'wooden' tradition, either because it is coming to a close or, more probably, because its Apollonian will to order seems fossilised in comparison with the Dionysian flux of an East whose god 'Sees through everything, while everything / Flows through him'. The speaker's Orientalism, however, registers not only a perturbed fascination with the East but also that familiar high modernist preoccupation with the collapse of tradition – the temple of Angkhor Wat is a ruin, a monument to a civilisation, the Khmer Empire, long since perished. The exotic unfamiliarity of the 'dung-filled jungle' signifies an undifferentiated, teeming present:

> A fling of flowers here
> Whose names I do not know
> Downy, scarlet gullets
> Green legs yielding and closing

Devlin's persona in this poem curiously resembles the character of Fernand in Olson's 'The Kingfishers', who, Olson's narrator recalls, 'had talked lispingly of Albers & Anghor Vat' the night before:

> He had left the party without a word. How he got up, got into his coat,
> I do not know. When I saw him, he was at the door, but it did not matter,
> he was already sliding along the wall of the night, losing himself
> in some crack of the ruins.[18]

Fernand, as Sherman Paul has persuasively argued, is a man possessed by an awareness of the ceaseless erosion of traditions and civilisations in the Heraclitean flux of time. Conscious of avant-gardism (he talks 'lispingly' of the Bauhaus and Black Mountain painter Josef Albers), he nevertheless fails to embrace 'the will to change' advocated by Olson's 'The Kingfishers' (and 'Projective Verse') as the spur to human creativity, remaining instead a 'dilettante who despairs and loses himself in the past'.[19] Devlin's speaker, confronted by the likeness of Buddha, is also 'losing himself / in some crack of the ruins' at Angkhor Wat: 'Let us lie down before him', he exhorts his companion, 'His look will flow like oil over us'. Fernand and the protagonist of 'Ank'hor Vat' share an Eliotic predisposition to 'surrender' to Tradition, the fragments of which they thenceforth can shore against their ruins. Olson's poem is indeed a direct reply to Eliot, its title alluding to Eliot's *Burnt Norton* –

> After the kingfisher's wing
> Has answered light to light, and is silent, the light is still
> At the still point of the turning world – [20]

which takes its epigraphs from Heraclitus, and to the Fisher King of *The Waste Land*. Olson's commitment to new beginnings, his declaration that 'the present is prologue, not the past',[21] is at one with the open verse advocated in 'Projective Verse'. Devlin's 'Ank'hor Vat' neither endorses

Olson's post-modernism at the level of theme nor in its formal treatment of its subject-matter. Like 'Lough Derg', and again after the practice of Eliot, it is structured around a symbolist dualism between speaker and a subjectively charged environment, the ruined temple in the midst of the 'dung-filled jungle'. Devlin's symbolic jungle thus differs from Olson's projective reworking, in 'The Kingfishers', of the jungle in Pound's Canto XX: 'Jungle: / Glaze green and red feathers, jungle, / Basis of renewal, renewals':[22]

> When the attentions change / the jungle
> leaps in
>   even the stones are split
>   they rive

Olson's jungle is not an objective correlative of the speaker's thoughts and feelings, but an object within the field of the poem, the rhythm of which – as in these lines – should register through its open or projective form a reality governed by process or change.

The close resemblances between Devlin's non-projective verse and Crane's symbolism is apparent from a comparison of 'Lough Derg' with Crane's 'For the Marriage of Faustus and Helen'. Devlin's condemnation of the contemporary Irish Catholic sensibility as 'doughed in dogma' echoes Crane's earlier portrayal of the spiritual apathy of modernity:

> The mind has shown itself at times
> Too much the baked and labeled dough
> Divided by accepted multitudes.[23]

Likewise, the urban setting of 'For the Marriage of Faustus and Helen', the literary antecedent for which is Eliot's London in *The Waste Land*, possesses a comparable symbolic import to the otherwise dissimilar locale of Devlin's text:

> Numbers, rebuffed by asphalt, crowd
> The margins of the day, accent the curbs,
> Convoying divers dawns on every corner
> To druggist, barber and tobacconist,
> Until the graduate opacities of evening
> Take them away as suddenly to somewhere
> Virginal perhaps, less fragmentary, cool.

Nevertheless, while the movement of Crane's poem (as opposed to Eliot's) is the transfiguration of the 'fragmentary' cityscape and the spiritual malaise of its multitudinous inhabitants through the visionary potential embodied in the speaker's unification with the Helen of the poem's title, 'Lough Derg' charts a failure to transcend the quotidian:

> Behind the eyes the winged ascension flags,
> For want of spirit by the market blurbed,
> And if hands touch, such fraternity sags
> Frightened this side the dykes of death disturbed
> Like Aran Islands' bibulous, unclean seas;
> *Pietà*: but the limbs ache; it is not peace.
> (*CP* 135)

In contrast to Crane's enthusiastic faith in an 'imagination [that] spans beyond despair, / Outpacing bargain, vocable and prayer',[24] Devlin views the modern mind's potential for ecstatic release with despondency, its 'winged ascension flags'. Whereas the imagination for Crane 'spans beyond' material constraints, Devlin acknowledges the 'want of spirit' in a society whose values are coldly caricatured in the 'jobbers', 'pink bank clerks' and 'tip-hat papal counts' who make 'their rosary rounds' at Lough Derg (*CP* 132).[25] Human freedom has been 'blurbed' by the very same 'market' that is exuberantly, though uneasily, championed by the sender of the 'Memo from a Millionaire':

> What jugs, what knives, what cups for drinking in!
> My keys! my watch! my silk-protected skin!
> Ginger and orange glowing, mouse-foot peas,
> My princely delft!
> (*CP* 140)

The millionaire is the veritable personification of an existence deformed by commodification. His claim, 'I am more than you by what I give to you', has to be held against his acknowledgement that his is consequently a 'stunted' life, 'with the dust of my possessions, / Unmoistened mortar, mending Time's abrasions' (*CP* 141). 'Lough Derg', in contrast to 'For the Marriage of Faustus and Helen', offers no panacea for the stultified lives of its pilgrims. Yet the difference between the two poems in this respect overlays their similar diagnosis of autonomous art in a society dominated by exchange-values. That side of Crane which smacks of hand-me-down romanticism, as in the high claims made at the close of 'For the Marriage of Faustus and Helen' for the transformative powers of the poetic imagination, is better viewed as an expression of the emancipatory promise of art in commodity capitalism. Art's functionlessness ('Outpacing bargain, vocable and prayer') silently bespeaks a freedom from the emptiness of the exchange-relations depicted in the 'Numbers' who 'crowd / The margins of the day'. In such a society, of course, art too is a commodity, a fact registered in the poet's apostrophe to his muse, Helen, whose 'hands', we learn, 'count the nights / Stippled with pink and green advertisements'.[26] But it is only through the fetish of art, *l'art pour l'art*, Crane implies, that commodity-fetishism can be seen for what it is. In Adorno's words:

The truth content of artworks, which is indeed their social truth, is pre-
dicated on their fetish character. The principle of heteronomy, apparently
the counterpart of fetishism, is the principle of exchange, and in it
domination is masked. Only what does not submit to that principle acts as
the plenipotentiary of what is free from domination; only what is useless
can stand in for the stunted use value. Artworks are the plenipotentiaries of
things that are no longer distorted by exchange, profit, and the false needs
of a degraded humanity. . . . Although the magic fetishes are one of the
historical roots of art, a fetishistic element remains admixed in artworks, an
element that goes beyond commodity fetishism.[27]

The abstractness of the autonomous artwork, as witnessed in Crane's
convoluted, discomfiting diction, imagery and syntax, is an indictment of
a society that has stripped art of use-value and an auratic dimension, the
very 'vocable[s]' of Crane's poem frantically gesturing towards a freedom
from their own compromised status.

Devlin's 'vocable[s]' in 'Lough Derg' and elsewhere draw attention to
themselves as much as Crane's: both poets load every rift with ore,
creating a poetic language that foregrounds its textuality. It is precisely
this quality that drew the ire of Randall Jarrell in his vituperative review
of Lough Derg and Other Poems: 'There is something rhetorical, unevenly
assertive, collage-y, sophisticated about the poems; the poet is extra-
ordinarily conscious of surfaces – as a child he must have mirror-fought
as other children pillow-fight.'[28] Randall's delightful picture of the boy-
Devlin's mirror-fighting is acutely apposite to the poetry's self-reflexivity,
which renders the poetry's mimetic impulse, or referential dimension, of
secondary importance beside its status as a self-regarding verbal artefact.
The result is an orientation towards the message which is definitive, in
Roman Jakobson's view, of 'the poetic function' – a foregrounding of an
utterance's formal devices to the point at which the 'roughened' or
defamiliarised texture of the language 'deepens the fundamental
dichotomy of signs and objects'.[29] The poetic function is arguably not so
much the essence of literariness, as Jakobson contests, as a theoretical
justification for some of the procedures of modernism. (Jakobson's
argument has its origins in his, along with other Russian Formalists',
championing of Russian Futurism in the first two decades or so of the
century.)[30] As construed by Jakobson, the poetic function is indebted to
Saussure's structural linguistics, in which the representational capacity of
language is extraneous to an account of the internal workings of the
linguistic system. In its emphasis on the hermetically sealed structure of
language, Saussure's Cours de linguistique générale dispassionately delin-
eates an auto-referentiality that equally informs, though usually less
sanguinely, the poetic presuppositions of many high modernists.[31] Devlin's
Lough Derg and Other Poems shares the autotelism common to the

theories of Jakobson and Saussure, and to the New Criticism, yet the title poem chooses to refocus the problematic relationship between signifier and signified, signified and referent, in religious rather than poetic terms:

> We pray to ourself. The metal moon, unspent
> Virgin eternity sleeping in the mind,
> Excites the form of prayer without content
> (*CP* 135)

A high modernist detachment from praxis, as evinced in the elevation of formal devices to fill a space once occupied by social content, finds a spiritual corollary in a prayer the religious significance of which has gone, leaving only its 'form' as solace. Devlin's pun on 'content' in this quotation keenly realises the speaker's distress. While the stanza's metre and rhyme-scheme demand that the final line signify his spiritual dissatisfaction (or discontent), the proximity of 'form' to the line's concluding noun inescapably suggests the emptiness (the contentlessness) of his worship. The purposelessness of prayer is therefore articulated in a language that foregrounds its vocables (as in the pun on 'content') to the point that the poetic device threatens to compose the text's principal import, its form constituting its significant content. Devlin's poetry, in other words, displaces its own functionlessness onto the spiritual inefficacy that comprises its ostensible pretext. And in this respect, Devlin's resignation to 'the form of prayer without content' is simply the flip side of Crane's flailing desire to transcend 'bargain, vocable and prayer'. Both Devlin's capitulation to 'form . . . without content' and Crane's frenetic, imaginative 'Outpacing' are tacit admissions of autonomous art's inherent uselessness.

At this juncture, it is worth noting that both Crane and Devlin contributed to Eugene Jolas's magazine, *transition*, an important forum for innovative writing from the late 1920s to shortly before the war. Jolas's theoretical pronouncements on the need for an 'American Romanticism' found powerful confirmation in Crane's work, especially in the mythos and techniques of *The Bridge*.[32] Crane's style, even at its most refractory, differs from the work of fellow contributor, Gertrude Stein, in its determinacy. For this reason, Crane, as Paul Giles observes, should be viewed in the company of Malcolm Cowley and Matthew Josephson, each 'attempting to build a bridge between the innovatory aesthetics of Europe and the traditional ethics of America'.[33] Devlin's trajectory, from his flirtations with Surrealism to the New Critical qualities of *Lough Derg and Other Poems*, charts a related arc to Crane's, but one lacking the American's pressing concern with national identity.

Devlin's contribution to *transition* is a single poem, collected in *Lough Derg and Other Poems* under a new title, 'Celibate Recusant'.[34] In publishing in *transition* Devlin was following the example of not only Crane but also, among his countrymen, Joyce, MacGreevy and Beckett. Both MacGreevy's and Beckett's names are appended to the *transition* 21 manifesto, 'Poetry is Vertical', the theory of Verticalism superseding as it encompassed the ideas expressed in the famous 'Revolution of the Word' manifesto of *transition* 16/17. Whatever the relevance of the later manifesto's statements to the work of MacGreevy and Beckett at this date, 'Celibate Recusant' is rewardingly read in the context of Verticalist principles. Verticalism builds on the restless experimentalism advocated in 'Revolution of the Word' but differs from the earlier position in explicitly lambasting classicism, promoting the 'orphic forces' of the poet, which stem from his or her mediumistic character, and claiming that, in the words of the manifesto, 'Poetry builds a nexus between the "I" and the "you" by leading the emotions of the sunken, telluric depths upward toward the illumination of a collective reality and a totalistic universe'.[35] As Douglas McMillan states: 'It was clear now that *transition* was seeking God – if not an orthodox God, at least the God of theological existentialists like Martin Buber.'[36] 'Celibate Recusant' is included in a section of *transition* 25 headed 'Vertigral', the term, first present in *transition* 22, further linking Verticalism to the idea of religious quest through its incorporation of the German word *Graal* (grail).[37] The style of Devlin's poem has the Surrealist inflections of many of the poems collected in *Intercessions*, and thus consorts comfortably with other contributions to the issue (which includes work by Dylan Thomas).[38] Under its original title, 'You Don't Know a Good Thing When You See It', the poem establishes a distance between its author and its speaker, the persona repudiating an airborne 'Virgin' who 'planes down over [him]':

> I jerk out what comes next
> In the ritual of slaves of slime,
> My fear all unstrung:
>
> 'Touch me not!' to the unsexed,
> Abstract, furious Virgin hung
> Above me, time after time
>
> And like a great, dull fish
> She floats on: 'It's as you wish'.
> (*CP* 186–7)

The poem depicts its speaker, a man of the early Christian era, as deaf to the good news, unable to understand 'the signa fish were / In the incoherent catacombs'. As the Virgin descends, his pagan celibacy is threatened: 'Endymion and the Moon I see.' With delicious irony, his *noli me tangere* constitutes an unknowing perversion of Christ's words, in

John 20.17, to Mary Magdalene outside the tomb prior to his ascension to heaven. The poem's revised title reinforces our sense of the persona's obduracy: he is a recusant as well as a celibate, that is, like an English Catholic of the sixteenth through the eighteenth centuries refusing to attend services of the Church of England, he is unwilling to submit to the alien religious authority embodied in the floating woman. From another perspective, and considering the poem's context in *transition*, one can perceive in Devlin's persona an 'anti-Vertigralist', whose recusancy is directed at the Verticalist call to poetical-spiritual ascension, the quest for the avant-garde *Graal*. This is not to suggest, absurdly, that Devlin's poem is an explicit intervention in the aesthetic debates of *transition*. Rather, the poem attests to the saturation of Devlin's work in the problematics of modernism and avant-gardism in the inter-war period. Read in this fashion, the poem reveals the extent to which Devlin's poetry, in the 1930s, is drawn towards the 'orphic forces' Jolas and others claimed for the avant-garde artwork, an attraction which leaves its imprint on the poems collected in *Intercessions*. His persona's abjuration of the 'Abstract, furious Virgin', however, may also be seen as a tacit acknowledgement of the theoretical insubstantiality of the often wild pronouncements of the avant-garde, from those of Dada and Surrealism to the not unrelated claims made on behalf of Verticalism and Vertigralism. With the outbreak of the Second World War, ideas of poetry forging a 'nexus' between poet and other – or between Buber's 'I' and 'thou' – in the service of illuminating 'a collective reality', must have seemed nugatory. At any rate, their vacuity for Devlin is apparent from 'Lough Derg'.

There, as we saw, the speaker's poetic dilemma finds a corollary in his spiritual predicament, the latter finding expression in a Jansenist stress on the lack of observable divine justice in human affairs:

> Not all
> The men of God nor the priests of mankind
> Can mend or explain the good and broke
> (*CP* 135)

Devlin's Jansenism can be put down to psychological predispositions reinforced, as I argue in the next chapter, by the poet's experiences as a civil servant in the Department of External Affairs during the inter-war years.[39] The origins of Jansenism lie in the seventeenth century, as a spiritual outlook developed by the French aristocracy in compensation for its loss of temporal, that is, political, authority. In 'Lough Derg', Pascal's silent God, whose voice 'no longer sounds out above the march of human destiny',[40] is a singularly appropriate deity for a world plunged into the violence of total war. At this moment of history, the platitudes of orthodox faith seem almost laughable: 'With mullioned Europe shattered, this Northwest, / Rude-sainted isle would pray it whole again'. Such a religious mindset is crudely superstitious, a degraded version of Jansenism overly preoccupied with sin, particularly those of the flesh:

> All is simple and symbol in their world,
> The incomprehended rendered fabulous.
> Sin teases life whose natural fruits withheld
> Sour the deprived nor bloom for timely loss:
> Clan Jansen!
> (CP 132)

Devlin's own Jansenist leanings do not, however, escape self-scrutiny. 'Jansenist Journey' is one of a number of poems begun in the early 1930s that in earlier, unpublished versions bear the title 'Adventure'.[41] The adventure of 'Jansenist Journey' leads the speaker and his brother, riding donkeys and escorted by their 'back-faced scapegoat, Guilt', to the 'Gospel gates' where they are greeted by 'Mother and sisters':

> The mother gave us a diamond each,
>
> Casketed, shut with a miser's clasp.
> I said to my brother: 'Life, the diamond,
> is locked inside hard and fast.'
>
> 'Yes?' he said, putting his down
> Indifferently. I opened mine:
> It was a gold ball. It was sundown,
>
> We entered cloisters with a priest,
> Sat on the stone wall, listening
> To his plans for our retreat,
>
> Black-face forgotten, the diamond too,
> And the mother and sisters. No rapture;
> The plain virtue of the chosen few.
> (CP 145–6)

The 'cloisters' to which the adventurers attain can be contrasted with 'the bombed cathedral town' of 'From Government Buildings' (CP 138) and the devastation of the Second World War – 'mullioned Europe shattered' – that comprises the backdrop in 'Lough Derg' to the pilgrimage taking place in neutral Ireland. 'Lough Derg' makes plain what is merely implied at the close of 'Jansenist Journey', that prayer has no impact in an unjust world: 'We pray to Ourself', the speaker of that poem gloomily concludes. Likewise, in 'Obstacle Basilisk', the persona's quest (on horseback rather than by donkey) takes place in a vaguely medieval landscape gripped by war – 'A mile below is a breastful of warships / In a heroic harbour, menacing, tight' – and in which a priest's cries of 'Halleluia! halleluia!' are rendered ridiculous by his 'fractious dance / His legs curve[d] like a weak smile' (*CP* 188). Stan Smith suggestively places the speaker's distress in 'Obstacle Basilisk' in a Jansenist framework, as representative of the fears 'of [a] recusant minority in a squalidly hostile environment, careful of a spiritual election which is also its guarantee of class superiority'.[42] In this respect, 'Obstacle Basilisk' makes clearer the more subdued irony of 'Jansenist Journey', the persona of which finds in those 'cloisters' a spiritual hideaway from the violence and injustice of mid-century Europe. In other words, the Jansenist is deaf to the self-condemnatory, but self-revelatory, close to 'Lough Derg'; his 'adventure' consists of an all-too sudden release from the 'black-faced scapegoat, Guilt', and his 'retreat' becomes the occasion for a spiritual smugness analogous to the self-satisfied religiosity of the 'Clan Jansen!' satirised in 'Lough Derg'. Such self-delusion is made manifest in his mistaken claim that the casket his mother gives him contains 'Life, the diamond', when, upon opening it, he in fact finds 'a gold ball'.[43]

The fact that 'The Statue and the Perturbed Burghers' (reprinted in *Lough Derg and Other Poems*) is another in the 'Adventure' series of poems brings into focus the relationship between 'Jansenist Journey' and Devlin's poetics. In the previous chapter, I argued that the former poem affirms an implicit rupture with the aspirations of the avant-garde in a fashion reminiscent of Stevens's ruminations in the opening two parts of *Owl's Clover*. Stevens's defence, in 'Mr Burnshaw and the Statue', of the functionlessness of art (the statue) against a vulgar Marxist (Mr Burnshaw's) demand for social relevance finds, as we saw, a parallel in Devlin's injunction that the statue 'disdain' its bourgeois consumers. Yet in embracing the very uselessness to which a burgherly world has consigned it, the artwork confesses its social and political irrelevance. It is thus noteworthy that the donkey-riding adventurer of 'Jansenist Journey' differs from, even as he resembles, Stevens's similarly mounted quester, 'Mrs Alfred Uruguay'. The titular woman in Stevens's poem represents a commitment to 'the real' that Stevens contrasts with the questing 'figure of capable imagination', a noble rider 'Rushing from what was real' as he spurs his horse to 'the imagined land'.[44] (Even Mrs Alfred Uruguay's trudging donkey 'wished faithfully for a falsifying bell'.) Devlin's donkey-borne pilgrim is a figure of a discapacitating imagination: while his adventure succeeds ('We bested the last lingering hill / Of life'), and Mrs Alfred Uruguay's apparently fails, the anticlimactic conclusion to his quest, seated in the raptureless cloisters of his faith, cannot be construed as an heroic transcendence of reality after the fashion of Stevens's noble rider.[45] After all, the poverty of reality, for Devlin, is not so much its want of

imagination, as in Stevens's poem, as it is a literal condition – a world in which 'the wretched', in the words of 'Encounter', 'Hold out their begging-bowls at the wooden gates, / Too poor to weep, too poor to weep with tears' (*CP* 136).

These words are spoken in reply to an Englishman's vaunting of his nation's poets, specifically Milton and Blake, 'Who would rib men with pride against the spite / Of God'. The Irishman's response is that 'Milton and Marvell, like the toady, Horace, / Praised the men of power for the good / They happened on, with bible and sword'. His indictment of Marvell's 'An Horatian Ode upon Cromwell's Return from Ireland' invokes the Renaissance poet's apparent equation of power and justice in Cromwell's sure grasp of *Realpolitik*:

> Though justice against fate complain,
> And plead the ancient rights in vain:
>   But those do hold or break,
>   As men are strong and weak.[46]

But for all Devlin's sympathy in 'Encounter' and in 'Lough Derg' for the 'desperate', those 'who have been robbed, their wasting / Shares in justice legally lowered' (*CP* 134–5), his poetry abjures commitment to their cause. If Milton, Marvell, and 'the toady, Horace' allowed their work to be harnessed to political ends, in declining any such engagement the speaker of 'Encounter' can express merely baffled anger, just as the persona of 'Lough Derg' can articulate only inefficacious prayer. In the most searching review of *Lough Derg and Other Poems*, Vivienne Koch characteristically drew attention to the way in which Devlin's poetry focuses on 'the subjective power of religion and the social powerlessness of poverty': 'mediation enters when the poet . . . attempts to show up a conflict, not necessarily causal, but, rather, antinomial in its nature.'[47] In 'Encounter', the antinomy between 'the subjective power of religion' and 'the social powerlessness of poverty' finds no resolution. Indeed, the impasse is clearer in the version of 'Encounter' published in 1944 in *Urbana*, in which the 'wretched' are said to be 'Too poor to weep, even with the tears / That you and I have wept for them'.[48] It is a predicament unsatisfactorily defused by means of the words of the Frenchman, 'François from Touraine', who advocates a form of wise passiveness: 'Patience; listen to the world's / Growth, resulting in fire and childlike water!' The possible vacuity of the Frenchman's attitude is intimated in the beautiful vignette in the poem's final stanza:

> Boxflower scent. Fumes of burgundy.
> Nagging children at the tables
> A dream's remove from their fathers smoking
> Along the boulevard laid with yellow evening.

François's trusting innocence is gently upbraided by the presence of the 'Nagging children', whose intrusive voices are mildly reminiscent of the implorations of 'the wretched' invoked by the Irishman. The poetic debate conducted by the colloquists of 'Encounter' recalls the discussion held by Stevens's 'diplomats of the cafés' in *Owl's Clover*;[49] but unlike Stevens's diplomats – who 'expound: / Fromage and coffee and cognac and no gods' – Devlin's triumvirate reach no agreement. In both Devlin and Stevens, an attempt is made to negotiate a relationship between art and a poverty-striken reality that is personified, in Stevens, as the 'destitute' female in the first section of *Owl's Clover*, whose 'bitter mind' figures as an obstinate reminder of the penury (imaginative and literal) with which the artwork (Stevens's statue) is confronted:

> The mass of stone collapsed to marble hulk,
> Stood stiffly, as if the black of what she thought
> Conflicting with the moving colors there
> Changed them, at last, to its triumphant hue,
> Triumphant as that always upward wind
> Blowing among the trees its meaningless sound.[50]

If *Owl's Clover* strives to move beyond this impasse, 'Encounter', in line with the bulk of *Lough Derg and Other Poems*, does not. In this regard, the old woman in Devlin's 'Royal Canal', whose 'fingers / Feather the keyboard' (*CP* 142), is valuably read as a revision of the spinet-playing 'sister' of 'The Statue and the Perturbed Burghers'. Whereas the latter is indifferent to the burghers, her 'silk music' played behind 'scented shutters', the former hides in 'Terror', shielded by her window from a world of 'gruff mongrels in aimless exercise / With boys shouting'. Her music, in contrast to the spinet-player's, is 'A perspicuous storm of chords / She finishes nothing'. The disharmony of her playing appears to be concomitant with the lack of reciprocity between the woman and 'The world plunged in the evening light' beyond her window: there exists 'A costly silence between enemies'. The disturbing conclusion to the poem delineates an environment onto which the woman's feelings of alienation have been projected, a landscape which, as a consequence, emits a 'meaningless sound':

> The druid elms, closed in their lost language,
> Their shoulders heavy
> With a menace not their natural own
> Rest in panic on the still canal.

The woman's panic, for Stan Smith, 'is the friction of an unrealized act: a deadlocked hysteria, a congealed subjectivity that cannot break out of its own sealed petrifaction'.[51] Such a coagulation of consciousness is comparable to the 'rupture of the lines of communication' of which Beckett speaks in 'Recent Irish Poetry'. In Devlin's poem, 'the breakdown of the object' explored in Beckett's essay leaves the woman helplessly confronting a world as alien, and as apparently uninterpretable, as a 'lost language'.

The miserable plight of the estranged pianist of 'Royal Canal' is counterpointed, in *Lough Derg and Other Poems*, by Devlin's portrayal of the titanic struggle of Michelangelo in 'Casa Buonaroti':

> He struggled all life with pigment, rock, chisel and sun
> To put God in matter, magnify himself;
> Worked against Time, rhetorical skull on the shelf,
> To muscle in stone ideas by Time undone:
> And skull's grin, that long bogy, would outrun
> His work yielded to Time: why God made Hell:
> The inch to retreat to from the daring ell
> Of giving his image the risk of being none.
> (CP 147)

The octave of Devlin's sonnet depicts the Italian artist as poised on a cusp in the history of art, between art as courtly and bourgeois. The courtly art of the Renaissance is distinguishable from the sacral art of the medieval period in that it lacks the latter's immediate functionality in institutional religion. As the product of the individual artist rather than collective craftsmanship, courtly art foreshadows bourgeois art's overriding emphasis on individual production.[52] Devlin's Michelangelo, though seeking 'To put God in matter', is the epitome of the individual 'genius', whose 'struggle' with the materials of his art 'magnif[ies] himself'. In this respect, Michelangelo's work presages the autonomous art represented by the sculpture in 'The Statue and the Perturbed Burghers', which, in mute outrage, stands apart from the burgherly mores of its consumers. The sestet of 'Casa Buonaroti' turns its attention to those consumers, by moving from the horizon of Michelangelo's artistic production to the horizon of its reception:

> Not devils but the meek minimize the great
> Who bind their eyes as likely as not
> So not is like what they would like it were.
> Samson they enhance us whom our flaws deflate:
> Yet God, from the refuge of his comic thought,
> Moves the momentary tourist with his fear.

These lines recall a poem Devlin admired, 'Under Ben Bulben', in which Yeats's hieratic speaker declares:

> Michael Angelo left a proof
> On the Sistine Chapel roof,
> Where but half-awakened Adam
> Can disturb globe-trotting Madam
> Till her bowels are in heat,
> Proof that there's a purpose set
> Before the secret working mind:
> Profane perfection of mankind.[53]

The visceral response of the 'globe-trotting Madam' to the roof of the Sistine Chapel is close to that of the 'momentary tourist' in Devlin's poem, both over-awed by Michelangelo's achievement. The intensity of her gut-reaction suggests that the art of the 'great' possesses the ability to 'move', as Devlin's poem also argues, its casual consumers to the point of illuminating their lives (either in a 'Profane' or spiritual fashion). The experience of art like that of Michelangelo's thus contains a utopian dimension. The Samson-like blindness of art to the poverty of reality originates in its distance from 'the wretched' and 'desperate' invoked in 'Encounter' and 'Lough Derg'. Yet, paradoxically, it is precisely in their seemingly misleading ability to 'enhance us whom our flaws deflate' that major artworks barely manage to intimate a condition beyond poverty, one in which 'not is like what they would like it were'.

'ADAM'S DREAM': THE LOVE POETRY

A large proportion of the new poems collected in *Lough Derg and Other Poems* are love poems. In his love poetry, Devlin's object of desire is a completeness of being which 'From Government Buildings' refers to as a condition in which 'want and have are equal' (*CP* 137). Nevertheless, in virtually the entirety of these texts such a goal is shown to be elusive. The poems frequently address an absent other and thus reinflect, in the realm of the erotic, the isolation experienced by Devlin's Jansenist persona and the predicament of the purposeless artist. In poem after poem, the speaker invokes a desired woman whose ontological status, and hence her ability to allay his solitariness, is revealed to be highly problematic. While the women represented in these poems have their origins in a literal woman, Devlin's personae are painfully aware that the lovers they imagine are their own creations, desperately spun out of their poetic entrails in an attempt to overcome their feelings of privation.[54] This is an issue that Devlin will examine at greatest length in *The Heavenly Foreigner*, but it is already central to a poem such as the scrupulously self-reflexive 'A Dream of Orpheus':

Low and knelt on my heels at the blank bed in moonlight
Listening with sidelong frightened eye to the forms of the table
Twitching out of inanimate wood, all form erratic,
Night-risen mineral and plant loose from man's neat dominion,
I stroke and stroke the sheets murmuring the old endearments:
'Little mouth of honey! thyme breath! lamp of my comfort!'. . .
But here's a ghost's hand only I hold; and heartsick I think of
Your eyes' Cyprian charm from sacred, ivory centuries,
We lying, balanced in night's blue hammock in bright upset
And earnest lark singing so brilliant to faint-come sun
I willed them both in my arms
(CP 217)

Of course, despite the speaker's 'will[ing]' he cannot breathe life into the 'ghost' for whom he longs, and the 'sheets' he strokes and entreats remain those of a forlorn 'blank bed'. Nevertheless, he can imagine another nocturnal moment, when her 'Cyprian charm' lay beside him in 'night's blue hammock', and, in so doing, the blank sheets (both of bed and text) find themselves overlain by her form. His solace in sexual fantasy, however, is checked by his recognition of the unreality of the fantasised woman: 'Orpheus I am not whose grief sang so melodious, / . . . / and singing / Conquered back his Eurydice murdered'. Orpheus is a 'Priest with power over words', whose ability as a singer is such that his words have 'power over things' (CP 218). But Devlin's speaker can 'dream' only of Orpheus's 'power'; his words are empowering merely at the level of wish-fulfilment, in the sphere of daydreams not reality. Orpheus's poetic harrowing of hell 'persuade[s] the dead beloved back', although he fatally loses Eurydice to Hades owing to his failure to observe the warning not to look back, to 'Turn from her yet the terror of human eyes' (CP 218). For Devlin's persona, Orpheus thus stands as a figure of the poet whose tropes exert an authority over the referential world denied his own metaphors: 'Little mouth of honey! thyme breath! lamp of my comfort!' In the sexual politics of patriarchal love poetry, Orpheus's 'power' is the epitome of male mastery of the represented female object, as the close to Devlin's poem makes clear:

Orpheus
Grieves for her still; in the shell and web of her body, beauty
Dreamt the forms his love made substance of and that she dreams in him.
(CP 219)

Devlin's moving depiction of Orpheus's grief has to be set beside his speaker's curious and revealing interpretation of the classical myth. For the persona, Eurydice's innate 'beauty' is made substantial through the medium of Orpheus's love, a love which the poem hears in his songs about her beauty. As a result, she paradoxically becomes dependent on him and his poetry for knowledge of her beautiful form, dreaming of those 'forms' 'in him'. There are, then, two dreams of Orpheus in this poem: that of the speaker and that which the speaker ascribes to Eurydice, and both should be viewed in the light of the anxiety exhibited in the text with regard to its own enfeebled textual prowess.

A similar scenario to that of 'A Dream of Orpheus' occurs in 'From Government Buildings', the speaker of which, confronted by a spiritually enervated and war-blasted Europe, turns for sustenance to an unspecified and absent other:

> You, you I cherish with my learned heart
> As in the bombed cathedral town, doubly
> A tourist trophy now, the dean shouted: 'At last!
> At least and at last we have stored the windows away,
>
> The fabulation of my Lord's glory, by
> Seven and by seven and by seven multiplied!'
> So is my care though none your mystic I,
> Nor you like the painted saints but breath and more.
> (*CP* 137–8)

There is more than just conventional flattery lying behind the extremity of the poem's juxtaposition of the addressee with the stained glass's 'fabulation of my Lord's glory'. In 'stor[ing] away' those precious windows, the dean exercises a 'care' comparable to that of the persona's 'cherish[ing]' of his beloved's image in his 'learned heart'. First published in 1945,[55] Devlin's poem can be read alongside Beckett's 1946 quatrain, 'Saint-Lô', in which the subject sees in the bomb-damaged city of the title an intimation of the imploding disintegration of his selfhood:

> Vire will wind in other shadows
> unborn through the bright ways tremble
> and the old mind ghost-forsaken
> sink into its havoc[56]

'From Government Buildings' resists the fate that awaits Beckett's Cartesian subject by the invocation of those ghosts who forsake Beckett's speaker. For although the desired woman is literally absent, in the persona's imagination she stalks phantasmally through his empty room:

> And do not pace the room haunting the future
> But be my insular love; and I would have you
> Fingering the ring with its silver bat, the foreign
> And credible Chinese symbol of happiness.

The 'you' of this poem can be viewed, in Sartre's terms, as an imaginative negation of reality. Unable to bear existential isolation, the speaker's 'malignant waiting' is partially countered by that which, strictly speaking, is the creation of a *no-thing*. In *The Psychology of Imagination* Sartre comments: 'However lively, appealing or strong the image is, it presents its object as not being. . . . [W]e seek in vain to create in ourselves the belief that the object really exists by means of our *conduct* towards it: we can pretend for a second, but we cannot destroy the immediate awareness of its nothingness.'[57] In Devlin's poem, the addressee, however 'appealing', is merely an image in the speaker's consciousness, a fact of which he is all too painfully aware. In this respect the properties attributed to the ring he wishes her to finger more properly apply to her. She is, like any product of the imagination, both metaphorically 'foreign', in that she is without empirical substance in the poet's present surroundings, yet 'credible' to the extent that she can be visualised or projected as an intentional image.

Such intentionality is also present in 'Farewell and Good', the speaker of which is forced to acknowledge the fact that 'She I loved so much will not appear again' (*CP* 213), except in imaginary form:

> At any time of the day and night, struck by a wind-flash
> In snood of leaves or in phantasms of sleep assembling her form,
> I restore my kingdom in her, the real that deepened the dreamed-on
>
> Ritual loves of legend women admired in childhood:
> Then remembrance stings my reason, both entangled in
> Grief which webs movement and is merely want.
> (*CP* 213–14)

These lines movingly reiterate, in the context of sexual desire, Sartre's claim that in imagining another's presence we are forever aware of the nothingness of the image: 'assembling her form', the speaker is conscious of the 'want' that informs his 'grief' over her literal absence. Without the 'real', the 'dreamed-on . . . women' – those idealised love-objects of his youth – are insubstantial, and the possession of imaginary 'legend women' meagre compensation for the impossibility of fully mastering the originary, literal object of desire. 'Farewell and Good' concludes:

> Still the complaint, still no comfort to her and me split
> Like a glass, like life spilt by some Sistine hand,
> Our life that brimmed over like diamonds in our light.

The allusion in 'Sistine hand' to Michelangelo's depiction on the ceiling of the Sistine Chapel of God's creation of Adam is interpreted by Dillon Johnston as an ambivalent image of individuation. In the light of the fact that, as represented by Michelangelo, God's hand 'separates from, as it creates, Adam', and given Devlin's movement in the tercet from shards of glass to 'the beauty of faceted diamonds', Johnston opines: 'Because in their split they realize their distinctive selves, this Fall is both tragic and fortunate, as the title "Farewell and Good" implies.'[58] Yet the echo in the title of a line from 'Communication from the Eiffel Tower' – 'Farewell and good to the dead leave us reproached' – might suggest that the phrase has a more defensive tone than Johnston's reading would allow it. Furthermore, a draft of the poem, simply entitled 'Farewell to Her', disconsolately concludes: 'Still talking, still no comfort to her and me split like a gourd.' Rather than documenting the maturation of a 'distinctive' selfhood, the poem's imagery of splitting and spilling serves to emphasise the speaker's feelings of irrevocable loss.[59]

The sequestered self of Devlin's love poetry is equally central to his religious poetry (indeed, the two poetic sub-genres will fuse in *The Heavenly Foreigner* and 'The Colours of Love'). The speaker of 'Meditation at Avila', confronting the 'waste and magnificence' of the 'star-quartz universe', also addresses another with the aim of surmounting his solitude:

> Soul, my dear friend,
> Welcome as always;
> Fibrous listener in the darks of mind
> Till my confession
> Articulate your silence,
> Pallas Athene through my beating temples . . .
>
> If I could not talk to you
> Fear would oppress me.
> (CP 162)

Introducing this poem at a reading at the Writer's Club of the Library of Congress in 1946, Devlin said that 'the conversation is supposed to build up a role for the soul, which is a mixture of consciousness and persistence'.[60] In 'build[ing] up' the soul's 'role', this one-sided 'dialogue' of self and feminine soul is comparable to that between the speaker and the love-object of 'From Government Buildings': the soul, as Stan Smith observes, 'is *constructed* by the mundane self out of a dialogue in which one side is always silent'.[61] Hence the likening of the soul to Pallas Athene, who sprang, fully grown, from the 'beating temples' of Zeus. The 'conversation' of self and soul is succeeded in the poem by a genuine dialogue between the persona and the wife of a Moroccan traveller, an encounter spiced with sexual *frisson*:

> The traveller's housewife
> Like a wife too long shut away in a new suburb
> Chatters: through her inept words, the epileptic
> Sacrifice of black bulls; almond blossom, oranges,
> Anxious cultures among the wide, bronze, mountainous wastes,
> The sigh-spent wavetops of sierras;
> Dance, the shellfish eaten, dance, the stertorous heels,
> Sensual asserveration of bare thigh:
> I stored her joy in my breast against the future.
> (CP 162–3)

This sexually charged atmosphere nevertheless dissipates, as the wife 'Goes to [her husband], sleepy and reluctant. / Contempt falls like a shadow between us.' The intercourse between self and soul inverts that between the babbling traveller's wife and voyeuristic poet, as the feminine soul becomes the 'Fibrous listener' to the speaker's 'confession'. In the Sartrean terms of the present discussion, the soul is a negation of that which the self literally perceives (the 'traveller's housewife') by an image, one which intermittently brings 'Comfort, my viaticum, journey-food'. In this respect, the relationship between the two achieves a consummation, of an imaginary kind, denied the poet in his encounter with the literal woman.

The poem's interlarding of carnal and spiritual desire is at one with its rejection of a religious attitude identified with Santa Teresa, 'Covetous burning virgin!'

> Scorning to nourish body's
> Farmlands with soul's
> Modulating rains
> (CP 163)

However, in tune with the love poetry elsewhere in the collection, the poet's projection of a wish-fulfilling image (the soul) is a hollow compensation for his isolation. The second part of the poem centres on the yawning need experienced by the speaker for imaginative 'comfort', his soul perceived to be the 'seed of my suffering, seed / Of my want', rather than its cessation. What terrifies the poet is the prospect of death, imaginative and literal, of which the poem grants a frightful vision:

> Do you remember how, one night,
> Staring up at the Milky Way,
> Simplified like a parish registry recording only life and death,
> With an ink-dim memory leafing back the centuries,
> I watched the innumerable, witless cortege of the dead
> Floating mute and baffled, they had died
> All their desires fresh on their hastening lips,
> They had gone out the door of life between two calls
> (CP 165)

The likening, in the first half of this remarkable passage, of the night sky to the prosaic details of a parish registry serves to strip life to those facts – of birth and death – that the imagination cannot gainsay. It is thus of consequence that, after confronting this appalling vista, the self turns away to see his soul 'Toothless, bald and smiling' (CP 166), that is, bereft of its fictitious consolations.

In a memorable moment in this poem, Devlin likens his construction of the soul to Adam's parthenogenetic conception of Eve:

> With fruitful diminution of my light,
> Like Eve accomplisht out of Adam's side,
> Soul glides, a glow of flesh, from out its packing.
> (*CP* 164)

Keats famously found in the sleeping Adam's 'conceiving' of Eve a parable of creativity. In a letter to Benjamin Bailey he follows his observation that 'What the imagination seizes as Beauty must be truth' with the reflection: 'The Imagination may be compared to Adam's dream – he awoke and found it truth.'[62] Imaginative truth in Keats can be defined in circular fashion ('Beauty is truth, truth beauty', the Grecian Urn tells us) without, it appears, becoming a cause for anxiety: make-believe or Fancy possesses its own requirements for what shall count as true. Surrealism reiterates, after its own fashion, Keats's understanding of truth: in Paul Éluard's poetry the imagination seek to revivify existence through an extremely intensified language of love. Devlin's translation of Éluard's 'Celle de toujours, toute', 'She of always, all of her', contains an interesting syntactical deviation from the French text that warrants attention in this context. Éluard writes of a woman 'Qui supprimes l'absence et qui me mets au monde'. In Devlin's rendition it is the female addressee rather than the male speaker who is set or put in the world: 'O thou that suppressest forgetfulness, hope and ignorance, / That suppressest absence and that *I* put in the world' (*TE* 166–7; my italics). Roger Little, in an informative introduction to Devlin's translations, notes the discrepancy between original and translation, but rests content with claiming that Devlin has 'misinterpret[ed] the clause' (*TE* 12). Little's point is trivially correct, but fails to grasp the significance of a possible Freudian slip in an otherwise scrupulously literal translation. Devlin retains Éluard's speaker's supplicatory attitude before the woman while foregrounding an element possibly absent from the French poem. For Devlin's addressee suppresses absence through wish-fulfilment, transforming – in the terms of Beckett's 'Recent Irish Poetry' – 'the space that intervenes between him [the artist] and the world of objects' into some kind of 'Hellespont'.

In this manner, Devlin's version of Éluard's text implicitly makes the woman a creation of the speaker, thus linking the translation to 'From Government Buildings' and 'Meditation at Avila'. The same form of self-empowering creativity is also present in 'Eve in My Legend', if in a slightly different form from the previous two poems. The lyric tells of the poet's infatuation with a woman who, in this case, seems more substantial than the aforementioned objects of desire. However, 'Once [he] had kissed her', she undergoes the following metamorphosis:

[The] air whose sunny tongues are birds
Bore with ease our heavy words

As she from my drugged side took life.
I feel like Adam who in sleep
Gave birth to Eve, daughter and wife
Whence his far brood would sow and reap,
Half monster, half philosopher,
Movement by mood conceiving her.
(CP 206)

Adam's dream, here, is an image for a re-conception of reality or, in André Breton's term, the creation of a '*surreality*', as the desirable other now '[takes] life' from the poetic subject, thus enabling him to overcome his Adamic loneliness. Devlin's interest in the poetry of René Char, one presumes, sprang from a recognition of the French poet's comparable faith in the transformative power of the mind. For instance, Char's prose poem 'Partage Formel', which Devlin translated, proclaims the poetic transmutation of the base metal of reality:

> Imagination consists in eliminating many incomplete bodies from reality, so as, with the help of the magical and subversive powers of desire, to secure their return in the guise of a presence totally satisfying. It is then the unquenchable uncreated reality.
> (TE 209)

The 'reality' on which this passage concludes is as 'real' as the products of Keats's imagination are 'true'; satisfaction is achieved through a combination of the subversive magic of desire and imagination. That Eve's 'birth' is analogous to imaginative 'conceiving', to what Sartre called the 'magical' act of producing 'the thing one desires, in such a way that one can take possession of it',[63] is suggested by the unusual manner in which the speaker of Devlin's poem seduces the woman. He does so through a metaphor:

> The world turns round and leaves the sun . . .

> Today we passed from a yellow street
> Into a black one, high and cold
> I said to her, I turned it neat,
> 'Your hair's the sun now, warmth and gold.'

This verbal conquest is developed at greater length in a prose version of this poem, 'Benidicta', in which the male says to the woman: 'I have always in the end in my relations with people, found the phrase exactly suitable to overturn them, they had never heard it before, and they were mine.' The woman's scepticism is put to the test when, finding herself in a darkened street, he counters her complaint at the dreary surroundings by quipping: '"No it's bright . . . your head is the mobile sun." I should explain that she is blond. I knew that Helen was the sun risen by some miracle in the south in Faust II but she did not. She turned and looked half-conquered and considering' (*HF* 46). This curious little narrative links the poet's dexterity with language (his ability to coin phrases which those he desires 'had never heard . . . before') to sexual conquest and thence to control of others. She becomes Eve in *his* legend, a figure in his private mythos. It is a strategy further present in an untitled piece of writing in prose and verse among Devlin's papers:

> I will know everything of her hands, the beat of her body in the air, every-thing. I will circumscribe, yes, so that if I were a creator I could make her. Single shuttling limbs, white forest-star, amba thleca. Yet thou are not my god but a goddess, not my image but a rib taken from me who am an image. (*HF* 50)

This disturbing passage desperately conflates creativity and mastery of the desirable woman: to 'circumscribe' her is to 'make her'. As Anne Fogarty has observed, this crucial dimension to Devlin's love poetry can be seen as an instance of that which Alice Jardine terms, 'gynesis', 'the putting into discourse of woman', a procedure in Devlin 'emblematic of the operations of the imagination as a whole and of its attempt to compensate for the rifts in being':

> The riddling declaration that closes ['Eve in My Legend'] indicates that the woman who can only be depicted metonymically as 'blond laughter' is a shifting horizon of meaning rather than someone tangible and concrete. The process of knowing devolves into an endless series of displacements. Moreover, the attempt to imagine the perspective of the other, what the woman might know, founders. In the end, it is the self's failure to grapple with anything outside itself that becomes the only thing that can be imagined by this self-defeating ontology.[64]

Fogarty's reading is truer to the sexual politics of Devlin's poem than Lorna Reynolds's sanguine belief that, at the end of 'Eve in My Legend', 'each [lover] is all to the other'.[65] On the contrary, the substitution of the literal by the figurative woman forestalls in advance any knowledge of the other as a 'tangible and concrete' human being, and, as a result, Devlin's speaker's is left with epistemological confidence in naught but his intentional images.

In the most dazzling instance of such rhetorical conquering, 'Welcome My World', the plethora of images becomes increasingly overdetermined. The speaker's 'world' is predominantly described as female, as 'A baffled virgin', a 'witch', a 'Marble protectress with vigilant breasts':

> My Olive naiad in Ionian creeks,
> My ballad maiden raped in Highland forays,
>   World all in fable speaks,
> My gun-flanked heroine of detective stories.
> (*CP* 191–2)

The abrupt metamorphosis of one female figure into another 'type-symbol'[66] has an almost frantic air. The urgency of the speaker's negation of reality by means of his imaginary 'world' has a vertiginous quality to it, as the 'World all in fable speaks' because the speaker recreates it in the fabulous forms of his imagination. To this degree, the relationship between poetic subject and female object is that of, in the words of the title to another poem, 'Poet and Comic Muse'. She is comic in the sense that her reality is aestheticised; her 'Twittering proliferation pruned to style', she is 'bunted out in borrowed quips'. (*CP* 195). This latter poem suggests hopefully that only through the mediated 'rite' of art, the acting of the text's extended metaphor, can her reality be comprehended:

> On fiction fixed, the general, vague drouth
> Is slaked by the neat passion we do:
> And winning them I can approach you.
> (*CP* 195)

But male desire in these poems is asymptotic: 'On fiction fixed' it 'approach[es]' a woman whose literality recedes into infinity.

Devlin's representation of women, in these poems, arguably shades into the pornographic. By this I do not mean to suggest that women in Devlin are portrayed as the culpable victims of male violence, but that the representation of women in his love poetry is governed by a principle of domination that Susanne Kappeler, in *The Pornography of Representation*, describes as follows:

> Turning another human being, another subject, woman, into an object is robbing her of her subjectivity. The systematic representation of women-objects is not a question of a single subject representing to himself another subject, who happens to be a pretty woman, as an object. In cultural historical terms, it is the male gender, unified by a common sense, who assumes the subject position: as the authors of culture, men assume the voice, compose the picture, write the story, for themselves and other men, and *about* women.

In Kappeler's view, pornography cannot be identified solely with the visual or literary content of a given cultural artefact (hence the notorious difficulty of distinguishing 'acceptable' erotica from pornography proper). Of equal, if not greater, significance is the 'structure of representation' that governs the pornographic scenario, and which underpins patriarchal culture's depiction of women in general: 'For in terms of representation, and with respect to the objectification of the female gender, the porno-grapher only reproduces, on a less elevated level and within a less exclusive circulation, what the artist does in the esoteric fields of high culture'.[67] Devlin's love poetry, to my mind, is narcissistically preoccupied with establishing and asserting the (albeit precarious) identity of the male subject; an identity, moreover, achieved through the representation of woman as object rather than as a complementary female subject. There is no genuine intersubjective communication in these texts. Rather, they reveal the connection Naomi Schor draws between 'male narcissism and fetishism', which constitute 'the very foundations of the representational system elaborated by patriarchal society'.[68] While the narcissism of Devlin's poetry, as Fogarty argues, is apparent in its intense preoccupation with the ontological status of its (male) personae's representations, its fetishism is most apparent in its metonymic reduction of women to body-parts, principally, though not exclusively, hair. The speaker of 'Edinburgh Tale', for example, fragments his companion on Princes Street through his hyperbolic praise of portions of her anatomy: 'I love your eyelids, leaves landing'; 'Your eyes lit up like a theatre'; 'I love your hands of a drowning man gripping a spar' (CP 203). Such metonymic appropriation, as these examples make clear, is closely aligned with Devlin's metaphorical posses-sion of the female body. As Helena Mitchie contends, for many feminist poets, including Adrienne Rich, 'metaphor and figuration' are 'the iden-tifying marks of patriarchal discourse. . . . The abstract and the figurative distract the reader from physical reality; feminist poetry becomes a reinscription of the literal.'[69] From this perspective, Devlin's intentional imagination, despite its pathos, is enmeshed within patriarchal discourse: its figurative recollection of women, to paraphrase Char's 'Partage Formel', consists in eliminating the literality of *female* bodies from reality.

Yet such synecdochic and metaphorical subjugation of the female is fraught with apprehension, as the 'Ballad of Mistress Death' illustrates. Confronted by the sexually active 'redhead Sally', the speaker's trepi-dation is clearly conveyed in his transference of her lasciviousness onto the object world: 'The sea's blue maw glittered / Like a fat, barbaric queen's' (CP 157). Indeed, in a sense she *is* objectivity, the reduction to which, in death, the speaker resists through transmuting his 'darkhead' in a fashion comparable to the metamorphic possession of the woman charted in 'Eve in My Legend':

> 'Yes, I've found out your secret,'
> Said I to my darling,
> Walking the dark streets
> Through leaf-shaken lamplight.
> 'I never will be jealous
> Nor you numb or nag at me
> I'll name you the world's most beauty
> Yellowheaded Helen
> And no lie be telling;
> No woman will disprove it.'

The imagination, in short, exercises power over one's environment. It is a means of restoring communication with the object world through destruction and projection, making 'reality', in a quasi-idealist fashion, dependent upon the creative mind. Yet the darkness of objectivity presses hard on the poet. 'She held me like nightfall', says the male balladeer, attesting to his thralldom to a reality the brute facticity of which is a threat to his imaginative powers: 'Her breath came like knives'. Devlin's loose appropriation of the ballad form in this poem contrasts sharply with Yeats's radicalisation of the same form in sequences such as 'A Woman Young and Old' and the Crazy Jane poems from *Words for Music Perhaps*. As Elizabeth Butler Cullingford convincingly demonstrates, in those ballads in which he ventriloquises female sexual experience, Yeats powerfully 'reinforces his attempt to displace the romantic male self: as anonymous compositions constantly modified by the women and blind men who primarily transmitted them, the ballads provide an appropriately non-canonical form for a man trying to speak as a woman'.[70] In 'Ballad of Mistress Death', Devlin's male speaker attempts to shore up rather than 'displace' his selfhood by means of his Adamic naming of the woman as 'Yellowheaded Helen'. In contrast to Yeats's adoption in a number of poems of the perspective of a woman, Devlin's poem objectifies the female through exactly the same structure of representation as found in 'Eve in My Legend'. Along related lines, one could also compare Devlin's crossing of sacred and profane love in *The Heavenly Foreigner* with Yeats's 'Supernatural Songs', in which the 'hybridization' of love and divine poetry, according to Cullingford, 'challenges the frigidity of contemporary Holy Rome by exposing the erotic foundations of religious power'.[71] While Devlin's own generic 'hybridization', in *The Heavenly Foreigner*, does not mount a direct 'challenge' to the orthodoxies of Catholicism, it is well-nigh as sexually charged as Yeats's sequence. Its spiritual erotica are grounded in the same narcissism and fetishism that underpin the sexual preoccupations of the love poetry of *Lough Derg and Other Poems*, but are elaborated at far greater length and in a more involuted fashion than the concerns of the earlier lyrics.

4

'HEART-AFFAIRS DIPLOMAT': LATER POEMS

'A MODERN *DÉLIE*'? *THE HEAVENLY FOREIGNER*

The Heavenly Foreigner, first published in full in 1950 and later revised, represents the high-water mark of Devlin's religious and erotic poetry. In its final version, the poem is divided into eleven sections, each of which takes its title from a specific locale, in most cases a cathedral, and all focusing on the speaker's relationship with an unnamed woman. The poem's origins lie in the mid-1930s, in an unfinished prose piece called, at various times, *Benedicta* and *Beata*.[1] One undated typescript bearing the latter title begins with a *dizain* from Maurice Scève's *Délie* (1544), and continues with a passage in prose subsequently reworked in *The Heavenly Foreigner* as the conclusion to 'St Malo' and opening of 'Wells', the first and second sections respectively of Devlin's poem. The *dizain* quoted is number 367 in Scève's *canzonerie* of love poems:

> Asses plus long, qu'un Siecle Platonique
> Me fut le moys, que sans toi suis este:
> Mais quand ton front je revy pacifique,
> Sejour tres hault de toute honnestete,
> Ou l'empire est du conseil arreste
> Mes songes lors je creus estre devins.
>   Car en mon corp: mon Ame, tu revins,
> Sentant ses mains, mains celestement blanches,
> Avec leurs bras mortellement divins
> L'un coronner mon col, l'aultre mes hanches.
> (*HF* 57)[2]

Bereft of his lover for a month that weighed 'longer than one of Plato's ages', Scève's persona greets her return 'in my body: my soul', 'Feeling her hands, hands heavenly white / With their mortally divine arms / One crowning my neck, the other my thighs'. The passage in *The Heavenly Foreigner* which corresponds to the prose immediately following these lines in the typescript centres on a similar paradox to Scève's, the 'mortally divine' dimension to the desired woman:

> It was being in the making of heaven, intoned in the terrestrial
> Rehearsal of the faithful, being with her,
> The red-cheeked faithful, busy with hope. Yet
> If in that heaven my difference should compose,
> And in such temporal harmony of health and harm,
> Flood of perfection flood back over me, there,
> There, in that bubble I'd exaggerate
> A wet miniscus of discontent,
> And all my activity lie
> Chaffing between diameter and arc.
> Time virtual is what keeps me in Time:
> Leave me in abeyance.
> (CP 261)

Devlin's geometrical image for his predicament, 'Chaffing between diameter and arc', recalls the 'asymptotic gasps' of the male godhead of 'Est Prodest'. In both cases, the speaker recognises the inescapable fact that human faith is inseparable from its temporal context, the lived experience of the 'faithful' – in the words of the earlier poem, 'He must be proved in time' (CP 83). In Scève's *dizain* the presence of Délie enables the speaker to find proof of the divine, within time and the compass of her arms, 'by giving', as Odette de Mourgues argues, 'to the flesh the immortal quality of the soul (*bras divins, mains celestes*) and to the soul a physical power of touch (*mon Ame . . . sentant ses mains*)'. However, de Mourgues adds, this is a 'momentary and precarious perfection: for while the lover reconciles the bodily quality of Délie's arms with the divine element, he does not forget their inevitable fragility (*bras mortellement divins*), and we may even suspect that the celestial quality of her hands is due to their earthly whiteness'.[3] In *The Heavenly Foreigner* Devlin explores the possibility – again strongly reminiscent of 'Est Prodest' – that the 'temporal harmony' found in his love for the woman may allow for a refracted apprehension of the atemporal divinity of the titular figure. This vaguely Neoplatonist element to *The Heavenly Foreigner* may owe something to Devlin's knowledge of the Petrarchist tradition in French Renaissance poetry. (Among his translations are poems by Joachim Du Bellay and Pierre de Ronsard.)[4] Whatever its origin, in the lines immediately prior to the above passage, the speaker's recollections of the woman move swiftly from an image of her carrying 'an idol' to how 'she startled, at evening',

Out of the bloody underbrush
After the badger's death, being after being –
Being after being of light, on wings and with one sound (rising which
    sounded Beauty! Beauty! and falling Faith! Faith!) and out there
    between the sea and the sun, some love-goddess clung like a lark to
    the clear air.
(*CP* 260–1)

The idol-bearing woman mutates into 'some love-goddess' as she becomes the means by which the male speaker briefly transcends a world of becoming, of which the dead badger is the grim totem, to a realm of being, an intimation of which is granted in the marvellous sight of the birds' flight seaward from the animal's corpse.[5] Nevertheless, the 'heaven' that ensues for the persona while 'being with her' is short-lived: it is a 'perfection' as fragile and precarious as Scève's, a 'temporal harmony' which inevitably collapses due to the persona's half-resisted, half-accepted 'abeyance' in time. While the ambivalence of the phrase 'Leave me in abeyance' leaves the reader in doubt as to whether the speaker, at this point in the poem, is willingly suspended in time or not, the remainder of the text shows him progressively 'Chaffing' at this existential bit.[6] This has led Brian Coffey to surmise that in the persona's increasingly frantic reaction to his temporal 'abeyance', and to his consequent inability to apprehend directly the Heavenly Foreigner, lies the chief difference between Devlin's poem and Scève's *Délie* (the above *dizain* of which, Coffey notes, Devlin at one time had intended using as the epigraph to his poem). Coffey's commentary on *The Heavenly Foreigner* in relation to *Délie* emphasises Scève's sequence's heavily qualified Petrarchanism, its ultimate refusal to forsake profane for sacred love:

> Scève's world contains ideally two beings, namely Délie and the poet. Devlin's world may have appeared to him, for a while, 'an instant preconising eternity', as one reduced to the essential abstract couple of theoretical love, absolute pain-in-joy. But the world he experienced with increasing honesty while he aged could not be refined down to a couple . . . there was a third, not in third place, to be preferred before both idol and poet. . . . The Devlin known to the writer never could have accepted the everlasting tears and fire which were Scève's lot, nor could he reasonably, truthfully have judged that the place where Scève suffered the fascination of Délie might be made to contain the multitudinous universe of beings – among them a woman hoped preeminent and himself (both, like them, to themselves insufficient) – which he continuously experienced intensely.
> (*HF* 8–9)

As Coffey's comments imply, Devlin's enthusiasm for Scève, which Coffey dates from 1933, clearly drew upon biographical circumstances of 1930–31. The woman represented in *The Heavenly Foreigner* is yet

another instance in Devlin's poetry 'of woman as exemplified in one par-
ticular woman', as Coffey puts it (*HF* 8).[7] Likewise, Scève's persona's love
for Délie is generally assumed to reflect the author's relationship with the
poet Pernette Du Guillet. In this fashion, both *Délie* and *The Heavenly
Foreigner* rely on the reader discerning or rather reconstructing their
'narrative pre-text[s]' – those *fabulae* which, as Doranne Fenoaltea argues
in relation to *Délie*, tie 'the work to the human and literary intertext and
thus to the narrative pre-texts of other lyric collections'.[8] Further speculation
on the biographical context, if not the literary intertexts, of Devlin's poem
is largely irrelevant to its understanding, for – to quote I. D. McFarlane's
words on Scève's *Délie* – 'literary traditions and [the poet's] own creative
urge have transformed it [the stimulus of a real love] so much that there
is little excuse for treating the text as autobiographical evidence'.[9] Devlin's
responsiveness to Scève was due, I would hazard, as much to the sixteenth-
century poet's attractiveness to a reader attuned to French modernism as
it derived from recent events in his love life.[10] Indeed, if Devlin had
originally 'a strong conscious intention to write a modern *Délie*' (*HF* 9),
as Coffey maintains, the presuppositions of his modernism pull his poem
into the orbit of the epistemological and representational issues that we
have seen dominate both his religious and love poetry.

Scève's *Délie*, Dorothy Gabe Coleman argues, is 'sufficiently ambivalent
to suggest the chaste, pure, uncarnal love Scève sings of and yet, contra-
dicting and interwoven with this is the perennial hope, the physical desire
and, in rare moments, the physical satisfaction of the poet, his continual
perseverance in "taming" Délie by his *service d'amour*'.[11] Devlin's *service
d'amour*, Coffey observes, while as ambivalent as that of Scève's speaker,
is not confined to a woman but extends to the Heavenly Foreigner. He is
the third figure of 'Wells', 'The thing behind your elbow' (*CP* 261),
whose elusive yet insistence presence recalls the ghostly figure of Eliot's
The Waste Land ('Who is the third who walks always beside you? /
When I count, there are only you and I together').[12] So too, in 'Irvine', the
speaker says, 'Something there was other / Always at my elbow' ('Irvine',
CP 272), and the female figure of *The Heavenly Foreigner* becomes the
contested site of the poet's struggle to apprehend this 'other' being. Both
Devlin's dependence on and divergence from *Délie* can be registered in
the lines in 'Irvine' which recall Scève's description of Délie's 'mortally
divine arms' while deploying the allusion to specifically spiritual ends:

> The world glows with mortal divinity;
> The red turns grey,
> The ash creeps up on the flame
> O Heavenly Foreigner! Your price is high.
> (*CP* 273)

Devlin's male speaker is fixated with this oxymoronic quality of the woman, her 'glow' of 'mortal divinity'. His memories of her constitute nuclei around which he weaves imaginative conjectures, making the remembered woman, in the words of 'Geneva', 'his emblem / Making her the absolute woman of a moment' (CP 266). That the poet pledges to genuflect before this 'absolute woman' suggests that she is, in a loose sense, a Marian figure, that is, an intercessor with God on the speaker's behalf. This aspect of the woman is developed in a humorous episode (subsequently titled 'Munich') in the Beata prose-work. The passage's narrator expresses a desire 'to be assumed into the love of a celestial lord', a wish he immediately counters with the reflection, 'But I cannot for the heavens do not open as far as I can see'. These deliberations take place, the reader is suddenly made aware, while the narrator is dining with a female companion. She offers him a way of attaining his wish, in his words, 'by implication':

> I kneel down in the restaurant, not minding the amused diners near by
> and lace her shoe and elected gallant of other times.
> 'Do you like doing this?'
> 'Yes.'
> and I blush with delight and shame that she may not like the affectation
> making her the absolute lady of a moment.
> (HF 42)

As a 'gallant of other times', the man's *amour courtois* introduces into this discussion of *The Heavenly Foreigner* the importance of troubadour poetry to Devlin's representation of femininity in the poem and in other, related texts. In an exquisite prose draft of the opening of the poem, the sight of a girl's blonde hair 'brings back the noon, all that placid gold over all that pellucid shadow, like medieval poems over the keeps' (HF 62); an association that strongly suggests the importance to the sequence of Occitan literature of *fin'amor* ('true' or 'pure love'), Devlin's interest in which is attested to by Coffey.[13]

In the context of literary modernism, Devlin would almost certainly have been cognisant of Pound's championing of the troubadours; indeed, there is the flavour of Pound's belief that 'the Middle Ages did not exist in the tapestry alone . . . but that there was a life like our own'[14] in the modern gallant's actions in *Beata*. The gender-relations of *The Heavenly Foreigner* themselves bear some resemblance to the structure of the troubadour lyric. Rouben C. Cholakian summarises the 'love story' told in the Provençal lyric as one 'whose personae are an enunciating lover, more unloved than loved, and an unnamed woman, more unloving than loveable. The plot includes also a third male party who is by turns a slandering eavesdropper (*lausengier*), a jealous rival (*gilos*) or a neutral companion. Critics have seen in this amorous tale the very "invention" of the basic love story, or a least the beginnings of a long European tradition of love poetry.'[15] While the three parties (poet, woman and Heavenly Foreigner) of *The Heavenly Foreigner* obviously interact in different ways from the dramatis personae Cholakian delineates in the Occitan *canso*, they nevertheless make up a comparable *ménage à trois* of lover-poet, beloved-woman, and 'third male party'. More significant is the resemblance between Devlin's depiction of the woman and that in the troubadour lyric. Cholakian notes the way in which 'Descriptions of . . . "individual" women blend together, losing particularity', in the poetry of *fin'amor*, and that this composite female figure becomes the site of various patriarchal responses to femininity: 'Is she a feline monster or is she a near-divinity? Is she a distant beauty or a wily seductress, who needs to be tamed into marital submission? Is she forever *pre*text, no more than an inspiration for poetic achievement, or is she the interceding, holy Mother of mankind? In any case, from our postmodernist perspective we must see her as *constructed*, not *real*.'[16] The female figure in *The Heavenly Foreigner*, despite her basis in an extra-textual woman, conforms to several of these constructs, especially that of 'interceding, holy Mother of mankind'. In this context, it is worth noting the faint echo of the Occitan *pastorela* and the *pastourelles* of the *trouvères* in the occasional conversations between poet and beloved in Devlin's poem (in 'Chartres' and 'Geneva'), which distantly recall the converse held between the male knight and shepherdess in, among other Provençal lyrics, the poetry of the late troubadour, Guiraut Riquier. The parallel with Guiraut is all the more apparent in the way in which *The Heavenly Foreigner* attempts, like some of Guiraut's work, to see in the speaker's female colloquist a mediatrix.

The relationship between troubadour poetry and the cult of the Virgin Mary is a matter of some debate among scholars and critics of Occitan literature. Marina Warner, in her study of Mary, *Alone of All Her Sex*, argues that the appropriation of troubadour poetry by Mariology allowed 'the Virgin . . . . to assume so much of the character and functions of the original beloved of Languedoc poetry and to rob it and its many descendants of its dangerous hedonism and permissiveness. . . . The introduction of the Christian ascetic ideal into Provençal poetry created a particular sentiment that was a travesty of the original wanton temper of the troubadours but was to prevail as the very fibre of lyric verse.'[17] In *The Heavenly Foreigner*, Devlin's deeply felt Mariology lies cheek-by-jowl with a sensuality redolent of the troubadours' 'dangerous hedonism'. The young poet who had published a translation of Louis Le Cardonnel's 'Prière du soir d'été', as a 'Prayer to Our Lady', in the *Missionary Record of the Oblates of Mary Immaculate* (1929; see *TE* 49), was, after all, the same man who, during the composition of *The Heavenly Foreigner*, chose to translate Paul Verlaine's Decadent sonnet 'Parsifal': a highly eroticised account of the eponymous knight's ascetic renunciation of his 'fleshly leanings' towards 'pretty babbling and light breasts', his vanquishing of 'the Woman, beautiful, subtle-hearted, / Spreading her breast and fresh arms' (*TE* 41). In 'Ile-St-Louis' femininity is associated with precisely this Wagnerian form of seductive enchantment, 'the sorceresses whispering / Wind in the wood', while the woman herself becomes the occasion for a rapturous outburst that rapidly shades into sexual perturbation:

> Oh, cling
> Close to the world and her; she crowns
> This moment with the diadem of her Time, and waves
> The floral barge into a frame of trees;
> Her eyes darken with the music,
> Darkness lies against her mouth,
> There is a sharp wind between laugh and cry.
> (*CP* 264)

This passage is plainly reminiscent of Enobarbus's depiction, in *Antony and Cleopatra*, of Cleopatra's barge, swathed in the music of flutes, its tackle handled by her handmaidens' 'flower-soft hands, / That yarely frame the office'.[18] But the shadow that falls over the woman in the passage also brings to mind Eliot's own ironic deployment of Enobarbus's speech in the second part of *The Waste Land*, in which the allusion to Cleopatra on her barge modulates, via a reference to the myth of Philomela's rape, into an atmosphere charged with repugnance at female sexuality. While femininity in *The Heavenly Foreigner* is largely unattended by the squeamish distaste for women one finds in Eliot's poem,[19] the counterbalancing of the Marian dimension to the female in Devlin's poem with a 'darker' side creates an all too familiar patriarchal construct. Furthermore, the idealisation of the woman as an 'intercessor' is compromised by the literal woman's sexual 'darkness', which renders her inadequate, in the speaker's mind, as an image for the Heavenly Foreigner. On the one hand, the construction of the ideal woman can be construed as an attempt to lessen the threat to the male persona posed by female sexuality. In this aspect of the poem's Mariology we find another link to the troubadour Guiraut, whose representation of women Cholakian sees as governed by a desire for patriarchal mastery: 'Transformed into *the* depersonalised female, contained within the spiritual cosmos governed by the father, it is she who surrenders and he who enters into the male community of power and mastery. In that framework, rivalry is ended, the victory is won.'[20] On the other hand, however, *The Heavenly*

Foreigner contains its own critique of this process of idealisation, periodically turning on its depersonalisation of the woman in an urge to retrieve the specificity of her sentient being. Hence the poet's declaration, in 'Sirmione', that 'The woman' is 'No Lady of the Sonnets, no Cathar':

> No need to make of her
> Any invisible, ideal vampire
> Sucking my cells that water anyway.
> (CP 270)

If the literal woman is vampiric on the speaker, the idealised woman bleeds dry both the male lover *and* the literal woman on whom the 'ideal' is dependent, draining away that which a manuscript plan of *Benedicta* calls 'Unique love-love of one person' (*HF* 39). More alarming still, at least for the persona, is the danger that the woman's role as an image for the inexpressible Heavenly Foreigner, her metaphorical intercession, will result in verbal idolatry:

> Young men will not name the beloved object for fear of degrading it.
> Mental prayer is the highest . . . And just at that point
> Which is only, and nothing else, Yourself
> Is that point, is that which I love
> With no words for it.
> (CP 270; Devlin's ellipsis)

Not the least of the paradoxes in *The Heavenly Foreigner* is its lushly metaphorical argument that the images or 'words' denoting the woman constitute a fetishistic symbolism. As 'Chartres' argues:

> Whereas, O my term, my unavoidable turnstile
> In the cathedral porch, I call you these things,
> Term itself, apse itself, had you but come,
> Our absolute Lord had not been me, not me or you,
> But an instant preconising eternity
> Borne between our open eyes,
> With no perceptible bank of land between,
> Nor oblique eyesight deciding other objects were there.
> (CP 262)

The persona's fond hope that if the woman were present the relationship between them would lead to an apprehension of their 'absolute Lord' recalls the injunction in the manuscript plan to 'Est Prodest': 'Let us be content with what we learn by looking at one another, reality be made by the connecting line between us' (*HF* 39). But the woman's literal absence in 'Chartres' defers the 'instant preconising eternity' – a moment redolent of Eliot's epiphanic 'still point of the turning world' in the *Four Quartets* – [21] precisely through her obtrusive presence in the speaker's imagination. Calling her 'Term itself, apse itself' somehow prevents the speaker ingress to the body of the church and its apse, leaving him stranded on the threshold, 'In the cathedral porch'. In addressing her as 'my term' the persona suggests that his recollection of the woman sets up a limit or boundary of some sort, 'an unavoidable turnstile' that, taking into account the architectural meaning of 'term', is also a bust (like that of the god Terminus in the temple of Jupiter Optimus Maximus in Rome), an idol barring his entry to the cathedral's nave. She becomes the 'bank of land', as it were, that lies between male poet and the Heavenly Foreigner, prompting the anxious question raised in the poem's 'Galway' section: 'How I might make my soul / In a freedom that might destroy it?' (CP 268). As in Devlin's other love poems, the imagination in The Heavenly Foreigner possesses a Sartrean freedom vis-à-vis the material world: 'The faint breath of life we breathe into [our imaginings] comes from us, from our spontaneity.'[22] But such 'freedom' has a price: that which 'our spontaneity' constructs has a doubtful ontological status, and therefore the danger, as the speaker sees it, to his 'soul'. Time, in the words of 'Dublin', 'is volumed round me, thick with echoes, things / I cannot see throughout' (CP 269). Those 'echoes', those 'things', are the memories to which he obsessively returns, leafing vainly through the voluminous library of the past for insight, realising that 'The already is my present unresolved'. The subject's existence in the here-and-now is as an echo-chamber of his past, and this prompts an epistemological problem: the 'knowledge' of the Heavenly Foreigner granted by the woman he recalls is, perhaps, knowledge of nothing more than his own mental images of that love-object.

If a phenomenological conception of the imagination posits a self 'volumed round' with images, then the danger of such a process is that, in the terms of Beckett's 'Recent Irish Poetry', in 'stating the space' intervening between himself and the world of objects in this manner, poetry collapses into self-referentiality. Stan Smith has argued that, for Devlin, 'In language alone can the anxious self be guaranteed a breathing space, a cordon sanitaire within which to construct its negotiations with an alien and always potentially destructive world'.[23] But, by the same token, language becomes a Nietzschean prison-house, in which a personal style chatters away to itself, speaking of nothing but its own private creations. The most striking occurrence of this dilemma occurs in the final section of The Heavenly Foreigner, 'Notre Dame de Paris':

How she stood, hypothetical-eyed and metaphor-breasted,
Weaving my vision out my sight,
Out of my sight, out of my very sight,
Out of her sight,
Till the sight I see with is blind with light
Other than hers, other than mine;
Till it unravels
And there's only a light smoke in my hands.
(CP 273)

The first line of this quotation hyperbolically announces the imagination's destruction of the literal woman and her recreation in non-perceptual form, projecting her as a 'hypothesis', an image or 'metaphor'. While it is common practice in patriarchal love poetry to liken the female anatomy to a host of desirable objects, Devlin's image is unusual in that it simply foregrounds the act of comparison, the substitution involved in metaphor of one entity for another. Devlin eschews a specific metaphor, instead identifying the woman with figurative language in general. This strangely transmogrified creature initially appears revelatory, but in the end she reveals nothing, pitching the speaker into blindness, unravelling the vision she had appeared to be weaving:

And this is where, O bed of beds!
Tiger, rough of skin and smooth of eye!
She is my loss and my lost one
And I will possess and dare, cannot possess
This other one, this similar, this One.
(CP 274)

Devlin's writing is at its most compressed in these lines, and one needs to turn elsewhere to find a purchase on their densely woven texture. In a prose manuscript, *Benedicta*, so finely wrought it stands as a prose poem to the verse of *The Heavenly Foreigner*, Devlin writes of 'a human being of the female sex wet violet-eyed tigersmooth armed' who, clearly enough, prefigures the female of 'Notre Dame de Paris'. The caveat which follows the prose's unusual description helps to elucidate the speaker's experience of loss in the lines quoted above: 'doubtless, such epithets though they add to her body, do not belie my vision of her and therefore herself too since she is what I make her – but O bed reality! she is yet at bottom a woman like others, and this I possess not this I have not, is only a brilliant thought slipping through my fingers, a poor fish!' (*HF* 46).[24] As I understand it, the prose argues that any figurative depiction of the woman does not 'belie' his imaginative vision of her, since that vision is of his own making. But 'epithets' allow only an illusory possession of the woman. Faced with her physical absence the passage develops into an invective against 'the books . . . of the masters of love' with 'their idealisation; their lamps of truth, their transformation of essence, their alteration of the she to a stimulant of virtue, a path to heaven, a reward for disappointment'. However, all such idealisations lead to the 'loss' of the literal woman, 'since the herself is gone'. Poignantly, the speaker says: 'What lack to me her two hands and her two feet, her head of sun, her mouth to touch, her all I could wish for. Just this, her.' A corresponding movement is traced in *The Heavenly Foreigner*. A tortuously heightened poetic language conceives of the woman as a metaphor for the Heavenly Foreigner himself: 'This other one, this similar, this One'; but the similarity is, possibly, a self-deluding 'epithet', an 'alteration of the she to a stimulant of virtue, a path to heaven' and thus a loss of the 'bed reality' of the woman in the gaining of an idealised yet inadequate image. The poem concludes with the imagination in possession of naught but its own similitudes, with the 'I' obsessively meditating on its own no-things, fearful of their inability to transport him beyond the limits of consciousness:

> There is none but You I think of.
> I know there is one thing, which is You, it is the unique
> Which also in part is she,
> You, not seen by her,
> You, not to be reduced by my eyes' famine of her . . .
> As I know You, there, behind my back. As I know as far as I can
>   think and have thought You.
>
> There is none so much as You, none You, I think of.
> (CP 274)

Condemned to think of and thus to imagine what is literally unthinkable and unimaginable, the female provides Devlin's persona with an image which, however credible, betrays the absolute otherness of the Heavenly Foreigner. The lame syntax of the final line signals the contortions of the speaker's conceptual struggle, introducing a cluster of ambiguous notions. The clause, 'There is none so much as You', reinforces the sense of the previous lines that nothing resembles the Heavenly Foreigner, that no image can provide an adequate metaphor of him. The parenthetical, 'none You', adds to this, but raises the disturbing suggestion that the second-person pronoun has no referent, that it is non-existent, a non-You. The final words, 'I think of', loop back on those preceding, but fail to stabilise fully the jostle of meanings arising from them. Indeed, by concluding on a dangling preposition the poem, in a sense, severs the act of conceptualisation from the unknowable, unthinkable object, 'You'.

Seamus Deane has claimed that Devlin sought to 'achieve a poetry in which the fission between word and referent would be cancelled or overcome . . . [this being] an analogue for religious faith in which the believer and that in which his faith is vested become incarnated in one'.[25]

Yet that search, culminating in the powerful symbolism of *The Heavenly Foreigner*, is blocked by the 'fission' between intentional image and a referent ('that in which his faith is vested', in Deane's words) which cannot be stated, not even as an imaginary nothingness. If there is, as Deane believes, an analogical relationship between the aims of Devlin's symbolism and his religious faith, both aims are undone owing to the paradoxes at the heart of Devlin's poetic modernism. The literal woman behind the female figure of *The Heavenly Foreigner* acts, in fact, as an 'analogue' in the sense that Sartre gives that term: she is the reality corresponding with, or analogous to, her imaginary embodiment in the poem, the latter 'outside the real, outside existence'.[26] As we have seen, the 'bed reality' or analogical status of the female figure in *The Heavenly Foreigner* disappears in the nothingness of her imaginary realisation, yet this does not lead to a comprehension of the 'unreal' Heavenly Foreigner. It is precisely because of her figurative status that the female figure can never symbolise that which is perceived as lying beyond all linguistic representation, including symbolism.

DISSOLUTE FRAGMENTS AND PLAINSONG: 'THE COLOURS OF LOVE' AND 'THE PASSION OF CHRIST'

The Heavenly Foreigner's deconstruction of the very symbolism on which it is premised is the impasse beyond which Devlin's poetic cannot progress. Such symbolism has its origins in Devlin's early and formative interest in the French *symboliste* poets, which Lorna Reynolds and William G. Downey see as at least partly deriving from his contact as a student with Roger Chauviré, Professor of French at University College Dublin, whose literary enthusiasms also included Racine and Montaigne.[27] Devlin shared his professor's admiration for Montaigne, on whom he wrote his MA dissertation, and the self-interrogation of his symbolist practice may well be coloured by the exploratory, sceptical character of the *Essais*. Certainly, this is how Robert Welch reads Devlin's relationship to the French essayist:

> Like Montaigne Devlin confronted the actual, head-on. There are no fantasies, no alternative worlds, absolutely no visions. Despite the lyric intensity for which he is often praised, the dominant mood of Devlin's poetry is a hard-edged attentiveness to how things are in time; his prosody, a flexible instrument, opens and contracts to accommodate this frank engagement, which is asymbolic, unvisionary, almost scientific.[28]

Welch labours the comparison in terming Devlin's poetry 'asymbolic'; it is rather a symbolism the transcendent aim of which founders on the rocks of its temporal context, an 'anguished communication' (CP 274) aware that its desired object, the divine other of *The Heavenly Foreigner*, cannot be identified with or through the figure of the woman: 'You, not to be reduced by my eyes' famine of her' (CP 274). For this reason, Daniel Murphy's claim that 'issues of faith', for Devlin, 'must be explained finally through analogical relation', while not wrong, manages to deprive Devlin's recourse to symbolic 'analogies' for the Heavenly Foreigner of any sense of desperation.[29] Murphy does, however, usefully introduce the pertinence of Allen Tate's theory of a 'tension in poetry' into a discussion of Devlin's poetry from *Lough Derg and Other Poems* on, quoting from Tate's 1938 essay of that title: 'The metaphysical poet as a rationalist begins at or near the extensive or denoting end of the line; the romantic or Symbolist poet at the other, intensive end; and each by a straining feat of the imagination tries to push his meanings as far as he can towards the opposite end, so as occupy the entire scale'.[30] Tate's theory is a defence of the New Critical verbal icon. Poetry, for Tate, necessarily comprises 'a unity of all the meanings from the furthest extremes of intension and extension', its 'tension' residing in 'the full organized body of all extension and intension that we can find in it':

> The remotest figurative significance that we can derive does not invalidate the extensions of the literal statement. Or we may begin with the literal statement and by stages develop the complications of metaphor: at every stage we may pause to state the meaning so far apprehended, and at every stage the meaning will be coherent.[31]

What Murphy fails to note is the degree to which 'tension' in *The Heavenly Foreigner* stems not from its 'balance of modes', as Murphy contends,[32] but from the manner in which the poem opens a fissure between extension and intension, the literal and the figurative, as the woman's real and symbolic identities are inexorably prised apart. The analogies fail Devlin's persona, as the urge to find a *symboliste* correspondence between the woman and the Heavenly Foreigner is undermined by a quizzical, Montaigne-like interrogation of the ground of the comparison. In I. A. Richards's influential distinction, one adopted by the New Critics, the vehicle of the poem's central metaphor fails to carry its tenor, and the comparison thus, as the persona laments in 'Notre Dame de Paris', 'unravels / And there's only a light smoke in my hands'.

'The Colours of Love' (1952), the composition of which would appear to be roughly contemporaneous with that of *The Heavenly Foreigner*, opens with a restatement of this recurrent conundrum in Devlin's later poetry:

> Women that are loved are more than loveable
>   Their beauty absolute blows:
> But little, like the urgent, carnal soul,
>   More than its leaves so mortal in the rose.
>
> O rose! O more than red mortality!
>   What can my love have said
> That made me her imagine more than be?
>   Her mind more than mind, blood more than red?
> (CP 275)

In a fashion familiar from other love poems by Devlin, the glimpse of 'absolute' beauty in the phenomenal beauty of 'Women that are loved' is due to the latter's reconfiguration by the imagination, which negates the literal woman so that she seems 'more than red mortality'. The poem as a whole charts the speaker's ambivalent response to his having 'her imagine[d] more than be' in a process of self-interrogation and self-reproach, inaugurated by the question nagging the speaker in the second stanza quoted above. As in *The Heavenly Foreigner*, this aspect of the poem is indelibly entwined with its relation to the conventions of *amour courtois*, which Coffey reads the poem as renouncing: 'although [it was] not written out of the tradition of courtly love (of which, like so many of the Gaelic Poets, Denis Devlin was well aware), ["The Colours of Love"] might well sum up the European sentence upon the extraordinary phenomenon: Better no love than love, which, through loving leads to no love: the poet seems to free himself from his conflict in its overt form, and thus, mature, turn inward to the personal life out of which issued *The Passion of Christ*' (CP [Coffey] xiii). Coffey's opening proviso notwithstanding, the poem refracts its autobiographical pretext through the prism of literary convention. Devlin's persona initially pledges allegiance 'to that mistress planet, / Venus', believing that her 'hunting priests explain / My heart and the rush of legend on it'. The poem's collage of lyric passages, drawn, as the successive drafts of the poem demonstrate, from a substantial sheaf of discrete poems, comprises a series of responses to this opening declaration. The effect of this structure, as in the similarly constructed 'The Passion of Christ', is to exert pressure between the traditional stanzaic form of the individual parts and the fragmented nature of the poem as a whole. It is a structure at one with the poem's vacillatory stance towards the temptations of both venery and its literary representation:

> Voices from the shrubbery nearby:
> 'Smile with your eyes,' one says, 'what sweet invention!'
> What did that Mediterranean nymph reply?
> 'Smile with your fables and their sweet intention.'
> (CP 276)

These voices speak of the allure of 'invention' and 'fables' as much as the seductiveness of eyes and smiles; while that 'Mediterranean nymph' draws both lyric subject and reader back to the shores of Occitania and the pleasures of *fin'amor*. Dillon Johnston, taking issue with Coffey's interpretation of the poem's response to *amour courtois* sees the possible influence of the *stilnovo* poets on Devlin's treatment of love. Disputing Coffey's claim that 'Devlin pronounces "sentence upon" courtly love, or that he slackens that cord between carnal and spiritual love, on which he plays', Johnston contends that the poem 'might even be read as a playful extension of the *dolce stil nuovo* with its emphasis on eyes and smiles, in the manner of Guido Guinizelli'. This suggestive point can be linked to Johnston's observation that, in the central sections of the poem, the persona 'imagines his own Dantean exile within an Irish setting'.[33] The relevant passage concludes:

> I saw him move among the iron leaves
> Which were to carbonise through his love's breast.
> Hers, and the graves of lechers, louts and thieves,
> Would sag and musty change be all their rest.
>
> When leaves have fallen and there's nothing left
> But plainsong from ascetic bony birds,
> I say a prayer for all who are bereft
> Of love, of leafy summer, of loving words.
> (CP 278)

The striking image of the 'iron leaves' among which the unnamed figure moves brings to mind the simile Eliot deploys in *Little Gidding* to describe the approach of 'a familiar compound ghost', Eliot's confrontation as a whole modelled on Dante's meeting with Brunetto Latini in Canto XV of the *Inferno*:

> I met one walking, loitering and hurried
> As if blown towards me like the metal leaves
> Before the urban dawn wind unresisting.[34]

Devlin's dead leaves, like Eliot's, find an echo elsewhere in the *Inferno*, in Canto III, in the account of the damned souls on the banks of Acheron: 'As in autumn the leaves drop off one after the other till the branch sees all its spoils on the ground, so the wicked seed of Adam fling themselves from that shore one by one at the signal, as a falcon at its recall.'[35] The figure moving 'among the iron leaves' in 'The Colours of Love' is a 'compound ghost' in which the shades of the troubadours, Guido Guinizelli and the Dante of the *Vita Nuovo* can all be faintly glimpsed – not so much through specific allusions as through the overdetermined quality of the writing. Overdetermination arises from the text's belatedness,

its self-conscious evocation of a tradition of amatory verse the delights of
which haunt the speaker even as they give rise to feelings of guilt. This
aspect of the text entails that its autobiographical pretext, like that of *The
Heavenly Foreigner*, cannot be disentangled from its literary pre-texts; the
poem, after all, details the *colours* of love rather than love itself, and the
palette with which Devlin paints his erotic experiences is that of courtly
love and its variants:

> Remember! do you think I could forget?
> The pigeons growl like dogs in sleep remote.
> Yet now if you should ask, I could not yet
> Forswear that fascination, break that note
>
> Which death in his lush garden exercised,
> The habit of repentance feeds the sin
> (*CP* 276)

The sinfulness of the persona's desire for the woman, and that of its
representation in the 'note[s]' of verse, reminds us of Dante's judgement
on the poetry of Guinizelli and that of the troubadour Arnaut Daniel, the
two poets grouped with the penitent sexual sinners in *Purgatorio* XXVI,
where it would seem that both the lusts of the flesh and the Barthesian
pleasures of the text can be purged by fire. However, we can detect a
crucial difference between Devlin's relationship with his precursors, in
this text and elsewhere in the later poems, and Dante's in the *Commedia*.
Dante's treatment of his poetic predecessors in *Purgatorio* XXVI can be
allied to the 'transumption' evident in, for example, his troping of the
dead as autumnal leaves, an image which subsumes and enlarges, even as
it alludes to, related metaphors in the sixth books of the *Aeneid* and the
Iliad. Harold Bloom argues that the 'strong' poet's successful transump-
tion of his precursors, as in this instance, produces the disorientating
effect of reversing the chronology of literary history, so that 'the influence
process uncannily flows backward', Dante becoming, it would seem, the
literary progenitor of Virgil and Homer.[36] By way of contrast, Devlin's
dependence on the poetic traditions Dante respectfully yet firmly consigns
to purgatory is a recognition of his poetry's belatedness, which it neither
seeks to overcome nor deny. Bloom's claim that 'Transumption does not
murder precursors, but rather drives its projective violence *against time*'[37]
simply has no relevance to Devlin's poem (and little either, one feels, to
Eliot's use of Dante in *Little Gidding*), which is dominated by a sense of
the lateness of the hour for *amour courtois*. In 'The Colours of Love' the
weight of tradition does not prompt an Oedipal struggle with poetic
forebears; instead, recovering momentarily from his fear that 'leaves have
fallen and there's nothing left / But plainsong from ascetic bony birds', the
speaker takes succour from a troubadour-like 'kinsman':

as he sang my courage grew,
It was about betrayal and disgrace,
He said 'Love fails but love of love stays true.'
(CP 278)

The persona draws strength as much from the literary conventions of the
kinsman's song as from its aphoristic wisdom: 'Singing in vain and formal
in the shade / The noble poverty those houses made.' A somewhat
threadbare version of Stevens's singer in 'The Idea of Order at Key West'
(for whom 'there never was a world . . . / Except the one she sang and,
singing, made'),[38] the kinsman makes structures that offer shelter of a
kind, however much their original nobility is now striken by 'poverty'.
Looking back both on the love of his 'young year' (CP 280), and at the
distant origins of his love poetry, the poet breaks briefly with his obsessive
attachment to the past, his fixation with lost love and eroded poetic
forms, only to reaffirm his anguished commitment to 'love of love':

> When Spring with her lambs and sea-cries rises,
> Her fluent fantasy makes a mock of me;
> I throw off my absolutist devices
> And dissemble in the loose, resplendent sea:
>
> Yet think on how San Juan, bitter and bare
> Wrapt in his drama, sent his cry above
> And though, through layer on suffocating layer
> Nothing came back, he loved; and so I love.
> (CP 279)

San Juan performs the same consolatory role as the kinsman, even as he
draws the poem's concern with human love into the orbit of the trans-
cendental. San Juan's mysticism proved attractive to many modernists,
including Eliot, whose *East Coker* draws upon his notion of the *noche
ocura*, or Dark Night. (Devlin alludes to the same experience in
'Transfiguration', the closing lyric to 'The Passion of Christ': 'As if dark
were light / . . . /The torsion and the tension of that Night!' [CP 294].)
Closer to the general practice of Devlin's religious poetry is the manner in
which the Spanish poet, after the example of the *Song of Songs* and its
medieval interpretations, deploys human love as a vehicle for the
inexpressible mysteries of divine love, sublimating profane desire into
the search of the soul for God, as in the *Cántico espiritual*. San Juan's
visions are glossed by Evelyn Underhill – in a book of 1911 that
impressed Eliot and many of his contemporaries – as not 'objective', but
'forms of symbolic expression': 'Visionary experience . . . is a picture
which the mind constructs . . . from raw materials already at its disposal.'[39]
Such, of course, is Devlin's asymptotic approach to the Heavenly Foreigner,
as he constructs a relationship to a deity out of the 'raw material' of the

desire for a literal woman. San Juan's 'visionary experience' becomes, in 'The Colours of Love', an exemplary artistic performance, the poet 'Wrapt in his drama'. This immediately raises the spectre of an essentially solipsistic imagination, one which, *à la* Sartre, projects its subjective fantasies onto the world through negation: 'drama', after all, carries connotations of histrionics, of self-dramatisation. Driven back into self-communing, the self grows narcissistic as its contemplates its own imaginary constructs, and, unlike Sartre, Devlin views such freedom not as existentially liberating but as a 'suffocating' deprivation of objective knowledge of God.

The poem can find no resolution to its yawing trajectory; instead, it reaches closure of a kind through a highly ambivalent renunciation of its problematic premises:

> At the Bar du Départ drink farewell
> And say no word you'll be remembered by;
> Nor Prince nor President can ever tell
> Where love ends or when it does or why.
> (*CP* 279–80)

In these chasteningly beautiful lines, Devlin would appear to say 'farewell', firstly to the woman the memory of whom dominates his love poetry,[40] secondly to the tradition of 'courtly love' poetry of which 'The Colours of Love' is a self-consciously belated example, and thirdly to the 'hypothetical-eyed and metaphor-breasted' (as *The Heavenly Foreigner* describes her) female figure who emerges in his work out of the confluence of auto-biographical and literary pretexts. Yet the poem does not conclude on a sustained note of resignation, regardless of Coffey's claim that, with this poem, Devlin brings a certain phase of his work to an end:

> Down the boulevard the lights come forth
> Like my rainflowers trembling all through Spring,
> Blue and yellow in the Celtic North . . .
> The stone's ripple weakens, ring by ring.
>
> Better no love than love, which, through loving
> Leads to no love. The ripples come to rest . . .
> Ah me! how all that young year I was moving
> To take her dissolution to my breast!
> (*CP* 280; Devlin's ellipses)

Even as the rings of memory and those of a particular literary tradition gradually 'come to rest' there is, as Johnston notes, 'a final ripple in the poem's movement', as 'that young year' stubbornly reasserts itself in the persona's consciousness.[41] The eroticism of this resurgence is inseparable from its literary historical dimension: Devlin's characteristic bolstering of male subjectivity through an attempt to control a female other is equally his final negotiation with a crucial portion of the Western canon of (male) love poetry. The patriarchal underpinnings of Devlin's verse are apparent in the striking image in the final line, in which, 'moving' to embrace 'her dissolution', the speaker acts as if the woman's only guarantee against disintegration lay in her physical possession by him. Ironically enough, it is Devlin's usual practice to separate or dissolve the female body into its constituent parts through metonymy, as in the present poem's reduction of the woman to her 'blond haunches' (*CP*, 277). The image of 'dissolution' also reintroduces the poem's earlier concern with the sinful excesses of profane love, now predictably projected onto a alluringly dissolute, female partner. Such projection is further apparent in the transferral onto the woman alone of the persona's own doubts about love, as she becomes the embodiment of the 'dissolution' of love, the termination in love's failure that the poem records. The poem's preoccupation with the disintegration of love is reflected, at the level of form, in the lyric shards that make up the sequence, fragments which themselves comprise meagre precipitates of a tradition in a state of dissolution. To appropriate Eliot's words on his leave-taking of the 'familiar compound ghost' in *Little Gidding*, 'The Colours of Love' is 'a kind of valediction' to a specific love and to a body of love poetry.

The individual poems that make up 'The Passion of Christ' (1957), like those of 'The Colours of Love', were quarried out of a larger mass of material, and comprise a sporadic narrative spanning from the Fall to Christ's Ascension. The composite quality of the poem differs from the lyric dissolution and circularity of 'The Colours of Love' in its progressive sequentiality: the poems constitute, in Tim Armstrong's words, 'extended versions of the Stations of the Cross'. Whereas the lyrics of 'The Colours of Love' leach into one another, the poems of the later text are firmly demarcated and individually titled. Armstrong finds the text 'a dry performance', possessing a 'rigidity of form' possibly informed by the example of Tate, to whom the poem is dedicated, 'who was in that period busily writing himself into an American version of Eliot's Anglo-Catholic impasse'.[42] Certainly, in comparison to the hauntingly resonant music of 'The Colours of Love', the later text sounds like the 'Plainsong from ascetic bony birds' disparaged in the earlier. Following Armstrong's lead, one can trace this dimension of the text back to its dedicatee, and specifically, I would suggest, to his theory of a 'tension in poetry' discussed above. 'The Passion of Christ' can be read as Devlin's attempt to attain the kind of tension between rationalist and symbolist modes of poetry for which Tate argues in his essay – a strained endeavour to surmount the powerful proclivity of his poetry to peel apart the extensive and intensive properties of language, as in the wedge the heady symbolism of *The Heavenly Foreigner* drives between referent and figure. The poem circumnavigates this tendency by approaching its subject matter from the denotative or extensive end of Tate's scale of poetic language. The poem, in Tate's words, 'begin[s] with the literal statement and by stages develop[s] the complications of metaphor', principally, as we shall see, that of diplomacy. The result is a relatively terse, compressed diction, its imagery shorn of the Surrealist element that still enlivens *The Heavenly Foreigner* (and which was retained throughout Devlin's revisions to that poem).

Tate's theory, according to Radcliffe Squires, signalled a break with T. E. Hulme's classicist criteria for the successful poem, by means of which Tate opened 'a door to romanticism in his poetry'.[43] In Devlin's case, this door had been ajar since the early 1930s, as evinced by the symbolist and Surrealist dimensions to his modernism. Largely bereft of these constituents, the poetic texture of 'The Passion of Christ' has a crispness – or, if one inclines to Armstrong's view, aridity – new to his poetry:

> From what did man fall?
> From the Archangel Michael's irritated wing?
> Man is so small,
> Without him first the universe did sing,
> So fortunate since the Christ eluded his caul:
> Let us take on the whole
> Story in its negligence and passion –
> Archangel, we your images that fall,
> Dissolve and reassemble, session by session.
> You rise and rise, God's wasp, and sting!
> We fall and rise, God's instrument, and sing!
> (*CP* 286)

The almost curt opening is immediately lifted by the striking image of 'the Archangel Michael's irritated wing'. In Devlin's choice of adjective one can possibly detect the influence of Tate's 1944 religious poem 'Seasons of the Soul', the fourth section of which opens with a defamiliarising invocation of 'Irritable spring'.[44] Be that as it may, 'The Passion of Christ' shares Tate's poem's preoccupation with the desirability of God's intervention into history, that of the speaker and humanity as a whole. Tate concludes 'Seasons of the Soul' by beseeching the 'mother of silences' to intercede on behalf of its all-too-human speaker and his wartime contemporaries:

> Come, old woman, save
> Your sons who have gone down
> Into the burning cave . . .
>
> Speak, that we may hear;
> Listen, while we confess
> That we conceal our fear

That the poem's imploration goes unanswered also links it to Devlin's sequence, in which, in the words of 'The Good Thief', the 'reasons' for believing in Christ's divinity are grounded in the Jansenist paradox: 'You are there and are not there' (*CP* 292). The religious character of 'The Passion of Christ' can be glossed by a note in Devlin's papers, identified as his 'last statement': 'The poet justifies the ways of man to God'. The inversion of Milton's famous declaration of intent at the beginning of *Paradise Lost* is attendant on Devlin's religious views as developed from 'Est Prodest' through *The Heavenly Foreigner*. Given the epistemological uncertainty of his religious poetry, its fruitless interrogation of a Pascalian, hidden God, Milton's vaunting ambition is unavailable to Devlin. As 'images that fall', humanity in 'The Passion of Christ', as in Tate's poem, is doomed to a 'negligence' only Christ's crucifixion and resurrection can redeem. Consequently, the 'Story' the poem tells is studded with a sense of culpability in Christ's death, as in the section headed 'The Last Supper':

> None of us can remember without tears
> Nor asking with what faculty we failed:
> Was it the purse, or Peter's doubting ears?
>   Or the rash brethren jailed?
> (*CP* 288)

Devlin's familiar theme of the injustice of the fallen world is represented in the tableau of Christ 'Before Pilate': 'To flagellate, to crown with thorns, to make / A show of man who would Man create' is, the poem ruefully observes, 'Nothing much when Justice is at stake' (*CP* 290). If Pilate's world is one in which 'filthy, wine-lit bands / Forgive Barabbas who shed blood', it nevertheless is equally the world of 'Veronica's Veil', which depicts the faithful poor, 'Ragged mothers who give milk to their neighbours', as the inheritors of Saint Veronica, their actions at one with her merciful wiping of the blood from the face of Christ as he walked to Calvary:

> some holy women
> Will take their last white linen from the drawer
> And saying: 'God is ours as He is human,'
> Wipe the blood from the unbearable scar.
> (*CP* 290)

'Veronica's Veil' invites comparison with Yeats's 'Veronica's Napkin', in which the Christian legend becomes a vehicle for Yeats's late exploration of the bloody origins of human power and its seeming irreconcilablility with divine wisdom. Yeats's poem gnomically plays off arcane astrological and astronomical charts, which depict 'Symbolical glory of the earth and air', with 'A pattern on a napkin dipped in blood'.[45] The napkin's gory imprint of Christ's face becomes, in Yeats's hands, an image

of the blood's energies and desires – those fallible powers of the body –
that the Self, in 'A Dialogue of Self and Soul', yearns to recapture, to
'live . . . again': 'if it be life to pitch / Into the frog-spawn of a blind man's
ditch, / A blind man battering blind men'.[46] In Devlin, while the 'blindness'
of the human condition underscores the reasoning of 'The Bad Thief' –
who regards 'Men that torture knowing what they do' as the outcome of
a God who 'made it in our power / To destroy the World You saved us in'
(*CP* 293) – it also inspires the humility of 'The Good Thief':

> It is not right for me to talk to You,
> To wait on You with ministerial bow,
> To pray, or if I lived in higher merit
> To love even, or to adore, or care.
> (*CP* 292)

As J. C. C. Mays judiciously comments: 'The treatment of the two thieves
bypasses theology and frames the problem of divine justice in terms of
human understanding' (*CP* 32); that is, the good thief gropes towards the
same kind of understanding present in the words of the women of
'Veronica's Veil' ('God is ours as He is human'). Mays's claim that Devlin
chooses to 'frame' this central issue of his work through the 'syntax' of
the two thieves usefully brings together the question of the Tate-like
'tension' of the poem and its religious concerns. Mays contends that 'The
words of the bad thief are merely jumbled and confused' (*CP* 32); the
good thief, by way of contrast, develops a coherent image of himself as a
corrupt ambassador of Christ, commencing with the inappropriateness of
his 'ministerial bow' before Christ:

> My memory in lethargy turns sour
> All whence, my understanding, less imperious
>   Day by day and hour by hour,
>
> Loses whole continents where in my childhood
> I was Your Viceroy, and approved the Just
> And condemned my natural evil thoughts –
> Now, what has changed me? Is it the years
> You made and gave me, Lord? or am I prone to the evil
>   The masters dinned into my ears?
> (*CP* 292–3)

As Stan Smith observes, the diplomatic metaphors serve to defamiliarise
'the orthodox belief that original sin is a fall from the state of grace to the
state of nature': 'The poet's skill lies in playing up the statist metaphor to
the point at which he can speak of the "majesty of Christ" as that of
"God's son foreign to our moor".'[47] To this I would add that the 'playing
up' of the metaphor works in the fashion Tate identifies with the procedure

of the 'The metaphysical poet as a rationalist', who 'begins at or near the extensive or denoting end of the line . . . push[ing] his meanings as far as he can towards' the intensive end of the scale.[48] In this light, the metaphorical diplomat, disgraced and abject in his failure, complements the connotative, symbolic female of *The Heavenly Foreigner*, to the extent that in both figures Devlin represents his fraught relationship with God. In the end, the two approaches emphasise the highly mediated nature of that relationship. For if the Heavenly Foreigner eludes the grasp of the symbol, the imagery of diplomacy, as Smith observes, falls short of a God who exists 'beyond the compromising loyalties and betrayals of a fallen political world'.[49] In 'The Last Supper', God's 'world' is defined by the '*Absence* of principalities and powers' (*CP* 289; my italics), while in 'Ascension' Christ's bodily ascension into heaven leaves humanity with the double-edged knowledge of 'Life with its dark, and love above the laws' (*CP* 294). 'Ascension', in contrast to the close of *The Heavenly Foreigner*, is stoic in its acceptance of the inability of poetic language, whether in its extensive or intensive mode, to comprehend that love:

> It happens through the blond window, the trees
> With diverse leaves divide the light, light birds;
> Aengus, the God of Love, my shoulders brushed
> With birds, you could say lark or thrush or thieves
>
> And not be right yet – or ever right –
> For it was God's Son foreign to our moor

The speaker's perception of Christ is mediated ('It happens') through the 'blond window', an image imbued with the love poetry's 'Yellowheaded Helen', the woman of the 'blond haunches' who lies behind the ambivalent mediatrix of *The Heavenly Foreigner*. The image thus leads naturally enough into the reference to Aengus – the Celtic god conventionally associated with love – and his birds, which in turn foregrounds the interrelation of spiritual and secular love in Devlin's poetry. The subsequent lines admit that neither the symbolism of love (as in *The Heavenly Foreigner*), here figured forth in Aengus's birds, nor the imagery developed through the personae of the 'thieves' in 'The Passion of Christ' adequately conveys the utter foreignness of 'God's Son'.

EXTERNAL AFFAIRS: 'THE TOMB OF MICHAEL COLLINS' AND 'MEMOIRS OF A TURCOMAN DIPLOMAT'

Devlin's good thief speaks of 'The huge and foreign universes round me', an expression of his distance from God that chimes with the 'Alienation' which Tate, in 'Modern Poetry' (1955), saw as the condition of the modern poet and as partially explaining the incestuous relationship between twentieth-century poetry and criticism:

> Alienation as a subject for poetry seems to take two directions: first, the relation of the poet to the world – and this ranges all the way from a quasi-religious sense of man's isolation in the decentralized universe, down to the crass question of the poet's 'contribution to society'; and secondly, poems about the meaning of poetry itself. I suppose never before in the history of poetry in any language have so many poems been written, as in the American English of this century, *about* poetry.[50]

In the Hiberno-English poetry of this century, Devlin's exploration of 'Alienation', as defined by Tate (which we can see as compatible with the 'rupture of the lines of communication' Beckett discusses in 'Recent Irish Poetry'), addresses not only 'man's isolation in the decentralized universe', but also the 'crass question' of the poet's social role, in exactly the self-reflexive fashion Tate sees as characteristic of modern poetry. This dimension to his modernism finds a close parallel in the New Critical resistance to overtly political literature, as adumbrated by Tate in his 1950 essay, 'To Whom is the Poet Responsible'. In this essay, Tate makes the surprising claim that 'it would be better to suppress poetry than to misuse it [for political ends], to expect of it an order of action that it cannot provide'. The sole manner in which Tate is prepared to grant to poetry any political efficacy is through its capacity to make us 'more conscious of the complexity and meaning of our experience' which may have 'an eventual effect upon action, even political action'.[51] While Tate's argument is rooted in debates in America over the connections between literature and society, and between literary form and political relevance, that reach back to the 1930s, it is also germane to Devlin's political poetry.

I argued in chapter 1 that the political commitment of the cultural programme of the literary revival – its nationalist content – should be carefully weighed against its high modernist attention to literary form. The recurrent trope of the Western peasantry, for instance, both has a political subtext and, in its tendentious connection to the rural poor, is a manifestly *literary* device. Of the post-revivalist poets, Patrick Kavanagh stands as the most successful in breaking with revivalist idealisations of rural Ireland, a break enabled by that which Seamus Deane calls his 'revolutionary . . . regionalism'.[52] For Deane, Kavanagh's work marks the end of Irish poetry's involvement with politics, owing to 'the collapse of nationalism and [the] poverty of the period between 1930 and 1955'.[53] The regionalism of Kavanagh, the realism of his *The Great Hunger* and the 'parochial vision' he developed subsequently, turn against both the aestheticism and nationalism of the revival in favour of a 'clear and monochromatic' style of writing and a preoccupation with the local parish.[54] Deane sees Kavanagh's anti-nationalism as representative of Irish poetry in the mid-century: 'Only Denis Devlin in these decades attempts to make some reconciliation between poetry and politics in, for instance, his poem "On the Tomb of Michael Collins" – and that is a sad failure.'[55] If Devlin's poem (properly titled 'The Tomb of Michael Collins') fails as political poetry for Deane, in Austin Clarke's eyes it (happily) marked a *volte face* with Devlin's earlier modernism, in which he 'wrote strictly in the intellectual manner of modern French poets'.[56] Both of these claims require investigation. Devlin's text, I will argue, is most rewardingly understood in the light of a modernist attention to form and, its corollary, the severance of art from life praxis – an attention informed *by* Devlin's knowledge of French 'intellectual' or avant-garde poetry. As we shall see, read in this fashion the poem comes into focus as highly self-conscious of the difficulty of any 'reconciliation' of poetry and politics.

Deane's summary devaluation of Devlin's elegy for Collins, although unsubstantiated, may stem from the poem's apparent adherence to the popular mythology surrounding Collins. On a cursory reading, the poem seems to amount to little more than a versification of sentiments analogous to P. S. O'Hegarty's idealised memories of Collins. In a 1945 article for the *Sunday Independent*, O'Hegarty recalled that Collins 'was, in truth, as heroic and legendary as the stories make out': 'Out of the unknown he came, in the day of tempest, to sustain and lead this nation in a supreme hour, and across our history he flashed for a few brief years, like a sword, gay, laughing, generous, Irish and unafraid, and then again into the unknown.'[57] In like fashion, Collins in Devlin's poem is not only elegised but also eulogised; his shade, the speaker declares in the opening stanza, is manifestly different from 'the familiar and forgetful / Ghosts who leave our memory too soon':

> He was loved by women and by men,
> He fought a week of Sundays and by night
> He asked what happened and he knew what was –
> O Lord! how right that them you love die young!
> (CP 283)

In the tragedy of Collins premature death at Béal na bláth on 22 August 1922, the poem maintains, should be seen a final expression of his *sprezzatura*:

> Then came that mortal day he lost and laughed at,
> He knew it as he left the armoured car;
> The sky held in its rain and kept its breath;
> Over the Liffey and the Lee, the gulls,
> They told his fortune which he knew, his death.
> (CP 284)

That Collins died in the aftermath of a war of independence, in which he was a crucial strategist and negotiator for peace, is stressed in the elegist's platitudinous statement:

> There are the Four Green Fields we loved in boyhood,
> There are some reasons it's no loss to die for:
> Even it's no loss to die for having lived

As the above quotations illustrate, on one level the text adheres fairly closely to the traditions of the elegy as formulated from the seventeenth century on. The object of the elegy is mourned; his or her virtues are celebrated; his or her death leads into more general reflections on mortality and the cruel chances of time; and, finally, from the death of the individual is drawn strength for the living, including the elegist. The consolation to be drawn from Collins's death is stressed in the parallel the elegy's conclusion draws between the assassination of Collins and that of Lincoln (the poem alludes to one of Whitman's several elegies for the American president, 'O Captain! My Captain!'). Both men, we are told, 'have achieved their race' (*CP* 285).

Coffey finds in this treatment of Collins not 'a sad failure', but 'the personal reverence and affection of Devlin for a man who had been in his father's house', a response to 'the big fellow' that is not translated into political terms because of its 'remove from politics'.[58] The poem's success, in Coffey's eyes, lies in its exemplifying a tenet perhaps more central to Coffey's poetic than to Devlin's: 'to aim at poems . . . implies a freedom that neither reasons of state nor policing power can be permitted to restrain or constrain.'[59] One detects in Coffey's commentary the presence of his one-time doctoral supervisor, the neo-scholastic philosopher, Jacques Maritain, who argued that modernist poetry, while materially rooted in this world, is 'ordered to an object transcending man . . . whose fullness is without limit, for beauty is as infinite as being'.[60] For Coffey, in short, Devlin's poem makes no attempt at a 'reconciliation' between poetry and politics because the latter is subservient to poetry's transcendental ordering.

Nevertheless, for all the differences between them, Clarke, Coffey and Deane seem to me to short-circuit the wiring of this elegy by failing to explore its self-reflexive quality. In this respect, it is paradoxically Coffey's apolitical reading which allows us to broach the interrelationship between politics and modernism in Devlin's poem. Coffey's interpretation of Devlin's poetry as a whole is premised on his belief that it is characterised by what he identifies as Devlin's quintessential 'distance'. This 'distance', opines Coffey, can be broken down into three kinds: firstly, a 'reserve', a feature of his personality which endows his poetry with a 'specificity' or 'objectivity' based on 'respect for himself and others'; secondly, a 'syntax . . .

constructed to hold a subject-matter at the distance necessary for reflective empathy'; and, thirdly, his 'aim and search for what is most distant, most different and most distinct from us humans, and his attempt to bring that most distant beyond all sensible or imagined horizons into human proximity'.[61] Coffey's Devlin, in other words, is a classicist modernist who avoids 'subjective' expression. Experimental in method, he is thematically conservative, questing for transcendental values in a profane world. This, in essence, is identical to the reading of Devlin made by Terence Brown: 'Devlin seeks to . . . sustain a Christian tradition profoundly under threat in a modern world of political and philosophical nihilism.'[62] Coffey's reading also accords with Mays's opinion that 'Such poetry seeks to be classic. . . . It is impersonal, in that it abjures the sense of a lyric I', in support of which Mays quotes Devlin's comment to Coffey: 'I would like a discourse from which the middle terms have been dropped' (CP 42–3).[63] That quality of Devlin's poetry which Coffey calls 'distance' and Mays labels 'classic' and 'impersonal' would appear to bring Devlin into accord with Eliot's famous definition, in 'Tradition and the Individual Talent', of the 'impersonal' poet, whose 'progress . . . is a continual self-sacrifice, a continual extinction of personality'. Yet, as has been noted on many occasions, Eliot adds to this the qualification that, 'of course, only those who have a personality and emotions know what it means to want to escape from these things'.[64] In other words, an impersonal style, like a reserved social demeanour, may serve to conceal a depth of personality. Devlin's poetry chimes well with this view of the artist: in an Eliotic fashion his poems place the poet's personality, in Derridean terms, 'under erasure'; that is, an impersonal textual patina overlays an 'I' whose presence can, nevertheless, still be dimly apprehended.

In the light of the above, Coffey's error, to my mind, is to have failed to apply his general reflections on Devlin to this specific poem, a slip which causes him, in replying to Deane, to over-emphasise 'the *personal* reverence and affection of Devlin for [Collins]'. For the reverential tone towards Collins in the poem is mediated through two further voices or 'personalities'. Two of these voices are identified in a letter to Coffey, in which Devlin states that 'The popularesco repetitions "It is . . ." "It was . . ."' in the poem 'come, deliberately, from the Irish ballad, my aim being to make a ceremonial ode with country ballad elements' (quoted in CP [Coffey] xix). In other words, Devlin seeks, in Eliot's terms, to sacrifice his voice to the anonymity or 'impersonality' of the ballad tradition, while simul-taneously grafting that tradition onto the more elevated form or 'voice' of the homostrophic ode. The poem deploys several trans-national ballad elements: opening with a dramatic, and climatic, event, (Collins's death); moving abruptly from event to event; employing incremental repetition (that which Devlin terms 'popularesco repetitions'); and so forth. Alongside these, there are specifically Irish ballad features, as in the poem's reference to the 'Four Green Fields' quoted above and its role-call of Irish patriots from the past (preceded, in the following stanza's opening sentence, by an Hibernicism):

> I tell these tales – I was twelve years old that time.
> Those of the past were heroes in my mind:
> Edward the Bruce whose brother Robert made him
> Of Ireland, King; Wolfe Tone and Silken Thomas
> And Prince Red Hugh O'Donnell most of all.

Simultaneously, the ode-like quality to which Devlin also aspires can be heard in the poem's ambitious 'public' dimensions. Written in a largely Horatian manner, it frequently modulates into Pindaric enthusiasm, as, for instance, in the cry concluding the text's first stanza: 'Oh, what voracious fathers bore him down!'

The third voice of the elegy is the one the reader tends to identify with the author: the 'I' who dispenses autobiographical information, as in the above reference to the poet's age when Collins was shot ('I was twelve years old that time'). Yet this autobiographical 'I' is refracted through that doubled subject, the Horatian balladeer, the polymorphous tone of whom Devlin explicitly sought to evoke in writing the poem. The result is a compound elegist, the voice(s) of whom pre-empts any reading of the poem that would make of it a monody or elegy proceeding from a single voice (which, in the last instance, is the reading made by Coffey). One effect of this convoluted voice is precisely that 'distance' Coffey maintains is at the heart of Devlin's poetry, a distance that, I wish to argue, offers a quiet deconstruction of the poem's overt and intentional admiration for Collins.

This dimension of the poem is observable in its open allusion to Whitman's 'O Captain! My Captain!' The point easily overlooked in reading the final stanza is that the presence of Whitman's poem in *this* poem is as a 'lesson':

> Walking to Vespers in my Jesuit school,
> The sky was come and gone; 'O Captain, my Captain!'
> Walt Whitman was the lesson that afternoon –
> How sometimes death magnifies him who dies,
> And some, though mortal, have achieved their race.

As the punctuation of the final lines implies, the lesson taught by Whitman is not just that certain individuals, like Lincoln and Collins, alter a nation's history, but that such figures also may find a posthumous identity, henceforth becoming the nexus for political affiliation (or disenchantment). It is this process of 'magnification' that 'The Tomb of

Michael Collins' explores in a self-reflexive fashion, the poem's glamorisation of a boyhood hero inseparable from its exploration of the way in which romantic nationalism magnifies the heroic dead.

To this end, the text, in the course of what appears to be a straightforward celebration of Collins's courage, makes a revealing admission:

> He's what I was when by the chiming river
> Two loyal children long ago embraced –
> But what I was is one thing, what remember
> Another thing, how memory becomes knowledge –
> Most I remember him, how man is courage.

The parenthesis at the centre of this stanza is the structural axis on which the poem turns (and, significantly, comes at what is virtually the midpoint of the poem). On an obvious level, the parenthesis simply brings to light a discrepancy between the poetic persona at the time of Collins's death and the mature poet, thirty years later, reflecting on that earlier period of personal and national history. Yet it is less the difference between youth and maturity and more the impossibility for the mature poet of retrieving the reality of his youth that is under scrutiny. What the poet *was* is now present only through what he *remembers* he was, and the text is at pains to point out that these two phenomena are far from being the same thing. Indeed, a draft of the poem makes this explicit: 'But what I was is one thing, what remember / Another thing, how memory genders knowledge', and in the margin, with reference to the verb in the second line of this quotation, Devlin has written 'plays with'.[65] Even in its final form, the interjection has interesting consequences for how we interpret the final line of this passage, in that 'what' the speaker remembers has become, over time, a 'knowledge' representative of romantic nationalism's powerful tendency to solidify dead patriots into heroic types: 'Most I remember him, how man is courage.'

I am not suggesting that this poem is covertly revisionist in its intentions, a debunking of Collins or romantic nationalism as a whole (though another draft of the poem does refer to Collins, in life, as 'bland'). Devlin is no Roy Foster *avant la lettre*. While the poem's ambivalent attitude towards Collins was astutely noted in M. L. Rosenthal's early assessment of Devlin's work, Rosenthal went too far in asserting that this 'uninhibitedly emotional threnody' for 'a national hero' 'implies, though far more discreetly and tangentially than do several of Yeats's pieces, a revulsion against uncompromising nationalist ardor'.[66] Revulsion is, perhaps, wide of the mark; but Rosenthal was right to note the discrete and tangential qualifications in the poem's response to Collins. My own sense is that the poem is highly self-conscious of the idealisation of the heroic dead endemic to the romantic nationalist imagination (which one voice of the poem approves). That imagination, as we saw in the poem's invocation of Edward the Bruce, Tomás an tSioda (Silken Thomas), Wolfe Tone, and Hugh O'Donnell, is linked to a child's view of Irish history: 'I tell these tales – I was twelve years old that time. / Those of the past were heroes in my mind'. The boy's 'knowledge' of the Irish past constitutes a tableau of national 'heroes' who have undergone magnification through time. His vision of the 'past' lacks a diachronic dimension: history has become the telling of 'tales' stripped of their historical context (it is thus revealing that the above stanza's list of 'heroes' departs from their chronological order). Devlin's elegy, on one level, endorses this view of history as a synchronic gallery of heroic figures, a gallery in which the text proceeds to hang Collins's portrait. Yet, on another, the poem exposes the ideological distortions concomitant with such historiography. As its title suggests, 'The Tomb of Michael Collins', is a poem concerned with the enshrinement of heroes in the popular imagination, to which end it erects its own memorial. Yet it is simultaneously preoccupied with the ways in which such popular 'memory' 'plays with' and 'genders' a 'knowledge' that is distinct from historical fact. The poem's pastiche of Horation ode and popular ballad is not geared towards a 'reconciliation' of poetry and politics, as Deane would have us believe is Devlin's intention. Rather, the poem is indicative of Devlin's chariness towards 'committed' literature. In this respect, 'The Tomb of Michael Collins' can be rewardingly read in the light of the tenets of the American New Criticism (the poem, it should be recalled, like several of Devlin's later poems, was first published in *The Sewanee Review* in 1956).

The formal 'distance' of 'The Tomb of Michael Collins' from its emotive subject matter is close to the purported ontological status of the new critical 'verbal icon': 'an impersonal and ahistorical artefact', in Vincent B. Leitch's succinct paraphrase.[67] As Leitch emphasises, however, such an artefact was an ideal, the organic unity of which was prompted by, in Tate's words, 'the disunity of being which is the primary fact of the human condition'.[68] Tate's stress on the poem's compensatory nature in the face of material history, or the existential plight of humanity, is evident in his short sequence, 'More Sonnets at Christmas' (1942), dedicated to Devlin. The traditionalism of Tate's sonnets is at variance with, and seeks to circumscribe, their divisive subject matter – America's 'disunity of being' having increased with the end of isolationism and the country's entry into the Second World War:

The day's at end and there's nowhere to go,
Draw to the fire, even this fire is dying;
Get up and once again politely lying
Invite the ladies toward the mistletoe
With greedy eyes that stare like an old crow.
How pleasantly the holly wreaths did hang
And how stuffed Santa did his reindeer clang
Above the golden oaken mantel, years ago![69]

The final lines' force lies, as Radcliffe Squires has wittily perceived, in that 'their success is that they are the kind of verse no one in the twentieth century can successfully write'.[70] In other words, their wilfully gauche quality is counterpointed by the sestet's harshly ironic advice to the reader to 'pray most fixedly / For the cold martial progress of your star'. This combination of self-conscious naiveté, traditional form and irony are qualities also audible in Devlin's 'The Tomb of Michael Collins', though in a less exasperated tone and more mediated fashion than in Tate. In a related vein, the fact Devlin likened features of his elegy for Collins to aspects of the 'ceremonial ode' recalls Tate's strategies in his great 'Ode to the Confederate Dead'. Tate's recollection of the past in this poem is inseparable from an intensely self-conscious transfiguration and idealisation of that past in the light of a dissatisfying present. In the words of the Ode, while 'The headstones yield their names to the element' and 'The wind whirrs without recollection', the speaker finds this desolate graveyard a place where 'memories grow', sprouting 'From the inexhaustible bodies that are not / Dead, but feed the grass row after rich row'.[71] Tate's deployment of the classical ode to frame the fraught emotions to which his inheritance gives rise, chimes with Devlin's strategy in the elegy for Collins: in both cases, recourse to traditional form provides a solace that derives from their propensity to 'magnify' history. Yet, for both Tate and Devlin, such modernist mindfulness to the artistic medium does not preclude an arch knowingness about the mythologising attendant upon such traditionalism. In this respect, Tate's and Devlin's poems are equally conscious of the myth-making that often infuses the traditionalism of the American Southerner's and romantic nationalist's imaginations, the ideals of which, at one level, their poems respectively endorse.[72]

While Devlin's poem clearly bears the imprint of Tate, it is also marked by the poetry of Robert Penn Warren, to whom, in one draft, the poem was dedicated. This is of particular interest in that Warren, in *The Ballad of Billie Potts* (1943), had experimented with the ballad-form in a manner which bears some comparison with Devlin's attempt to incorporate 'country ballad elements' in 'The Tomb of Michael Collins'. As John Burt has argued, the 'studied artlessness' of Warren's poem 'aspires to the condition of the ballad, even as it recognizes that the ingenuousness of the ballad is not available'.[73] The casual brutality of the narrative stanzas of the ballad proper is spliced to a running commentary by the author. This formal device, in which the ballad loops back on and meditates upon its own story, is indicative of Warren's preoccupation with tradition and the narratives one creates out of that tradition. His work, as Richard Gray maintains, is dialectical in that its look to the past, to tradition, for values by which to live in the present, is inseparably bound to an awareness of how present experience shapes and changes those values.[74] *The Ballad of Billie Potts* indirectly prefigures Devlin's elegy in that both texts reflect upon their appropriation of a traditional medium, albeit in highly different ways, and interrogate in their respective fashions the significance their received subject matter possesses for the present.

If the Southern traditionalists' poetics can be related to the isolationist politics they held, then Devlin's modernism may well refract his experience of Irish foreign policy between the wars. Devlin was a junior member of the Irish delegation to the League of Nations in Geneva in 1935, at which Éamon de Valera (Taoiseach and Minister for External Affairs from 1932) was elected President of the Assembly. The failure of the League in that year to impose rigorously effective sanctions on Italy, which was threatening to occupy Abyssinia, would result in de Valera's growing disenchantment with the League's international role, and prompt Ireland's shift towards neutrality in world affairs. Initially a champion of the League, de Valera became sceptical of its ability to protect the rights of small nations, including, of course, Ireland. In a letter to Thomas MacGreevy, written on his return to Dublin from Geneva, Devlin expressed his own feelings about the League. 'I am very pro-Italian', he writes, 'I do not much care for being the ally of savages. And at present my work is the implementation of the sanctions agreed on at Geneva against Italy. Isn't it foul?'[75] Devlin's admission to being 'pro-Italian' does not, in itself, reveal any sympathy for Italian fascism; it is better viewed as a corollary of his letter's shockingly casual racism. Within a few short years, Devlin would find himself on Department business in Mussolini's Rome, and the evidence, as we shall see, would suggest that he had little time for the Duce's brand of politics. While Devlin's private feelings about the Italo-Abyssinian crisis were clearly at variance with his Department's, and the League's, official line, he clearly shared in the general sense of pessimism that had pervaded the Irish delegation to Geneva. Indeed, the failure of the League was all too apparent to Devlin when he wrote to MacGreevy: on 2 October 1935, just three days before, Italian troops had invaded Abyssinia. Hence, Devlin's pleasure in his 'marvellous recital' of MacGreevy's poem, 'Nocturne of the Self-Evident Presence', on a radio-broadcast for 2RN, is countered immediately by the reflection: 'I felt a fool broadcasting rimery [*sic*] during a war.'

Devlin's gloom was at one with de Valera's and the Department's growing dissatisfaction with the League's international role as a supposed broker for peace, a dismay that came to a head at the 1938 Assembly, at which attention was focused on the increasingly turbulent climate of Europe. Devlin dryly evokes this Assembly, and the extent to which it revealed the League's dismal record as an international body, in 'Anteroom: Geneva' (a draft of which is titled 'Anteroom: Geneva 1938'): 'The electorate at breakfast approved of the war for peace / And the private detective idly deflowered a rose' (*CP* 169). Michael Kennedy has cogently argued that Ireland's foreign policy between the wars was deeply coloured by a reaction to the violence of the First World War and that of the War of Independence through the Civil War. The politicians and diplomats of the Free State and, later, the Republic of Ireland, de Valera among them, were thus resolutely 'anti-violence'. Kennedy suggestively reads Devlin's poetry as representative of Ireland's attitude towards Europe during these years:

> Diplomat Denis Devlin's poetry is itself a curious allegory for the mindset of his department and colleagues. It was self-confident, definitely Irish, though unquestionably international. It sought to experiment with new ideas; as such it also mirrors what Irish diplomats were undertaking at the League.[76]

Devlin's openness to European and Anglo-American literary modernism, coupled to his resistance to the avant-garde's conjoining of poetic and political liberation in a 'revolution of the word', certainly parallels his Department's internationalism and the 'anti-violence' of Irish foreign policy. It seems inescapable that beginning the composition of 'The Tomb of Michael Collins' in Washington (to which Devlin was posted as First Secretary in 1940), 'With mullioned Europe shattered', Devlin had mixed feelings about the man whose military genius was crucial in the violent creation of the Free State, and who perished in the turbulence of the ensuing internecine strife. The poem's ambivalent attitude towards Collins is thus to be read not solely as an example of the irony and ambiguity beloved of the New Critics, and which was central to their own poetic practice, but also as the result of Devlin's experience as a diplomat in the mid- to late 1930s.

In 1950 Devlin was appointed Minister Plenipotentiary to Italy and, in 1958, a year before his death, he became Ireland's ambassador in Rome. In these years Devlin's home became a meeting-place for a number of Italian writers, including the neorealist novelist Ignazio Silone (the pseudonym of Secondino Tranquilli), to whom the published version of 'The Tomb of

Michael Collins' is dedicated. Silone's subject matter is the oppressed Italian peasantry, exploited, in his best-known work *Fontamara* (1933), by the fascists, and, in *Una manciata di more* (1943), by the equally abusive machinations of the Communist Party (with which, in the intervening years, Silone had decisively broken). Silone's neorealist engagement with recent Italian history, with the forces of revolution and reaction, is inseparable from the search for a literary medium, both popular and 'epic', appropriate to such national material. In this regard, Devlin's poem's ambivalent representation of its West Cork hero can be read as a tribute and, one suspects, a mildly quizzical response to the neorealist's idealisation of the Italian peasantry. [77]

Devlin's pre-war diplomatic posting to Mussolini's Rome, as part of the Irish legation from 1938 to 1939, would appear to have not only modified his 'pro-Italian' stance of 1935, but may also have left its mark on the poem completed during his later term in the city, and whose dedicatee was resolutely anti-fascist. In a reminiscence of Devlin, the Irish novelist and playwright Mervyn Wall recalled a night in Rome, in the spring of 1939, in which he and Devlin found themselves, 'after sundry glasses of wine', in the company of the Third Commercial Attaché from the British Embassy, the latter also half-cut and equally anxious about the volatile political climate in Europe:

> We had ourselves become depressed earlier that evening standing in the Piazza Venezia listening to Mussolini thundering from the balcony of the Palace, his harangue punctuated by shouts of 'Duce, Duce' from the enthusiastic crowd. It seemed to us, as to many, that the Europe which we knew was nearing its end, and that gas attack would decimate whole populations, and high explosives would shortly destroy the ancient capitals of Europe, but Denis suddenly thrust gloom aside and suggested that we should go to the Trevi Fountain where he would recite Yeats's last poem.[78]

At the Trevi Fountain Devlin read aloud to his tipsy audience:

> I do not know what the Third Commercial Attaché thought, probably no more than that the Irish were all mad. To me however the sonorous noble lines of the dying poet, read aloud and with emotion, seemed to express the courage and indomitability of the human spirit at that moment when beneath our feet earth's very foundations were preparing to take flight.

Wall's eloquent response to Devlin's performance is shot through by a revealing contradiction. His initially surprising interpretation of 'Under Ben Bulben' as an expression of the 'indomitability of the human spirit' is understandable, given the jaundiced portrayal of the narrowness of Irish Ireland in the years following independence to be found in Wall's fiction. Yet Wall's humanist generosity is unintentionally qualified by his supposition that the Englishman beside him – who, drunk or not, is presumably a fellow 'human spirit' – derives little if anything from this self-assertively Irish poem. A related irony permeates Devlin's recitation: dismayed by Mussolini's self-aggrandising nationalism, Devlin nevertheless chose to read Yeats's swaggering exhortation to the Irish poet to 'Cast your mind on other days / That we in coming days may be / Still the indomitable Irishry'.[79] It is an intriguing scene, the complexity of which provides a presentiment of the issues raised in 'The Tomb of Michael Collins'.

During his post-war period in Rome Devlin translated a number of sonnets from Joachim Du Bellay's world-weary sonnet-cycle, *Les Antiquitez de Rome* (1558). Du Bellay, a member of a wealthy family famous for its diplomats, visited Rome in 1553, and his sonnets record his disillusionment with Rome at the same time as they signal a severance of the sonnet from solely amorous concerns. While the evidence suggests that Devlin felt anything but the French poet's jaundiced attitude towards the city, Du Bellay offers Devlin a voice by means of which he can articulate, in a displaced form, the disastrous consequences for Italy of Mussolini's fascism. For example, Devlin's version of 'Nouveau venu, qui cherches Rome en Rome', given its post-war horizon of production, implies the collapse of a different Italian empire from that which Du Bellay had in mind:

> Look, what pride, what ruination; and how
> This mistress bent the world beneath the law
> To conquer all, she conquered first herself
> And then fell prey to Time, which all consumes.
> (*TE* 23).[80]

Du Bellay's rejection of Petrarchist conventions also parallels, broadly speaking, the trajectory of Devlin's poetry in his last years. It is a movement which culminates in 'Memoirs of a Turcoman Diplomat', published the year of Devlin's death, a sequence in which Devlin also deploys in a more developed manner the imagery of diplomacy that is fitfully present in 'The Passion of Christ'. The persona of the Turcoman diplomat shares something of Du Bellay's preoccupation with time's inevitable ruinations, if in a more self-mocking vein. He may also look back, in a serio-comic fashion, to Devlin's acquaintance with the poet-diplomat, Saint-John Perse (the pseudonym of Alexis Leger), whose poetic tetralogy, *Exil*, Devlin had translated, and seen published, in the United States during the latter part of, and shortly after, the war.[81] Perse's turbulent career prior to his exile to the United States has some bearing upon Devlin's 'Memoirs of a Turcoman Diplomat'. From 1933, Perse had been Secrétaire Général at the Quai d'Orsay, in which position he had resisted, throughout the years leading up to the German invasion of France, any appeasement with the Nazis. Dismissed in 1940 by the Prime

Minister, Paul Reynaud, he took ship to England after the fall of France. His nationality was withdrawn by the Vichy government in late 1940, by which date he had arrived in America, where he was to stay until 1957. Roger Little sees in Perse's actions as a civil servant a far-seeing internationalism bound to an implacable integrity of purpose in the midst of 'the shifting and often shifty policies of French Foreign Ministers after Briand': 'he had "l'attribut essentiel de l'homme d'Etat et du diplomate: le sens des possibilités." It was his sense of the possible, within the strict code of honour by which he lived, that allowed him to overcome the material and, more importantly, the spiritual deprivation of exile by turning to poetry.'[82] Devlin's Turcoman diplomat, who possesses his own somewhat tarnished 'code of honour', has also known exile of a kind: 'In the Foreign Office, they humorously ask my advice, / My father had money, I was posted from place to place' (CP 297); yet his deep sense of alienation is coloured primarily by the knowledge that he is an anachronistic hang-over in the Turkey of the modernising, 'Westernising dictator', Atatürk, who 'tumbled the chatterbox Greeks into the sea' at Smyrna (Izmir) in 1922 (CP 297). In the poem's first section, 'Oteli Asia Palas, Inc.', the diplomat ruefully outlines his present position:

> Evenings ever more willing lapse into my world's evening,
> Birds, like Imperial emblems, in their thin, abstract singing,
> Announce some lofty Majesty whose embassies are not understood,
> Thrushes' and finches' chords, like the yellow and blue skies changing place.
> (CP 295)

The Turcoman diplomat's recollections of an imperial past are poised between nostalgia and resignation. 'It is not now like when the century began', he muses, his reminiscences of the last days of the Ottoman Empire leading into thoughts of its long-vanished military might – when, with the help of 'the Sultan's battle horse', 'the Prophet conquered with murder in his hand and honour in his crescent lips' (CP 296-7). The persona's Islamic leanings, strongly discouraged under Atatürk's secularist drive, inform his xenophobia, directed primarily at the Greeks, but also at Europeans or 'Franks' in general: 'Moon! rest our emblem . . . not like Europeans / Whose stupid sun discovers all their dirt' (CP 298; Devlin's ellipsis). Yet the sensibility that exhibits nothing but disdain for Greek culture, 'those comedians with their epics' (CP 298), and the Frank at large, is a sensibility nurtured by a European education in Göttingen and 'by the vibrant Seine' (CP 296). His compromised position is concisely conveyed in his words in the Oteli Asia Palas, Inc.: 'I hold my stick, old-world, the waiters know me, / And sip at my European drink'. It is thus unsurprising that the Turcoman diplomat's nostalgia is coupled to a worldly awareness of the crude economic realities that underlay Ottoman expansion, as 'Our salaried Levantine admirals sank [the Franks'] trading ships' (*CP* 297). The Turcoman's pragmatism is most apparent in his self-serving view of the then current political situation in the aftermath of the Second World War, with which the poem concludes, in what may also be an allusion to the overwhelming defeat of the Republicans by the Democrats in the Turkish election of 1950. Declaring 'A truce to talk of genocide, and nation and race!' he urges his companion to

> Tuck in your trews, Johannes, my boy, be led by me,
> These girls are kind. And we're all the rage now, whiskey-
>   flushed men of our age,
> The callow and the shallow and the fallow wiped off the page!
> (*CP* 300–301).

Such an attitude to 'le sens des possibilités' might be held alongside Perse's combination of internationalism and patriotism, and the integrity displayed in his principled refusal to work for de Gaulle's self-styled Free French government in London because it was an unelected body.

While the Turcoman diplomat appears from one angle as a grotesque corruption of the diplomat Perse, he comes into view from another as a warped reflection of his creator, accredited as Minister Plenipotentiary to his nation in 1951. J. C. C. Mays has drawn attention to some of the similarities between recent Irish and Turkish history and to the fact that, in the light of these resemblances, Devlin's poem 'could indeed be the memoirs of a TD'.[83] Despite the neatness of this remark, it is of course a diplomat not a minister who speaks – a civil servant who holds in disdain a republic which was founded shortly after that of the Irish Free State, in October 1923, and which, like its European counterpart, emerged in the wake of a war of independence. Referring perhaps to Atatürk's successor as President, the far less charismatic Ismet Inönü, renowned for the strategic use of his deafness during awkward negotiations, the Turcoman diplomat derisively comments: 'The President of the Republic bends this way and that, / A bubble on the corner of his lips' (*CP* 299). This contemptuous attitude towards the Republic of Turkey is coupled to a distaste for its place within the United Nations, of which Turkey was a founding member: 'Now some international Secretary-General throws a lump of bait / And laughs and says my country's not my own' (*CP* 297). The Turcoman diplomat's political outlook would seem poles apart from that held by Ireland's Department of External Affairs, which, upon Ireland joining the United Nations in 1955, successfully defined a role in international areas such as peace-keeping and decolonisation. In this respect, the Department repeated its pre-war promotion of international cooperation on behalf of its country's Republican leader, de Valera. But the Turcoman diplomat's words find some rapport with the views

expressed in the coldly satirical 'Anteroom: Geneva', a poem which, as
I argued above, should be read in the context of de Valera's and the
Department of External Affair's waning of support in the late 1930s for
the United Nations' inept predecessor, the League of Nations:

> The General Secretary's feet whispered over the red carpet
> And stopped, a demure pair, beside the demure
> Cadet, poor but correct,
> Devoted menial of well-mannered Power.
> 'A word with you.' 'Yes, your excellency.'
> Excellency smiled. 'Your silk shirt is nice, Scriptor.
> But listen. Better not let these private letters
> Reach the President. He gets worried, you know,
> About the personal misfortunes of the people;
> And really, the Minister is due to arrive.
> It is surely most unseemly
> To keep the State in the waiting-room
> For God knows what beggars,
> For totally unnecessary people.'

Written subsequent to his posting to fascist Italy, Devlin's poem unob-
trusively yet mercilessly indicts an international body, including Turkey,
whose corridors of power failed to address adequately the 'personal
misfortunes' of, among others, the Ethiopian people and the republicans
in Spain. The Turcoman diplomat's words are not so much another
version of the sentiments of the earlier poem as they constitute their
perversion. From this perspective, the persona emerges as a device
whereby Devlin can externalise and dramatise his preoccupation with
the corrosive effect humans have on the very ideals by which they claim
to live. In this respect, the Turcoman diplomat is a reworking of the
persona of 'Old Jacobin', which precedes 'Anteroom: Geneva' in *Lough
Derg and Other Poems*. The old Jacobin recalls the corruption of his
revolutionary ideals when he 'wore the pandemonium of the heroes':

> But the antique stuffs I wrapt my virtue in:
> Porous they proved to the maleficent winds
> When prison walls
> Roared in my ears high and black like thunder
> The time I signed away the men I loved.
> (CP 167)

The old Jacobin is identified as Robespierre in one typescript, but in
versions entitled 'Fugitive Statesman' an Irish rather than a French setting
implies a Republican closer to home. Both the Irish Civil War and the
disastrous closing chapters of the history the League of Nations, in which
international cooperation collapsed in the face of nationalist aggression,
leave their impress on 'Old Jacobin': 'shout[ing] in the Assembly [while]

the deputies / Blushed in the drama', the surroundings of Devlin's persona flicker between eighteenth-century Paris and Geneva in the 1930s. Notwithstanding the many accomplishments of the Department of External Affairs between the wars and from 1950 on, and Devlin's own successful professional career within that department, 'Memoirs' atomises the venality of politics. To a certain extent, therefore, the Turcoman diplomat should be read as a self-parody. Devlin's poetry is unforgiving in its depiction of the estrangement from absolutes, ideals from which his poetic speakers nevertheless still fruitlessly solicit succour.

The Turcoman's reflections on his spiritual and political bankruptcy are a debased version of Perse's treatment of his literal exile as representative of humanity's alienated condition per se.[84] The difference between the two texts' response to such 'exile' is one of *tone*. The reference to '*some* lofty Majesty' in 'Oteli Asia Palas, Inc.' imparts to Devlin's recurrent image of a hidden God more than a touch of bathos – as Stan Smith observes, the diplomat is 'admitting good-humouredly that one is a precarious guest in the hotel of the world, as the evening itself is only one of many rooms in the father's house'.[85] This can be contrasted with the urgent voice of Perse's persona in 'Exil', gazing out over the sands at Long Beach Island, hoping to find in his peregrinations the wellsprings of poetic creativity:

> My fame is on the sands! my fame is on the sands! . . . And it is
> no error, O Peregrine,
> To desire the barest place for assembling on the wastes of exile a
> great poem born of nothing, a great poem made from nothing . . .
> Whistle, O slings about the world, sing, O conches on the waters!
> (*TE* 107; Perse's ellipses)

The tonal difference between Perse's and Devlin's poems is also, I would suggest, the difference between the ambitious rhetoric of *The Heavenly Foreigner*, with its occasionally Perse-like swells of movement, and the laconic digressiveness of 'Memoirs'. A further connection between *The Heavenly Foreigner* and *Exil* is their common image of feminine otherness. One of Perse's personifications of the poetry he seeks is a wandering female figure, of whom, in 'Exil', he asks: 'Which tall repudiated girl has gone, on whispering wings, to visit other thresholds, which girl, tall and crossed in love, has gone / At that hour when the lapsing constellations, whose language changes for the men of exile, sink into the sands in search of a place of purity?' (*TE* 111). The association of femininity with otherness in *Exil* is most clearly present in 'Poème à l'Etrangère', the Castilian immigrant of the title reinforcing, as Steven Winspur argues, the sequence's reiterated 'identification between the voice from another world and a feminine presence'.[86] Perse's extended meditation on the unrepresentable source of poetry deploys, among other devices, femininity as a trope for the foreignness of an ideal poetic language, an ur-language of thought in which, as Winspur puts it, 'words would not be exiled from their meaning' because they exist as signifieds shorn of the supplementary distortions of the material signifier.[87] If this finds a parallel of sorts in the gender-based symbolism of *The Heavenly Foreigner*, and the endeavour to depict the foreignness of God (the Logos) in words, it contrasts sharply with the Turcoman's emblematic farewell toast – made in an Asian version of the Bar du Départ – to female 'beauty', which may be viewed as bringing the ripples of 'The Colours of Love' finally to rest. As 'Evenings . . . lapse' like Perse's 'lapsing constellations', the Turcoman diplomat invokes 'women', albeit in a markedly dissimilar manner to Perse's querulous call for a 'tall repudiated girl':

> Ladies, I call you women now, from out my emptied tenderness,
> All dead in the wars, before and after war,
> I toast you my adventures with your beauty! . . .
> This woman who passes by, sideways, by your side:
> There was one you loved for years and years;
> Suddenly the jaw is ugly, the shoulders fall,
> Provoking but resentment, hardly tears.
> (CP 295)

In these lines, 'Memoirs' makes good the valediction that 'The Colours of Love' only hesitantly entertained. In the words of the poem's second section, 'The Golden Horn':

> We all have a magic kingdom, some have two,
> And cry: 'O my city on the Golden Horn, and O my you!'
> Discover, in the bee flaunting his black and gold among the
>   foliage in the frieze,
> You are not what you thought, you are someone like all these,
> The most ardent young man turn, at the drop of a black hat,
> Into some rabbity sort of clerk, some heart-affairs diplomat,
> A John of the Cross into a Curia priest.
> (CP 296)

The disparaging self-caricature ('some rabbity sort of clerk') recalls the 'white-collar clerks' in *The Heavenly Foreigner*, who 'sit alone over a thin drink', attempting to master, their 'provincial eyebrow[s] raised', 'The Essays of Sorel, the novels of Maxim Gorky!' (CP 265). Eliot's 'small house agent's clerk' in *The Waste Land* is perhaps the prototype for Devlin's clerks, who, as somehow synecdochic of the petite bourgeoisie as a whole, prompt in Devlin the same kind of disdain Eliot bestows on his 'young man carbuncular'.[88] In 'Memoirs', of course, the speaker's aspersions are directed at himself, and thus, at least in part, against the 'heart-affairs diplomat' behind the persona (the last line of the passage taking the reader back to San Juan's exemplary, though possibly self-deluded, performance in 'The Colours of Love').

Recognising the bathetic quality of 'Memoirs' goes some way to deflecting Mays's criticism of the poem as failing to bring to a 'successful resolution' its admixture of 'satire and praise'. Mays, I feel, misconstrues what he calls 'Devlin's demonstrable hope for his poem' as an attempt to move from indolent 'reflection' on 'the absolute kingdom far in sky' – a kingdom Mays delineates as 'beyond control and reason . . . magical and half-perceived' – to 'action'. 'Spectorial melancholy', Mays argues, is in the poem's final section 'energised . . . tak[ing] life from the accumulated energy of the poem's central movement', concluding with the speaker's exhortation to Johannes. As Mays points out, however, the actions of the persona at the end smack less of 'an outward-turning invigorated rhapsodist of life' than they constitute 'the half-mechanical lunge of an elderly roué on vacation'. Of the end of the text, Mays consequently asks: 'How many of us accept it as fulfilling the promise of the poem beforehand, and how many as an anti-climax?'[89] My simple retort to this is that it *is* an anti-climax, though intentionally so. Mays tries to circumnavigate such a reply by countering in advance that the poem, if accepted as ironic, does not rise above the level of crudely satirising its speaker. Yet this misses the target of the satire: the 'elderly roué' bathetically tropes on the heart-affairs diplomat of Devlin's later poetry, the effect of which is to give a sardonic rejoinder to the hyperboles of *The Heavenly Foreigner*, and a comical, even grotesque, twist to the belatedness explored in 'The Colours of Love'.

5

DEVLIN, 'THE THIRTIES GENERATION' AND NEW WRITERS

MICHAEL SMITH: SYMBOLISM AND THE NEW IRELAND

In 1967 New Writers' Press was founded by Michael Smith and Trevor Joyce. Initially largely a means of publishing poetry by young Irish poets, the press's policy had, by the early 1970s, been influenced by the ideas of Brian Coffey, with whom Smith had begun corresponding in early 1970.[1] The results of this contact are evident from a comparison of the editorials of the first four issues of NWP's magazine, *The Lace Curtain*. The editorial to the first number of *The Lace Curtain* (Autumn, 1969) speaks merely of Smith's and Joyce's desire 'to provide poets with a more immediate contact with an audience than, for the lucky few, a book every two or three years can'.[2] In the second issue (Spring, 1970), however, the editors take the occasion of Beckett's acceptance of the Nobel Prize as a platform from which to launch a polemical broadside at those who espouse 'the lie that Ireland is an incorrigibly literary country and that Dublin is an internationally important centre of literary activity'. For Smith and Joyce, that 'lie' is the product of 'the work of Bórd Fáilte admen, an indigenous multitude of tenth-rate non-poets and bombastic shamrock-nationalists (mostly, thank God, in exile)'.[3] Smith's antagonism is close in spirit to Coffey's jaundiced opinions on the insular preoccupations of much twentieth-century Irish writing. In the editorial, written by Smith alone, and choice of contents for the third issue (Summer, 1970), Coffey's influence is more palpable still. Taking as a springboard Brendan Kennelly's 1970 Penguin book of Irish verse, Smith attacks the erection of a 'National Irish Literature', founded by Yeats and the literary revival and subsequently buttressed by the work of Austin Clarke (in the early stages of his career), F. R. Higgins, Robert Farren, Padraic Fallon, Donagh MacDonagh 'and a forgotten host of others'. Common to this body of poetry is 'the myth of a national poetry', reinforced, according to Smith, by Kennelly's belief in 'a distinctly Irish tradition' in both Irish-language and Anglo-Irish poetry. That tradition, the editorial maintains, requires for inclusion that the poem possess 'an Irish content' or adhere to conventional, received forms.[4]

Central to Smith's argument in this editorial are those Irish writers from the mid-century whose work cannot be easily assimilated to this tradition owing to their refusal to conform to 'the provincial nationalism and false traditionalism of the time', among whom Smith lists Devlin.[5] The appearance in *The Lace Curtain* 3 of two previously unpublished poems by Devlin, alongside the reprinting of Beckett's review for *transition* of Devlin's *Intercessions*, and three poems by Brian Coffey, is indicative of the importance the 1930s modernists now possessed in Smith's developing views on Irish poetry. Their significance is even more apparent in the fourth number of *The Lace Curtain* (Summer 1971), edited by Smith with the assistance of Coffey, which is devoted wholly to the 1930s generation of Irish poets. Smith's editorial to this issue again castigates the revivalists and their critical progeny, those 'lovers of Anglo-Irishism [*sic*] in literature'. Certain poets of the 1930s stand apart from the canon of Irish poetry, in Smith's opinion, through their refusal to conform to conventions that smother individuality. These are poets who, in Smith's view, 'wrote their poetry out of what Wallace Stevens described, in a letter to Thomas MacGreevy, as "a feeling about the world which creates a need that nothing satisfies except poetry and . . . has nothing to do with other poets or with anything else".'[6] This commitment to individual expression is a quality that Smith, in an article published in same year as *The Lace Curtain* 4, identifies in James Joyce: 'His writing was a necessary and personal statement; his tradition that of writers like him, regardless of nationality.' The 1930s poets that Smith admires followed Joyce's rejection of cultural nationalism and wrote 'out of their *own* lives, without national props, out of their own individual self-awareness'.[7] Such critical reflections clearly derive much of their commitment to 'personal statement' and concomitant disenchantment with cultural nationalism, broadly conceived, from Coffey's own praise for Joyce's exemplary dedication to '*making* one's own work',[8] his belief in poetry that, addressing the individual, 'strips away the nationalist quality'.[9]

Smith's disparagement of the 'provincial nationalism' he descries in the bulk of Irish poetry written since independence, and his championing of the modernist poets of the 1930s, should be seen in the context of economic, social and cultural changes in Ireland during the 1960s. The year before the founding of New Writers' Press, Seán Lemass resigned as Taoiseach, to which office he had succeeded de Valera in 1959. Under

Lemass, Fianna Fáil had pursued an economic policy designed to substitute free trade for protectionism, a programme of modernisation inaugurated by the 1958 White Paper, *First Programme of Economic Expansion*, and underscored by Lemass's conviction that economic growth lay in industrial development encouraged by foreign investment, rather than improved agricultural performance. While the 1960s saw economic recovery and growth reduce emigration and raise living standards, it also witnessed industrial unrest and botched housing and commercial developments, particularly in Dublin. The gradual emergence, in the late 1960s, of group politics, most significantly that of the civil rights movement in the North, followed hard on the heels of the nationalist obesiance shown in the commemorations for the revolutionaries of the Easter Rising in 1966. The immense popularity of showbands in the decade, the influence of television after Radio Telefís Éireann began broadcasting in 1961, a sharp growth in tourism, are all indices of the sea change in Irish culture and society during the 1960s, as the country's economy increasingly interpenetrated with multinational capitalism. The aesthetic priorities of Smith and New Writers' Press mediate this process of modernisation in a contradictory fashion. Smith's polemics against cultural nationalism and his openness to the healthy influx of international modernism, an openness foreshadowed in the 1930s modernist poets, refract, on the level of poetics, Lemassian expansionist economics (though not Lemass's nationalism). Furthermore, his close identification of modernist artistic production with individualism consorts well with an entrepreneurial spirit deaf to certain self-satisfied shibboleths. However, in attacking the 'lovers of Anglo-Irishism in literature', Smith's target is not so much the Irish literary tradition itself as the transformation of that tradition into cultural kitsch. The nostalgic conservatism of those 'tenth-rate non-poets and bombastic shamrock-nationalists' Smith lambastes is, in this respect, merely the obverse of the 'progressive' philistinism of the developers who defaced the Dublin cityscape and the debased taste shown by the enthusiastic audience for Country and Western music.[10] In advocating, through New Writers' Press's publications and the pages of *The Lace Curtain*, a poetry that has learned from the example of high modernism, Smith's enterprise, in short, both reflects Ireland's modernisation and challenges it.

There is a parallel between Smith's reaction to 1960s Ireland and that of Thomas Kinsella, for whose work Smith has shown a qualified admiration. Kinsella's poetry, from *Downstream* (1962), through *Nightwalker and Other Poems* (1968), to *Notes from the Land of Dead* (1972), gradually dispenses with the lyric form in favour of a modernist sequential structure derived from Pound and Williams. As Steven Matthews

has observed, this shift in form occured as Lemass's policies were alter-
ing the fabric of Irish life, Kinsella's 'circling, open-ended, fragmentary
poetic . . . symptomatic of the modernization taking place in Irish
cultural, social and political life at the time'.[11] Kinsella's modernist
constructivism of the late 1960s and 1970s is thus implicated in, even as
it takes a stance against, the effects of economic expansion satirised in the
figure of 'Productive Investment' in 'Nightwalker', who 'beckons the
nations through our gold half-door'.[12] Kinsella's poetry from *Notes from
the Land of the Dead* through the early Peppercanister Poems, makes
increasingly hermetic recourse to Jungian analytical psychology and Irish
mythology in its search for the archaic roots of self and nation. It is a
strategy that is motivated by, among other impulses, outrage at 'THE
NEW IRELAND' as atomised in 'Nightwalker'.[13]

Nevertheless, despite the similarities, Smith and Kinsella part company
in the latter's qualified enthusiasm for Devlin and his ambivalent praise
for Beckett. Both, for Kinsella, 'wrote with an understanding of the oppor-
tunities in the new poetry of the time, but not always with an appreciation
of the related new demands'. The precise nature of those 'new demands'
Kinsella leaves his reader to infer. However, it would appear that Devlin's
and, in particular, Beckett's 'metropolitan' predilictions, as Kinsella has it,
are in the service of a poetry stripped of all but a concern with the
individual subject. Devlin's 'mixed achievement' consists of poems that 'were
often acts of will, without the "architecture" understood by Kavanagh,
which uses material – however accurately or elegantly realized – only
when it is essential'.[14] Again, Kinsella refuses to clarify his terms, though
Kavanagh's 'architecture' may refer to the nationalism that Kinsella
believes renders his work, like Joyce's, 'international, the universal resting
on the particular'.[15] If so, then Kinsella's description of Beckett's poetry as
'dramatic, but with only one main character; and directed inward',
suggests that it too lacks the 'architecture' of Kavanagh's. For the lacuna
in Beckett, Kinsella continues, is 'anything in the nature of a tradition. An
entire dimension is missing.'[16] Smith's interpretation of Devlin and
Beckett is surprisingly close in substance to Kinsella's. The difference
between them lies, of course, in the intense valorisation Smith, influenced
by Coffey, accords to the 1930s poets' supposed dismantling of the
'architecture' of the Irish literary tradition in pursuit of poetic authenticity.

Smith's poetry, in line with his prose, foregrounds the unique response
made by his poetic persona to various events, in a language carefully
constructed to eschew the ruralism Smith associates with the 'provincial
nationalism' of much modern Irish poetry. To this end, Smith's poems
look to the example of Baudelaire, for whom, in Smith's words, 'the
poet's function is to explore life and consciousness, confronting, with

passionate self-honesty and the wisdom of his own insights, the chaos of reality within and without'; put less grandly, the concern of the poet is 'the relationship, or the lack of one between himself and the world of his experience'.[17] The title poem of Smith's first collection, *With the Woodnymphs* (1968), prefigures this remark in its delineation of the relationship, 'or the lack of one', between its speaker and the titular mythological figures. His attention arrested by the sound of a dying ringdove, half-eaten by rats among the fallen leaves of a park, the persona comments:

> When the rats reach its underparts
> Death will be soon; but, before,
> Wingbeats unsettle the leaves,
> The feast moves a few more inches.
>
> What cause to leave the gravel path?
> Pity? where are the woodnymphs?
> When the rats are finished, in time,
> The wind will reshuffle the leaves.[18]

The poem's blunt depiction of the bird's fate is indicative of Smith's early concentration on decrepitude, decay and death. Yet the intense focus on the literal processes of destruction, here and elsewhere, serves as pretext for an implicit meditation on 'the poet's function' as Smith reads it out of Baudelaire. It is no coincidence that the bird of 'With the Woodnymphs' is precisely named: the denotation inescapably brings in its train the dove's poetic connotations in English-language poetry. The dove's reduction to a still-living 'feast' for the rats inhabiting the park is a judgement on the shallow consolations of a conventional poetic response to experiential reality. The Baudelairean 'self-honesty' of Smith's poem lies in its refusal to filter raw experience through a received tradition, the latter imaged in this poem in the classical woodnymphs. Smith's speaker tellingly stays firmly on 'the gravel path', his inability to find sufficient 'cause' to help the dying bird emblematic of a resistance to those beguiling but misleading figures of literature and myth.

The ironic undertones to 'With the Woodnymphs' are perhaps a little too knowing, and the poem, it should be noted, is not reprinted in either *Times and Locations* (1972) or *Selected Poems* (1985). Nevertheless, its programmatic nature is instructive in considering Smith's oeuvre to date, and helps the reader grasp the subtext to a poem such as 'Clare, October', also collected in *With the Woodnymphs*. Ostensibly a descriptive poem, the text on a deeper level works to undermine quietly and effectively that ruralism Smith identifies in modern Irish poetry ('a poetry of the parish pump', as he once caustically termed it):[19]

The orchard was deadly sick with a grey fungus
And the bark of the hazel was silver-grey.

The hair, skin, eyes, teeth of the old woman
Who polished my shoes for the dance, were grey.

Here in October dawn breaks in sheets of grey glass.[20]

The strength of this understated poem resides in its gradual blurring of rural landscape, hazel and putative *cailleach* into the same deathly hue, the process paradoxically leading, in the final line, to a clarity of vision unobstructed by such well-worn tropes and images. While many of Smith's poems have an urban setting, the treatment of Co. Clare in this poem explains Smith's reiterated and, initially at least, perhaps surprising, admiration for Kavanagh who, while clearly distinct from the 'European Irishmen', such as MacGreevy, Coffey, Beckett and Devlin, 'was as contemptuous of the phoniness of Irish literary nationalism as any of them'. The quality Kavanagh shares with the modernist poets of the 1930s, in Smith's eyes, is a desire to express an individual sensibility free from the clutter of poetic convention; the questions posed by Kavanagh's verse, argues Smith, are 'Is it sincere and, does it get at life?'[21] 'Clare, October' does not 'get at life' in the same way as Kavanagh's treatment of Monaghan in *The Great Hunger*, but both poems stand opposed to any easy romanticisation of rural Ireland, an antagonism continued in a number of poems in Smith's *Stopping To Take Notes* (1979). In the title poem of this collection, for instance, Smith refuses to idealise the West, instead deploying a poetic realism worthy of comparison with that of Kavanagh's poem:

In the ceaseless pour of rain
the miserable earth
seeps a black ooze
into ditch and pool[22]

Smith follows Kavanagh in questioning any facile conception of the West as the essential repository of Irish identity and culture. Kavanagh's effectively heavy-handed satire in section XIII of *The Great Hunger* has, of course, the revival as its main target, specifically its belief that 'Without the peasant base civilisation must die, / Unless the clay is in the mouth the singer's singing is useless'.[23] Yet his delightfully malicious reference to the 'travellers [who] touch the roots of the grass and feel renewed / When they grasp the steering wheels again' compounds his familiar *bête noir* with the tourists who batten on the Irish countryside,[24] prefiguring by nearly thirty years Smith's distaste for 'the Bórd Fáilte admen' and their glossy images of the Irish landscape. Smith's technique differs from Kavanagh's, but the end is the same: the speaker of 'Stopping To Take Notes' tellingly 'receive[s] no solace / from the cold sea and the islands'.

In a related manner, 'A Visit to the Village', from the same collection, begins by seeming to draw a distinction between the urban visitor to Connemara, for whom 'No ancestral bones of ours / roll like ivory dice / in that black sea', and those for whom life is supported by traditional 'local rites'.[25] Yet the poem concludes by pondering on the deeper similarity between the 'strangers' from 'the impersonal city' and the local inhabitants:

> We have come here
> to observe local rites
> learn new words for things
> and once again take note
> of human sameness
>
> Such roots as we have
> we carry with us
> in suitcases

The speaker, one of Kavanagh's 'travellers', finds in the West no 'roots' to his own identity as an Irishman. Rather, he perceives in this region an overriding 'sameness' to humanity, whether Irish or otherwise. The strong implication of this realisation is that identity is not a product of locality, region or (by extension) nation, but resides in individual existential choices (where one, as it were, decides to carry one's baggage) – and that this holds as much for the rural 'others' as the strangers from the city. Thus the pronoun of the final three lines may not signify solely those city visitors, but include within its denotation precisely those against whom the intrusive voice originally defined itself.

Smith's persona in this collection, and in *Lost Genealogies & Other Poems* (1993), elsewhere echoes that of the Baudelairean *flâneur*, whose attention is drawn by the sights and events of the modern cityscape, though Smith's own sense of evil is also mediated through the dark imaginings of the Dublin romantic poet, James Clarence Mangan (a *Selected Poems* of whom Smith edited in 1973). Mangan's presence in Smith's work dates from his first collection. In 'Long Lane', the scene is 'Just such a street as Mangan struggled down'; and the nineteenth-century Dubliner's fantastic appearance finds itself reanimated for the speaker in the 'silhouette of this club-footed man' he and his friends encounter on a lamplit evening.[26] This figure gives a nightmarish shape to the 'evening's academic talk / / Of black cold nihilistic visions'; that is, he personifies and objectifies the kind of chilling vision Mangan displaces onto the icy landscape of 'Siberia' and related settings of other poems – those works in which, in Yeats's words, 'Outer things were only to him mere symbols to express his own inmost and desperate heart. Nurtured and schooled in grimy back streets of Dublin, woods and rivers were not for him.'[27] However, whereas

Mangan's Siberian landscape is, on one level, a projection of his sensibility ('the sands are in his heart, / And the killing snows'), Smith's urban scenes shun the romantic pathetic fallacy. In this respect, the urban poems chime with the anti-romanticism of his poems about the West of Ireland in that, while the latter refuse to 'root' identity in locality or land, the former's Dublin subject matter stubbornly resists being an occasion for epiphanic significance. Hence the relevance to Smith's work of a passage from Whitman, which provides the epigraphs to two of his collections, *Times and Locations* and *Selected Poems*, is not as straightforward as, at first sight, it might seem:

> Locations and times – what is it in me that meets them all,
>   whenever and wherever, and makes me at home?
> Forms, colours, densities, odours – what is it in me
>   that corresponds with them?

The importance of these lines for Smith lies, I think, in their interrogative register. It is the *problematic* nature of the correspondence between the poetic subject and the object world that draws Smith's poetry on. Smith's personae, therefore, experience an environment of 'Forms, colours, densities, odours' in a different fashion from that of Baudelaire's *flâneur*. True, Smith, like Baudelaire, concentrates on the shifting experiences, the 'Locations and times', of modern city life, yet these do not impart or correspond to a metaphysical significance beyond their immediate reality. That is, while the persona of many of the lyrics in these two volumes wanders through Dublin in a fashion reminiscent of Baudelaire's peregrinations through Paris, the events and people that cause him to pause and 'take notes' do not generate the compensatory Symbolist consolations one finds in the French poet's work.

And yet those consolations haunt Smith's work if only in promissory form. In his words, 'If I had to say in one sentence what I have been about in poetry since I began writing it myself and translating it, I would say that I have been exploring the possibility of transcendence, almost in the theological sense of the word. . . . What matters to me is the *tension* involved in such an exploration.'[28] In this context, Smith draws attention to the following lines from 'Stopping To Take Notes':

> Before the high altar
> we watch dumbly
> the stained glass
> gloss the vacant air[29]

The '*tension*' here resides in the speechlessness of those confronted with a transcendental realm intimated by the windows' 'gloss', but which itself refuses to be directly known. Smith's poems equally constitute 'glosses' aware of their own 'stained' nature; moreover, that which they seek to 'gloss' itself may be illusory, merely 'vacant air'. In *Lost Genealogies & Other Poems*, the 'bent figure' in 'Woman Chopping Wood' prompts the questions: 'Witch of the wood? / Mother of firelight? / Crone of dereliction?'[30] The interrogative catechism humorously introduces the 'almost theological' dimension to Smith's 'possibility of transcendence', but that possibility significantly does not occur: the 'beam of the house', at which the woman chops, simply brings to the poet's mind a parodic 'gloss' of the crucifixion, as it 'stand[s] / cruciform with the chimney breast'.

Smith's interrogation of the transcendental in a language painfully alive to its material condition is not unrelated to his mistrust of the enfeebled literary conventions, as he sees them, of much twentieth-century Irish poetry. It is thus appropriate that *The Lace Curtain* saw the first reprinting of Beckett's pseudonymous 1934 article, 'Recent Irish Poetry', in which Beckett analyses the degree to which Irish poets 'evince awareness of the new thing that has happened, or the old thing that has happened again, namely the breakdown of the object, whether current, historical, mythical or spook'.[31] Smith's debilitated symbolism registers a 'breakdown of the object' to the extent that the given, in his poems, frustrates any intimation of transcendence, though the latter's possibility remains a necessary impetus to the creative act. Smith's *flâneur*, therefore, is also Beckett's expropriated individual, the 'man alone' in the epigraph to *Lost Genealogies & Other Poems*: 'The being in the street, when it happens in the room, the being in the room when it happens in the street, the turning to gaze from land to sea, from sea to land, the backs to one another and the eyes abandoning, the man alone trudging in the sand'. Smith's 'The Cottage' expresses an analogous sense of homelessness to Beckett's:

> The door is ajar, the curtain asquint.
> The dog on the threshold is real.
> Flowers, not smoke, bloom
> from the white-washed chimney-pots
> outside the door.
>
> This is the house they left,
> sons and daughters,
> the lost genealogies.
>
> Here she has always lived,
> and will live until the end.
> These things will hold till then:
> the caked lime, the door ajar,
> the real dog on the threshold.
>
> Don't cry now, you.
> From the darkness
> of this half-opened door
> we all walked away.[32]

Smith's insistence on the 'hold' the past exerts over the present is power-fully conveyed in the 'Forms, colours, densities, odours' of door, curtain, flowers and lime. Their particularity resists translation into symbolic meaning, though, metonymic of the cottage as a whole, they are redolent of a plenitude seemingly beyond recall. The manner in which the cottage hovers on the edge of figurative import, while retaining its stubborn literalness ('The dog on the threshold is real'), is typical of *Lost Genealogies*, particularly in the poems centring on 1950s Dublin. In this respect, while one inspiration for the sequence was Nevill Johnson's richly evocative photographs of Dublin in the early years of that decade,[33] the poems are perhaps more profoundly indebted to James Joyce's representation, in *Dubliners*, of petit-bourgeois life in early twentieth-century Dublin. Joyce's rigorous attention to the details of his Dubliners' lives functions as a counterbalance to the symbolist connotations of his narratives. To this extent, Joyce's early prose prefigures Smith's poems in its realist emphasis on the inexhaustibility of the quotidian by the symbolic meanings with which it, nonetheless, is deeply infused.

The quizzical cast of Smith's symbolism is at one with his inconoclastic reading of modern Irish poetry: a sceptical individualism underpins both his tentative exploration of 'the possibility of transcedence' and his firm rejection of the ruralism and conventionality he associates with the main-stream of modern Irish poetry. The Irish modernist poets championed in Smith's criticism are important to his own poetry less as formal models than as exemplary of the kind of 'self-awareness' towards which his writing strives.

TREVOR JOYCE: SPIRAL TO A QUESTION MARK

New Writers' Press's first publication was Trevor Joyce's *Sole Glum Trek* (1967), which was followed by a second collection, *Watches*, in 1969. Poems from both of these chapbooks, plus uncollected pieces, were reprinted in *Pentahedron* (1972). The publisher's blurb to *Pentahedron* describes the volume as 'a collection of experimental poems', an exper-imentalism that, elsewhere, Michael Smith has linked to the modernism of Devlin and Coffey.[34] Certainly, Joyce was familiar, through Smith, with the 1930s Irish modernist poets, but his early work is not particularly indebted to their example. Rather, Joyce's experimentalism in these pieces draws upon an eclectic number of writers and artists, including Empson, Holub, Rimbaud, Trakl and, perhaps most importantly, Klee.

In his 1924 lecture *On Modern Art*, Klee likens the artwork to the crown of a tree of which 'nature and life' are the root, the artist the trunk: 'Nobody would affirm that the tree grows its crown in the image of its root. Between above and below can be no mirrored reflection. It is obvious that different functions expanding in different elements must produce vital divergences.'[35] Some of the implications for the verbal arts of Klee's defence of non-representational modern painting are explored in an article published in *The Lace Curtain*, 'Considering a Poetic', jointly composed by Smith and Joyce (though credited solely to Smith). In the context of a discussion of Proust's 'involuntary memory', Joyce argues that representationalism in painting necessarily fails to the extent that 'No copy (insofar as it is a copy) can ever equal the original. . . . [A] rose pleases sight, smell and touch; but paint it and it feels like paint, smells of turps, though it may, if it is a competent job, bear a certain visual resemblance to the flower.'[36] The relevance of this to the poet or novelist is that words too cannot capture the quiddity of the non-linguistic, whether that of 'objects "out there"' or of those 'mental images' that make up memory and which possess a history and complexity of associations that defy smooth translation by the abstracting intellect into language. The result, for the writer, is a dilemma: 'Art must articulate the non-functional self, this self is revealed, described, defined, through involuntary memory, but the elements which invest such a memory with its significance for that person whose self it describes are incommunicable. What other solutions are available?'[37] The answer the essay provides is made apropos of Wyndham Lewis's claim that the artist 'transcends reality, dissolves it, in order to reveal what lies behind and inside it'. Here, Joyce writes, 'is Paul Klee talking': 'The artist has assimilated the world, and all that he wants to say is part of him, he cannot know what he wants to say until he has said it; there is no question of inspiration (inv. mem.), and then the necessity of applying another form of awareness (intellect) to that primary inspirational awareness. Manner and matter cohere, are one'.[38] Joyce's reflections echo Klee's statement that, 'standing at his appointed place, the trunk of the tree, [the artist] does nothing other than gather and pass on what comes to him from the depths. He neither serves nor rules – he transmits.'[39] Joyce, *à la* Pound, goes in fear of abstractions to the extent that he sees the artwork as rooted in experience, even though art cannot represent in its totality the manifold nature of that experience. As the crown to the tree, it creates an order that is distinct from the *materia poetica* from which it grows.

While Klee's ideas are far from being used programmatically in *Pentahedron*, the collection is usefully read as a series of forays into some of the issues raised in relation to the painter in 'Considering a Poetic'. In 'The Importance of the Bells (Meath St Church)', for example, Joyce disdains the transcendence proffered by orthodox religion in terms which are illuminated by the essay:

The bells are born and die
becoming part of history
along with
the French Revolution,
two world wars,
Lawrence of Arabia,
and the death of the cat
who is posing dramatically
in the gutter.

Acts are expectorated,
and when the spittle hardens
into facts, our lives
are emerald threads of mucous.[40]

The dead cat's dramatic pose aptly and bathetically prefaces the following image's equally reductive vision of personal experience. This concentration on physicality, characteristic of Joyce, leads into a dismissal of religion's redemptive possibilities:

The disembodied tones
finger carp on a slab
and the red necks
awry in a poulterer's window;
frenetic search for pattern
before giving up the ghost.

The pun on 'disembodied' and the ironic revitalisation of the cliché 'giving up the ghost' stress the inadequacy of institutional religion to 'reveal what lies behind and inside' nature, and thus transcend its hold. The religious aspiration towards a transfigured order or 'pattern' is constantly frustrated by 'the facts of life' the poem brutally foregrounds though references to dead cats, fish and chickens. Klee's aesthetic, of course, sees in art precisely the possibility of transfiguration that Joyce's text denies to religion, from an art which, like the bells, is 'part of history', rooted in nature. In *Pentahedron*, however, the formalism advocated in 'Considering a Poetic', in which 'Manner and matter cohere, are one', prompts an anxiety that art *betrays* the larger world through a disinterestedness consequent on the fact that there 'can be no mirrored reflection' between the two realities. In the words of 'Surd Blab':

This hour is delicate,
a pink-gold shell with an ocean in it,
a whorl,
a frozen whirlpool . . .

It is expressly mine
this whorling hour,
this iridescent spiral.

But who can bend a spiral
to a question mark?[41]

The delights of formal intricacy possess an inhuman coldness, a static 'frozen' quality, that do not address or interrogate the world, but mark a retreat from it. The final question thus haunts Joyce's densely patterned poems, which resist the strong appeal of a structuration akin to that which Joseph Frank termed the 'spatial form' of the modernist artwork, in which patterns of significance are generated by internal cross-reference rather than through reference to the extra-linguistic.[42]

Nevertheless, the question posed by 'Surd Blab' does not find an answer in that poem, though it is admitted to be a poetic imperative: 'That question is the present deed.' Its irresolution is present throughout *Pentahedron*, and is dwelt upon at length in 'Elegy of the Shut Mirror', the concluding poem to the collection and the last to be written. The elegy functions as a reply to the unconvincing assertiveness of 'Pentahedron', the fifth section or 'side' of which claims: 'I know these streets, / as crammed with dream as a clock with time.'[43] That this section is dedicated to Michael Smith is revealing, and suggests a defensive quality to Joyce's declaration. For Smith's poetry teems with human presences, while Joyce's, aside from its speaker, is largely depopulated. Joyce's assertion is an anxious corollary of his desire to bend the spirals of form to the world. Yet given the propositions put forward in 'Considering a Poetic', such epistemological certainty ('I *know* these streets') is far from self-evident, and its articulation in an artwork highly problematic. 'Elegy of the Shut Mirror' consitutes a poignant admission of the poet's inability to communicate to those others 'Pentahedron' had confidently claimed to 'know':

> A girl waits, lonely, on the bridge.
> can I tell her of remote roads
> where love, not knowing the shock of loss,
> has atrophied, and no-one sees
> how, at the desolate junctions
> the monuments of the old dead bleed
> with the green ichors of bronze[44]

The second half of this passage answers its initial question by turning on Horace's 'Exegi monumentum aere perennius'. The artwork, it would seem, blinds us to human suffering through its inability to represent mental states fully, as Joyce, in 'Considering a Poetic', had conceded. In the poem, however, the essay's somewhat unconvincing 'solution' to this problem (viz. art's assimilative, transcendent quality) provides no succour, reduced to the inhumanity of those 'ichors of bronze'. In short, the poem is an elegy to Joyce's early poetic, which, by 1972, had clearly reached an impasse.

Between *Pentahedron* and *stone floods* (1995), Joyce published *The Poems of Sweeny Peregrine* (1976), an adaptation of the medieval Irish work, *Buile Suibhne*. The composition of *Sweeny Peregrine* spans the decade 1966–76, and thus encompasses the years in which Joyce's poetry moves towards the aesthetic dilemma confronted in, if not resolved by, 'Elegy of the Shut Mirror'. [45] Read beside *Pentahedron*, Joyce's version of the Irish text can be seen, at least on one level, to constitute a commentary on his own early poetic. In this manner, Joyce's sequence bears some comparison with Seamus Heaney's adaptation of *Buile Suibhne*. In his introduction to *Sweeney Astray*, Heaney suggests that Sweeney, cursed by the outraged cleric Ronan Finn, is 'a figure of the artist, displaced, guilty, assuaging himself by his utterance'. It is, he continues, 'possible to read the work as an aspect of the quarrel between free creative imagination and the constraints of religious, political, and domestic obligation'.[46] Such a reading, of course, is conducive to Heaney in that it yields precisely the 'quarrel' that is at the heart of his own poetry during the 1970s and 1980s, and which finds its most extended prose elaboration in the lectures and essays collected in *The Government of the Tongue* (1988). Heaney's appropriation of the Irish-language text, despite its closer relation to its source material, is to this extent not dissimilar to Yeats's use of Irish myth and legend. Both writers take what Phillip L. Marcus, writing on Yeats, has called a 'personal' approach in their recasting of older material: the latter's function for the poet is as 'allegorical vehicles, sources of symbols, "objective correlatives" for his own feelings and ideas'.[47] In Heaney's case, this approach is particularly evident in his sequence 'Sweeney Redivivus', a series of variations on the original story that concludes his 1984 collection *Station Island*. In 'Sweeney's Returns', for example, Heaney reworks a moment from his source (here, the protagonist's loss of his wife, owing to his bird-like metamorphosis brought about by Ronan's curse) into a projection of the artist's condition:

> when I perched on the sill
> to gaze at my coffers of absence
> I was like a scout at risk behind lines
> who raises his head in a wheatfield
> to take a first look, the throb of his breakthrough
> going on inside him unstoppably[48]

The image of the scout behind lines foregrounds Sweeney's vulnerability and, by extension, implies the alarming isolation of the 'free creative imagination' in its 'quarrel' with 'religious, political, and domestic obligation'. Sweeney's plight thus provides Heaney with an appropriate vehicle in which to explore his contention, elaborated at length in *The Government of the Tongue*, that the importance of lyric poetry lies in the seeming irresponsibility of its 'untrammelled' utterance. In the 'jubilation and truancy at the heart of an inspiration' is a promise of autonomy 'in a world that is notably hampered and deprived'.[49]

For Joyce, the choice of Sweeny as a mask should be considered in the light of his comment, in 'A Note on the Text', that 'The relation in which the *Poems of Sweeny Peregrine* stand to the original Irish of *Buile Suibhne* may perhaps best be described by that phrase which Clarence Mangan used of his own inventive translations: they are "the antithesis of plagiarism".' Joyce's quotation from Mangan's 'impersonal autobiography' is on the face of it misleading, as, in context, Mangan is alluding to his practice of composing 'translations' for which in fact no originals exist, and obviously such is not Joyce's procedure in *Sweeny Peregrine*. However, the 'plagiarism' that Joyce may well be opposing is the straightforward romantic identification, present in Heaney's *Sweeney Astray*, of the translator's 'feelings and ideas' with elements of the source-text. While both poets defamiliarise their authorial selves by means of Sweeny, Joyce's self-projection is more ironic that Heaney's, constituting a critique of precisely the 'efficacy and resource' Heaney grants the untrammelled lyric poet: his 'power to open unexpected and unedited communications between our nature and the nature of the reality we inhabit'.[50] In Joyce's early work, poetry does not open that readily to a world beyond its involuted 'spirals'.

Sweeny's flight from the battle at Magh Rath and his subsequent deranged exile from humanity serve Joyce as an 'objective correlative' for his preoccupation with the relationship between poetic form and the non-linguistic world. The nausea experienced by the speaker of 'The Importance of the Bells (Meath St Church)' in contemplating the material world is grotesquely reiterated in the pursuit of Sweeny by five truncated heads at Sliabh Fuaid:

> The call of that hunt was the din and stridulation of stark terror and the hubbub of the chivvying spectres. They butted and plucked at his calves, ankles, shanks, shoulders and nape, clashing with branches, rocks, and each other like a flood unleashed and falling. At last he hid in the high gauze of the clouds.

The paucity of art's response to such 'hubbub' is evident in Sweeny's sojourn in Glen Bolcain, 'the resort of the Irish-turned-maniac', in a passage that gives a savage twist to Klee's image of the artist as the intermediary, the 'trunk', between nature and the 'crown' of art:

> Sweeny remained within the glen till one night when he roosted high upon an ivy-strangled whitehorn. He could not sleep there because each time he moved the wood tines stuck him, leaving his flesh split and specked with blood. So he went to where a single blackthorn limb spired above a briary thicket, rayed with fine spikes. He perched there, but the slender branch sagged beneath him and it snapped, throwing him into the thorny mass below so that his skin from heel to head was a crimson tracery. It was thus that Sweeny came to inveigh against thorns.

Sweeny, the mad bird-king, provides Joyce with an almost ludic trans-
position of the concerns of *Pentahedron* and 'Considering a Poetic', the
occasionally angst-ridden speaker of Joyce's early poems finding himself
parodied in the mock-solemnity of 'It was thus that Sweeny came to
inveigh against thorns'. Poem II from the Verse section succeeding the
Narrative of *Sweeny Peregrine* ventriloquises Sweeny's reported denun-
ciation, undercutting its speaker's magnificent hyperboles with an adroitly
placed bathos:

> The blackthorn drinks my blood again,
> my face bleeds on the sodden wood.
>
> Flood and ebb encompass me;
> lunar phases can't affect
> the homicidal iron I dread.
>
> Thorns lance my sores. I doze.

While the acute self-consciousness of Joyce's manipulation of Sweeny
as a mask resembles the proto-modernist personae in Mangan's trans-
lations (as analysed by David Lloyd), it is not, to my mind, as close to the
Poundian approach to translation as has been suggested. [51] As Stan Smith
has observed, translation is central to high modernist poetics to the extent
that it offers a means of recouping the past into the present, thus stressing
the continuity and timelessness of 'tradition'. It produces, in Smith's
words, 'the *illusion* of unmediated rapport with the dead', as in the
merging of Li Po's and Pound's voices in *Cathay*. Such immediate access
to the past, Smith argues, is illusory because the relationship that is forged
is a 'forgery' (mediated, in the case of *Cathay*, by 'an endless avenue
of scholarship'):

> A self-effacing modern voice speaks ventriloquially through the masks of all
> those *personae* assumed in the first wave of Modernist texts, constituting
> itself in its contemporaneity at the moment that it defers totally to the
> voice it revives. What we are aware of finally in reading such poems is not
> the felt immediacy of the past but our modern remove from such originary
> authenticity. [52]

Joyce's *Sweeny Peregrine* is at pains to foreground the process of mediation
that Pound's translations seek to conceal. The vagaries of transmission are
emphasised in the Narrative's closing reflections on its own truth-content:

> Moling it was who first recorded this tale of Sweeny, and noted his chants,
> but it is uncertain to how great an extent that saint expressed his reverence
> for the silent dead by emendation of a strange and confused history, and how
> far editors and interpreters have conspired with him, and time, and chance,
> to make corruption of the word outpace that of the flesh. Perhaps a final
> turn was added too, to make a palinode. May we, then, conclude just this:

that, after all, we have not here those words which Sweeny, between flight
and fall, spoke to the Man of the Wood.

If Moling's account forms the apocryphal basis for all subsequent
versions of Sweeny's tale, the cleric's possible 'emendation' of the story
prefigures the likely practice of later 'editors and interpreters', and
certainly Joyce's own: subtitled 'a *working* of the corrupt Irish text', his
text, moreover, was edited into Narrative and Verse sections by Michael
Smith. Interpretation, in this case, would appear to go all the way down.
Indeed, the only narrative credited at the close of *Sweeny Peregrine* with
pre-interpretative authority is, we learn, recounted by Sweeny in the
course of his wanderings to another madman, the Man of the Wood.

In the episode referred to, the Man of the Wood delays attending his
predestined death until, in Joyce's words, 'Sweeny had told him his own
tale just as it is set down hereinafter'. In this curious incident Sweeny
narrates the events of his life prior to their actual occurrence.[53] Joyce's
delight in this postmodern moment *avant la lettre* reflects his interest in
Borges and, to a lesser extent, Flann O'Brien's anti-novel *At Swim-Two-
Birds* (itself featuring Sweeny) at the time of composing *Sweeny Peregrine*.
But the scene's proleptic account is also valuable for understanding
further the relationship between *Sweeny Peregrine* and Joyce's early
poetics. Sweeny's ur-narrative can be read as constituting the absurd
extreme of Frank's notion of modernist 'spatial form': it is a text the
meaning of which would be independent, in the strongest sense imaginable,
of any pre-existent reality. Furthermore, its proleptic nature amusingly
rules out in advance the troubling opposition of involuntary memory
and intellect scrutinised in Joyce's contribution to the essay 'Considering
a Poetic'. Its 'matter' and 'manner' illogically but seamlessly 'cohere',
the speaker's 'mental images' of future events lacking that history of
associations which would problematise their representation in verbal
form. In contrast to Sweeny's ur-narrative stands Joyce's *Sweeny Peregrine*:
a 'working' of an always already reworked text, its highly mediated
quality implies the interpretative nature of art in general, its dependence
on a prior reality which it does not 'copy' but 'translates' and transforms
into new terms. The overdetermined figure of Sweeny is the veritable
embodiment of such translation and transformation. Physically metamor-
phosed, lacerated by wind, cold and thorns, the bird-man's poems show
him 'open' to and penetrated by a world from which, in his treetops, he
nevertheless remains estranged:

> Life is loud in the glen.

> Frail stag,
>   your cry has halted me;
> now I am sick with sudden longing

The Poems of Sweeny Peregrine, therefore, does not provide an 'answer' to the issues raised in *Pentahedron*. However, by distancing those same issues through a persona and through the medium of translation, *Sweeny Peregrine* emphasises to a greater extent than *Pentahedron* the 'corruption of the word' that is poetry. Joyce's poetics conceive of poetry as existing on the faultline between, on the one hand, an ultimately incommunicable sense of selfhood and, on the other, an object world the particularity of which cannot be adequately mapped by linguistic resources. To this extent, Joyce's poetic can be read as a late variation on the guilty aestheticism of certain high modernist poets, those who harbour, in Frank Lentricchia's words, a 'self-conscious recognition of a gulf between fictive discourse and being'.[54] In Joyce that recognition does not appear to find much consolation in the transcendental dimension Klee views as inherent in art's non-representational nature. Hence the guilt, absent from Klee, that shadows his aestheticist interest in the abstruse spirals of form and structure. An uncollected poem, published between *Sweeny Peregrine* and *stone floods*, bears this final observation out, while simultaneously pointing to a resolution to Joyce's poetic dilemma. In 'Mirror: Of Glazier Velasquez', the mirror's silvering, its 'enforced obscurity', is opposed to 'the menstruant whose searching gaze / strips the mirror of its validity':

> its silver and austere control being lost,
> the glass once more perspicuous,
> carved wood frames only chaos,
> and all slenderness and grace are gone[55]

While the urge of the 'menstruant' for an unmediated glimpse of nature is destructive of the aesthetic experience, art's 'silver and austere control' of 'chaos' is a lie against nature and time. To this extent, the poem's argument resembles that of Joyce's early poems: the silvering of art is a transformation of the chaos of reality. Yet the mirror, in the present text, is not a 'shut mirror':

> but this enlightenment gives shock
> as to see small private things
> of our familiar lives, estranged
> in the inverted vision
> of the encrypted dead.

These lines endorse a non-mimetic poetic, in which the text metamorphoses reality through mediating forms – interpretative structures in which it frames a 'chaos'. But the poem also claims that such 'estrange[ment]' is itself an 'enlightenment': that is, through its defamiliarising, 'inverted vision' of the world the poem remains, like Sweeny's body, open to the world.

Frames and chaos, closure and openness, are recurrent images in Joyce's *stone floods*. The volume is structured thematically around stasis and movement, control and transgression, around the recurrent images of stone and flood. The poems strive to inhabit both terms of these oppositions simultaneously, thus frequently referring to liminal spaces of one kind or another. It is of interest that Joyce has singled out Beckett's poem 'je suis ce cours de sable qui glisse'/ 'my way is in the sand flowing' as important to his own poetry.[56] As Lawrence Harvey has argued, the landscape in Beckett's poem is emblematic of its speaker's withdrawn mental state; locked into an undifferentiated and shrunken experience of time, he is drawn to a 'peace' identified in the text with non-being:

> my peace is there in the receding mist
> when I may cease from treading these long shifting thresholds
> and live the space of a door
> that opens and shuts[57]

Joyce's poetry is increasingly preoccupied with 'thresholds' and boundaries, with doors that open and shut. 'The Opening', the first poem in *stone floods*, invokes both boundaries and their transgression:

> You are reading this book
> On the table are letters a mirror some flowers
> from which a leaf falls down
> Behind is a wall in which there is no door
> but you have opened it
> and gone through
>
> You hear these words
> Your shadow moves across some photographs a leaf the threshold
> which is badly worn
> Beneath is the floor in which there is no chasm
> yet you have stumbled
> and dropped through
>
> I have shut the book
> and there is silence here
> Now by the window
> I look to the night
> which has begun to fall
> which will not be long now[58]

Although structured as an address from the poetic subject to another, the poem's references to communication in the first two stanzas ('You are reading this book'; 'You hear these words') yield, in the concluding stanza, to the failure of intersubjective intercourse ('I have shut the book / and there is silence here'). Coupled to this lack of interaction is the disorientating suggestion that the first- and second-person pronouns in this poem inhabit what appear to be different worlds: the addressee crosses thresholds hidden from the speaker in a disquieting, even ghostly, fashion, suggesting a freedom of movement the static speaker of the final stanza lacks. Yet the addressee's movement wants control. In the second stanza, we learn that s/he has 'stumbled / and dropped through' the chasm the speaker safely cannot perceive. Freedom seems allied to a disturbingly dangerous transgressiveness, control inseparable from a monadic stasis. The poem thus charts the collapse and the reinforcement of boundaries, the reaching for and the frustration of communication in a highly ambivalent fashion. As in Beckett's 'my way is in the sand flowing', boundedness is linked to being, but at the price of a dissatisfied longing for a breaching of the enclosed self, an opening associated with danger, possibly with non-being (the 'chasm' that swallows up the addressee). The formal properties of the poem reinforce its preoccupation with the threshold between chaos and control, boundaries and their collapse. Written in a relatively straightforward syntax, its declarative statements are nevertheless richly ambiguous, as evinced in the shifting pronouns, punning vocabulary and rapid changes in tense.

While such frustrated longing recalls 'Elegy of the Shut Mirror', the mirror referred to in the first stanza of 'The Opening' is closer to that in 'Mirror: Of Glazier Velasquez' than that in the early poem. For the mirror's presence identifies the addressee as not only a specific individual (the poem is '*for P. C.*') and the reader who has just opened *stone floods* ('*this* book'), but also the speaker himself ('I have shut the book'), narcissistically addressing himself in the second person. In this light, the poem/book is itself a 'threshold' (a reading reinforced by the pun on 'leaf' in the second stanza), one that opens the self to itself as another: self-estrangement, it would appear, is the self-knowledge poetic language grants its reader. While this recalls Joyce's preoccupation with the difficulty of linguistically representing mental states to oneself or to another in 'Considering a Poetic' and related poems, it also repeats the argument of *Sweeny Peregrine* and 'Mirror: Of Glazier Velaquez' in its insistence on the rewards imparted by poetic language. Poetry is open to a world it mirrors only by framing and transforming it, yet to which it nevertheless grants ontological priority, as the speaker's closing confrontation with the falling night, the book 'shut', strongly implies. This final observation is borne out by Joyce's first epigraph to *stone floods*, from the thirteenth-century Japanese poet, Dogen, which emphasises the relativity of our conceptual schemes, while maintaining a belief in a referential realm independent of those schemes: '*Dragons and fish see water as a palace, and it's just like human beings seeing a palace. They don't know it flows. . . . Still, there may be some dragons and fish who*

*understand that the columns and pillars of palaces and pavilions are
flowing water.*' Art's potential for making reality strange depends, in the
last instance, on its awareness that the 'palace' it constructs is a
transfiguration of a reality it can grasp only as if through a glass darkly.

The image of the mirror recurs in one of the most powerful poems in
stone floods, that from which the collection's title is drawn, 'The Turlough':

> London Bridge is falling down elsewhere
>
>
> Circuits and gates collapse
> in sand
> the face the glass
> composed breaks down
>
>
> Raw head finds bloody bones elsewhere
>
>
> Vast hands stop at the stretch
> knuckle
> of blazing gas
> and wrist of stars
>
>
> The gods explode this turn elsewhere
>
>
> Red giant and white dwarf
> come in
> in a blue shift
> Venus meets Mars[59]

The dissolution of the reflected image in 'the glass' is at one with the
poem's emphasis on the collapse of boundaries, from those of the
'composed' self to the very confines of the physical universe, the implosion
of which is the subject of the final lines. The entropy charted in the poem
is conveyed through images that, however disjunctive, follow an asso-
ciative logic. London Bridge's falling arches yield to the collapsing 'gates'
of computer circuitry which, through the reference to 'sand' (silica),
connect to the broken mirror. The decomposed face in the mirror's shards
leads naturally enough into the 'Raw head' and 'bloody bones', a bogey-
man, the *OED* records, used to frighten children, and whose presence
thus both recalls the nursery rhyme jingle of 'London Bridge' and
prefigures the anatomical images of 'knuckle', 'hands' and 'wrist'. These
'Vast hands' usher in the 'gods', who merge with the astronomical and
mythological portents of an incipient Big Bang. On the level of form, this
process of collapsing the divisions between scientific and mythological

discourses, technical and infantile registers, reiterates the poem's emphasis on the breaking of bounds, whether egoistic or cosmic. The titular 'turlough', a seasonal lake in limestone regions and thus 'on no map', is a highly suggestive emblem of Joyce's concern in this volume with fixity and fluidity, norms and their transgression:

> Vertical rivers reverse
> stone floods
> the karst domain
> each sink turns source

The syntax of these remarkable lines enacts their preoccupations: the phrase 'stone floods' is either the object of 'reverse' in the first line or itself the subject and predicate of a clause the object of which is 'the karst domain'. Such ambiguity is generated by Joyce's deployment of the Japanese *renga* form which, in a note to the poem, he describes as using 'systematic ambiguity to chain together a series of brief stanzas every one of which hinges both forward and backward'.[60] Closer to home, this form shows the influence of Empson, whose *Seven Types of Ambiguity* (rather than the poetry) Joyce has admitted informed his early interest in a dense poetic texture. In 'The Turlough' we have an instance of that which Empson labels 'double grammar', 'in which phrases will go either with the sentence before or after and there is no break in the movement of the thought'.[61] Empson's description of this as producing a 'fluid unity' is particularly apt to the movement of Joyce's poem, though elsewhere Joyce's deployment of this device produces a less unified verbal surface than that of 'The Turlough'.

In 'Chimaera' the *renga* form conjoins the voices of Richard Lovelace, Aloysius Bertrand and the Book of Lieh Tze to produce a dialogic verse reminiscent of its utilisation by Japanese poets in joint composition. Lovelace's easy egocentricity views nature in anthropomorphic terms ('then ah the sickle golden ears are cropped / dropping December shall come weeping in'), and as the vehicle for the surprising poetic conceit:

> such whose white satin upper coat of skin
> cut upon velvet rich incarnadin
> has yet a body and of flesh within[62]

Bertrand, by way of contrast, sees in nature a gross reminder of our physicality ('that creature fluttered free but voided in my lap / a maggot with a human head monstrous misshapen'), prompting his agonised reflections on the 'chaos of worlds' that threatens human order:

> souls of the dead like mountain oaks uprooted by demons
> souls of the dead like meadow flowers gathered by angels
> sun sky earth man all had begun all gone

Lovelace's self-satisfied, urbane wit and Bertrand's apocalyptic fore-
bodings of the levelling of all bounds are set against the Book of Lieh
Tze's acceptance of the provisionality of limits in nature, the fragility of
the ego and the interconnected diversity of the phenomenal world:

> cuckoos in due course again turn raptor
> swallows become oysters seashells hatch geese . . .
> apes grown of sheep fish that are rotten fruit
> flies born of roe such transformations are

It would be wrong, I think, to identify fully Joyce's beliefs with those
expressed by this third voice: Lovelace's verbal ingenuity and Bertrand's
nausea are also important aspects of Joyce's writing from *Pentahedron*
on. Moreover, the Book of Lieh Tze expresses an unboundedness that,
like Beckett, Joyce regards as the destruction of the individual being. In
this respect, therefore, 'Chimaera' ventriloquises Joyce's guilty aestheticism
through playing-off Lovelace and Bertrand against the Book of Lieh Tze.
Yet the poem can also be seen as Joyce's most successful attempt thus far
to straddle the 'gulf between fictive discourse and being' opened up by his
aesthetic assumptions. For the composite form of the *renga* provides Joyce
with a verse structure suggestive of the world's heterogeneity precisely owing
to its 'systematic ambiguity', as Joyce describes it.

GEOFFREY SQUIRES: FROM PROJECTIVE TO PHENOMENOLOGICAL VERSE

Geoffrey Squires's poetic career consists, to date, of two phases: the first
comprises *Drowned Stones* (New Writers' Press, 1975), *Figures* (1978)
and *XXI Poems* (1980); the second, *Landscapes & Silences* (New Writers'
Press, 1996) and *Poem for Two Voices* (1998). Falling between the two
groups is the recently republished (and retitled) *A Long Poem in Three
Sections*, first published in the *Irish University Review* in 1983.[63] *A Long
Poem* is pivotal in Squires's development in two related ways. It illus-
trates, on the one hand, his increased interest in certain ideas drawn
from the phenomenological tradition; on the other, it marks a break with
the disjunctive formal patterns of his earlier poetry in favour of a more
cohesive textual surface. As we shall see, however, these two aspects of
Squires's recent work are not so much a rejection of the concerns or even
the procedures of his earlier work, as they constitute their modulation in
a new direction. For linking both phases is the attempt to isolate formal
structures expressive of the interpenetration of subjectivity and the world,
the intercourse between an embodied consciousness and its material
environment.

Drowned Stones is a six-part sequence of poems and prose passages, a collage of materials that eschews the cohesion of a linear narrative. In the first part of the poem, the reader confronts a number of disjointed reflections largely on the subject's place of origin in Co. Donegal, a landscape viewed from the perspective of a mature self displaced from a once-intimately known locality:

> Turf dry and crumbling
> the inland lakes
> a dark shot troubled blue
>
> local people do not see
> what we see, landscape
> is already something
> you are outside of[64]

Squires's characteristic fidelity to the object world in the first three lines of this quotation is reminiscent of William Carlos Williams, who, with Charles Olson, is an important influence on *Drowned Stones*. In Williams and Olson the detailed rendering of a sense of place is inseparable from the realisation of personality. In epic proportions, Williams's *Paterson* and Olson's *The Maximus Poems* interrogate their respective authors' identities through close investigations of local history and geography, that of Williams's eponymous city and Olson's Gloucester. *Drowned Stones* lacks the ambitious scope of its American precursors, though it shares their impetus to explore a particular sensibility through an exploration of specific places and landscapes. In the above example, the 'troubled blue' of the lake illustrates the extent to which the environment is coloured by the perturbed emotions of its observer, for whom the landscape's significance is inevitably different from that of the 'local people'. Squires's partial indebtedness to Williams is suggested by the appearance, in Part I, of 'Patterson's dog' who 'used to stop / smell and piss':

> just once in each place
> and the same places every day
>
> a farmer stopped me once and asked
> what can that dog do[65]

Williams's *Paterson* also opens with a dog, whose presence invites from Williams's speaker a not dissimilar question to that of Squires's farmer:

> To make a start,
> out of particulars
> and make them general, rolling
> up the sum, by defective means –
> Sniffing the trees,
> just another dog
> among a lot of dogs. What
> else is there? And to do?[66]

After Williams, Squires implies a resemblance between dog and poet, the role of both (what they *do*) being the 'sniffing' out of 'particulars':

> Sand lizard, palmate and crested newt
> natterjack toad and edible frog
>
> a note as to how identity was established[67]

Nevertheless, in contrast to Williams, Squires makes no attempt to wrest a 'general' or national 'identity' out of his imaginative incursions into his past and region – indeed, the landscape of *Drowned Stones* is not constant, Donegal being only one of a number of locations in the poem. Rather, Squires concurs with and emphasises Williams's admission that the poet's lifeworld is one among many – he is 'just another dog / among a lot of dogs'. Landscapes in Squires are always 'something / you are outside of' in the sense that they provide sites in which consciousness becomes self-consciousness, in which the mind reflects upon its own mental landscape. They are the grounds of existential self-recognitions and their significance, therefore, eschews the regionalism attendant upon not only Williams's and Olson's, but also many Irish poets' – such as John Montague's and Seamus Heaney's – investigations of the local grounds to their identities.

The imprint of Williams and Olson on *Drowned Stones* is felt more strongly in the manner in which the sequence, as it progresses, increasingly transposes the poetic subject's voice with other voices, in verse and prose, and quotations from other texts (some parts of *Drowned Stones*, it is worth noting, are drawn from Squires's 1971 radio play for three voices, *Summer*). The deployment of found material from such source-texts as John Cunningham Lilly's *Programming and Metaprogramming in the Human Biocomputer* and Herbert V. Guenther's *The Tantric View of Life* strikingly foregrounds a major concern of the text: that there is 'a kind of permanent schizoid dissociation between two realms of reality'. The first is 'the public, quantifiable and therefore minimally intelligible but universally legitimate, language of official positivism'; the second 'is the relativistic domain of multiple, aesthetic, rich, and morally directioned private phenomenologies':

> The psychic premium in such a society would be on personalities that were
> flexible, unserious, not characterized towards integration of their being
> and perceptions, able to withstand a kaleidoscope of relativism by reducing
> most of it to play.[68]

The found materials of *Drowned Stones* stress the 'multiple' nature of reality and the partial, perspectival quality of our knowledge of the object world, the sequence as a whole exploring the 'domain' in which perception is relative to one's private phenomenology, itself a 'kaleidoscope' of shifting modalities:

> What is here is
> not time passing
> but time changing
>
> my mother growing
> old does not understand
> me growing old[69]

The mother's incomprehension deftly illustrates that 'reality' is produced by an experiencing consciousness, and thus conditioned by the forces that delimit that consciousness. The world, rather than subsisting independently of the human observer, as positivism insists, has moral and aesthetic significance only in relation to that embedded observer.

Formally, Squires's approach to this theme suggests the procedures of Black Mountain poetics. Squires has said that the first volume of Olson's *The Maximus Poems* (1960) influenced *Drowned Stones*,[70] and the poems are valuably read in the light of Olson's theories of 'open form' or 'composition by field'. In his seminal essay, 'Projective Verse' (1950), Olson argues that the poet engaged in 'FIELD COMPOSITION' is subject to the 'law' that 'FORM IS NEVER MORE THAN AN EXTENSION OF CONTENT'; in the *'process'* of the poem 'ONE PERCEPTION MUST IMMEDIATELY AND DIRECTLY LEAD TO A FURTHER PERCEPTION', to create a poetic field that has a solidity directly analogous to that of objects in 'what we know as the world'. [71] To this end, conventionalities of syntax and metre are 'broken open' by the 'front of syllable, line, field' in its creation of a poetic form that embodies 'objectism': 'Objectism is the getting rid of the lyrical interference of the individual as ego, of the "subject" and his soul, that peculiar presumption by which western man has interposed himself between what he is as a creature of nature (with certain instructions to carry out) and those other creations of nature which we may, with no derogation, call objects.'[72] If the polyphonic quality and found material of *Drowned Stones* downgrades the centrality of the lyric subject, this formal device is 'an extension of content', in Olson's sense, owing to the sequence's concern with our being in a world in which we too are objects or creatures of nature, among lizards, newts, toads and frogs. Objectism is present from the opening lines of the volume, in which the 'I' of Part I initially appears in the third person, as 'another': '(And all the trouble to learn him, the / strangeness of another, his turnings)'.[73] Placed in parenthesis and introduced by a conjunction, the self in these lines assumes a quality of 'strangeness'. The lyric I is, if not dissolved, then displaced as the governing centre of the sequence, such defamiliarisation functioning as the formal equivalent to the poem's resistance to the disembodied Cartesian subject. For, in Squires, existence is not reducible to 'a central point of identity and consciousness',[74] but a future-orientated and open-ended project:

> Where does the bee go
> with his honey-load
>
> through the open window of space
>
> sweetness of this universe
> being, infinite and not alone
> which draws bears on
> murmuring, through the night
>
> and the stars
> are light to fish
> as they rise[75]

Figures is a less ambitious collection than Drowned Stones but marks a change in Squires's poetic in that, whereas the earlier collection presents a multifaceted lifeworld through its utilisation of a range of voices and texts, the later sequence's constituent parts are themselves internally ruptured. To this extent, the poems register Olson's stress on the importance to field composition of one perception flowing onto another. The result is a series of often gnomic fragments, of which the following is typical:

> Two men and a girl
> down by the pier
> painting a dinghy
> well
>
>
> turn over a stone
> that elsewhereness
> bark of gulls
>
>
> that   elsewhereness
>
>
> the long strand
>
>
> and he never[76]

The form of these lines is an 'extension' of what the sequence later calls 'complex non-linear / memories / and whispers of composite faces'.[77] That is, the 'composite' nature of each fragment refuses the closure Olson identifies with 'The NON-Projective' lyric's encapsulation of the *'the private-soul-at-any-public-wall'*.[78] The lines quoted above refuse to allow the perception of the three figures painting a boat to stabilise and provide the ground for a lyrical mediation by *'the private-soul'* observing them, such conventional poetic closure disarmingly forestalled by the bathetic exclamation, 'well'. Instead, the reader or the speaker is enjoined to 'turn over a stone' in an openness to a new perception that echoes the projective ending to Olson's 'The Kingfishers': 'I hunt among stones'.[79] The 'elsewhereness' of the gulls' cry and the sight of the strand lead one from the other, and the poem concludes with a third-person pronoun that, if it denotes the poet, constitutes an act of objectism, as the speaker assumes his own 'elsewhereness' to himself. Whether in fact the pronoun refers to another or to the subject as an object within the landscape he perceives, the truncated syntax of the final line resists lyric finality in a fashion that anticipates the sequence's final fragment:

> Figures that dance wildly and then stop
> that makes as if to call out
> or cross suddenly[80]

These 'Figures' are both the 'composite faces' of the sequence and the poems themselves: just as the human figures abruptly cease dancing, so too the 'dance' of the sequence reaches no determinate conclusion, it simply 'stops'.

Squires's early projective verse has points of resemblance with John Montague's 1972 sequence, *The Rough Field*. While Montague's exploration of Tyrone is, on one level, deeply coloured by Kavanagh's Monaghan anti-pastoral, *The Great Hunger*, on another, it shows the influence of American and British poetic modernism, that of Williams, Olson, David Jones and Hugh MacDiarmid. In the most recent Preface to *The Rough Field*, Montague talks of being conscious, during the long gestation of the poem, of the 'debate on open-form from *Paterson*, through Olson, to Duncan', and of being 'equally drawn by rooted poets like MacDiarmid in *A Drunk Man*'.[81] Williams's influence on *The Rough Field* is palpable in 'the clean rhythm and ordinary language' of several poems, the Imagistic directness of others.[82] This approach produces some of the most memorable passages in the sequence, as in the understated but resonant conclusion to the opening poem of 'A Severed Head':

Like shards   ·
Of a lost culture, the slopes
Are strewn with cabins, deserted
In my lifetime . . .
Jamie MacCrystal
Lived in the final cottage,
A trim grove of mountain ash
Soughing protection round his walls
And bright painted gate. The thatch
Has slumped in, white dust of nettles
On the flags. Only the shed remains
In use for calves, although fuchsia
Bleeds by the wall, and someone has
Propped a yellow cartwheel
Against the door.[83]

If the presence of Jones can be sensed in Montague's interest in dis-
interring the cultural 'shards' of his region, the poem's representation of
MacCrystal's deserted cottage clearly bears the imprint of Williams in its
empathetic attentiveness to the quotidian (Montague's 'yellow cartwheel'
has a look of Williams's famous red wheelbarrow). The broader concerns
of the sequence are grounded in a landscape thus carefully perceived – as
'Bleeds', in the above passage, subtly introduces an allegorical dimension
to a firmly denoted landscape, the verb rendering the scene emblematic of
the violent history of Ulster charted in the sequence as a whole: 'All
around, shards of a lost tradition'.[84] More strikingly, in mapping the
rough field of the townland of Garvaghey, Montague makes use of
Elizabethan woodcuts and accounts of Ireland, political pamphlets and
letters, in a fashion reminiscent of Williams's and Olson's deployment of
found material in *Paterson* and *The Maximus Poems*. In 'The Bread God'
section of *The Rough Field*, for instance, Montague intersperses his lyrics
with loyalist documents and letters from his Jesuit uncle to produce 'A
Collage of Religious Misunderstandings'.[85] As Marjorie Perloff has
argued, collage, 'As the mode of detachment and readherence, of graft
and citation . . . inevitably undermines the authority of the individual self,
the "signature" of the poet'.[86] In the case of *The Rough Field*, this
modernist technique has 'the effect', in Dillon Johnston's view, of
'dissolv[ing] any sense of an authoritative causal history into separate
documents defining sectarian histories';[87] and, to this extent, the open,
hybrid form of *The Rough Field* is a brilliantly realised extension of its
densely conflictual content.

Nevertheless, in the light of Montague's attraction to the 'rooted'
nature of MacDiarmid's (and Jones's) modernism, Williams's and Olson's
importance to *The Rough Field* arguably lies as much in their localism as
in their exemplification of 'open form'. (It is of interest that Montague

was dissatisfied with the second volume of Olson's *The Maximus Poems*, *Maximus IV, V, VI* [1968], owing, one imagines, to its expansion of local preoccupations into mythological dimensions.)[88] In Montague, locality shades into nation, Ulster becoming a synecdoche for Ireland, in an inexorable movement from individual to regional to national identity. In formal terms, this aspect of the sequence finds expression in its lyricism (indeed, several of the individual poems were previously published independently). In contrast to Olson's projective verse, the autobiographical, lyric I is crucial to Montague's regionalist poetic. A non-projective endeavour at self-definition is inseparable from the poem's troubled nationalism – its reiterated attempt to define self in relation to place intertwined with its desire to reconceive place as a unified subject. Montague's bardic pretensions powerfully yoke his stammer ('some stuttering garb- / led ordeal of my own') to the national trauma of linguistic change:

> To grow
> a second tongue, as
> harsh a humiliation
> as twice to be born.[89]

The Rough Field draws its strength from its combination of lyric and open forms – a fusion of modes that derives from the sequence's focus on a discordant regional and national history coupled to a romantic nationalist emphasis on the culturally recuperative and restorative powers of the poet. In the words of the second epigraph to *The Rough Field*, taken from George Seferis, whatever 'wrong has been committed', 'The important thing is who will redeem it?'

Montague's interest in amalgamating open and closed forms is apparent in his 1973 article, 'The Impact of International Modern Poetry on Irish Writing'. Montague's high praise for Devlin in this piece rests on his conviction that 'he is the first poet of Irish Catholic background to take the world as his province', who drew poetic vigour from, initially, '*poesie pure* and surrealism', and, later, 'his American contemporaries', Tate and Warren.[90] Montague's own appropriation of poetic modes derived from other traditions than the Irish in *The Rough Field* obviously underscores his enthusiasm both for Devlin's 'internationalism' and Coffey's translation of Mallarmé's *Un Coup de dés*, the latter 'a possible example of non-iambic structure, of the use of the page in a kind of musical notation, all this before Charles Olson'.[91] Montague thus gently upbraids those Irish poets who, unlike Devlin, Coffey and others, write with an obliviousness to the formal innovations of modernist poetry, particularly those of Pound, D. H. Lawrence and Williams, and 'as though the iambic line still registered the curve of modern speech'.

Nonetheless, adducing *The Rough Field*, he claims that 'all true experiments and exchanges only serve to illuminate the self, a rediscovery of the oldest laws of the psyche'.[92] While as a generalisation this is debatable, it is entirely germane to Montague's own conjoining of projective and lyric forms. It also highlights the gulf between Montague's politically charged foregrounding of the self in *The Rough Field*, and Squires's phenomenologically conceived poetic subject, the 'illumination' of which becomes his chief preoccupation after *Drowned Stones*.

XXI Poems stands as a transitional collection in Squires's work. The harsh disjunctions of *Figures* are largely absent, replaced by a limpidity increasingly characteristic of Squires's poetry. A helpful gloss on this modulation in his work is Squires's distinction between poetry that is centrifugal and poetry that is centripetal. Prior to *XXI Poems* the poetry is centrifugal, the poetic consciousness a rim of fragmented voices and texts thrown out by the field of the poem. His subsequent poetry works centripetally in its emphasis on the individual as the determining centre of its world, a movement Squires identifies in Beckett's later prose and Coffey's major sequences. Such concentration on the subject, however, does not mark a turn towards the non-projective lyric. The subject's relationship to the world in which it is thrown is characterised by an openness of response that finds formal expression in Squires's use of the sequence. The poems that comprise Squires's recent collections are not closed lyrics; rather, they have a quality of provisionality, of being notations recording the ongoing and fluid relationship between subject and world. His sequences have the appearance of beginning and ending arbitrarily; they reach no crescendo, but maintain an insistent and hypnotic evenness of tone. They create, in the words of *Landscapes & Silences*, 'stories' that go 'off on tangents elaborate digressions / long parentheses each step growing / out of the one before'.[93] They ponder, meditate on, the poet's existential project, his being-in-the-world, and testify to Squires's deep immersion in phenomenology. For the poems articulate and inflect Husserl's dictum that to be conscious is to be conscious of something, that the world is 'intended' by the human mind. Hence the continuing importance of landscape in Squires's recent work: the natural world's perception by the subject becomes the object of the poem's ruminative stance. In Squires's words, 'Landscape not as conventional view but as test-bed of consciousness':[94]

> Claritas, detail, punctilious, bright
> now above all we are aware of the quality of the light
> that spreads itself, covering everything
> medium transmuting all objects and surfaces

> so it is, in such a landscape
> that the being of all animals and birds
> seems to be quick, animated and precise
> alert not from danger but from an innate
> keenness of perception[95]

The light's transformation of the environment requires a perceiving subject to establish a landscape of which one is 'aware', and to this extent the 'medium' of light explored in these lines is also the poet's 'keenness of perception', which 'spreads itself, covering everything'. Yet that same consciousness requires an object-world to exist, to be itself 'quick, animated and precise', and thus subject and object in these lines do not stand opposed but enter into a dialectical relationship.

This relationship is further scrutinised in Squires's *A Long Poem in Three Sections*, in the first section of which perceptual experience is shown to possess an irreducible openness:

> A leaf magnified
> endlessness of seeing of what is seen
> the world its strangeness the strangeness
> of small motions and of nearness
> and no interiority as such[96]

The 'endlessness of seeing of what is seen' is the theme of the entire poem, and of *Landscapes & Silences* and *Poem for Two Voices*. The 'what' of perception is dependent on the act of 'seeing', and that act will of course vary from occasion to occasion, from perceiver to perceiver – thus its 'endlessness', the constant 'strangeness' of the world in which humanity exists. The poem is, in this respect, indebted to the ideas of Merleau-Ponty, from whose *L'Oeil et l'esprit* it takes its epigraph: '*Après tout, le monde est autour de moi, non devant moi*'. Merleau-Ponty, expanding on Husserl's phenomenology, rejects the notion of a transcendental ego in favour of an incarnate subjectivity: a bodily self embedded within a 'phenomenal field' of which knowledge is necessarily perspectival. For Merleau-Ponty the perceiving body 'is caught in the fabric of things': 'vision happens among, or is caught in, things – in that place where something visible undertakes to see, becomes visible for itself by virtue of the sight of things; in that place where there persists, like the mother water in the crystal, the undividedness [*l'indivision*] of the sensing and the sensed'.[97] Squires's rumination on 'undividedness' develop out of the earlier poetry's 'objectism'; Olson's conception of 'the poem as field' modulates into a poetic investigation of the 'phenomenal field' in which the subject is situated. Indeed, in 'Human Universe', Olson himself employs the phrase 'phenomenal field' in the context of discussing 'the skin itself, the meeting edge of man and external reality', at which juncture the two entities are 'so involved with one another that, for man's purposes, they had better be taken as one'.[98] The concluding section of *A Long Poem* dwells on this Olsonian 'edge' to the 'fabric of things':

> Never for one moment does the attention falter
> or grow inward away from the surface of things
> waiting upon the slightest movement
> or hint of sound, so that what happens
> is sensed almost before it happens

Squires's forays into what this poem terms the human project of 'pressing forward' are continued in *Landscapes & Silences* and *Poem for Two Voices*. In the former sequence he speaks of the way 'the mind . . . moves over things':

> passing over them like a light shadow
> which darkens them for a moment only a moment
>
> and hardly at all[99]

The movements of the mind are the movements of perception, which create ever-changing figure-background structures: 'each time you look and nothing has changed / then suddenly it is different and you cannot say how'.[100] The object world is inseparable from these structures of perception, and thus, in the words of *Poem for Two Voices*, 'to say that it is visual does not do it justice   because that suggests something purely external   out there'.[101] Yet the object, as a thing-in-itself, possesses a stubborn particularity. The 'logic of things   unarguable objectivity of the world'[102] cannot be exhausted by or fully assimilated to the observing consciousness:

> green pendant luxuriant
> many-leaved many-layered
> things blurred too close to be in focus
> wet surfaces diaspora of light
> impossible to gather into perception
>
> all that we have[103]

The two sequences' attentiveness to this enabling interchange between subject and environment, between what *Poem for Two Voices* terms '*This reasoning*' and 'these surfaces which throw back the perception even the thought as if to say   it is so',[104] is reminiscent of Gary Snyder's exploration, in *Myths & Texts* and *Mountains and Rivers Without End*, of that which the American poet calls 'the very close correspondences between the external and the internal landscape' – Squires's poems, like Snyder's, 'moving back and forth' between the two.[105]

Coda

'NO NARRATIVE EASY IN THE MIND': THE IRISH NEO-AVANT-GARDE

The neo-modernism of the New Writers' Press poets examined in the previous chapter presents a variegated phenomenon. It is as varied as the modernism of the 1930s poets, whose respective oeuvres are ill-served by viewing them as possessing anything more than a shared receptivity to various currents of modernist writing of the early part of the century. The *direct* influence of the 1930s modernists on the poets associated with New Writers' Press is negligible, and what there is would appear to post-date their earliest work. Nevertheless, connections can be drawn. Trevor Joyce's preoccupation with liminality, for instance, bears fruitful comparison with Beckett's representation of thresholds and boundaries; Michael Smith's critical prose clearly owes its polemical stance to Coffey and Beckett, though his poetry arguably shares more with Devlin's hankering after a revelatory symbolism, albeit in an attenuated form; and Geoffrey Squires's recent ruminative poetry finds an echo in the meditative stance of Coffey's *Missouri Sequence* (1962), *Advent* (1975) and *Death of Hektor* (1979), and some of Beckett's later texts. If it is possible to detect a schism between symbolist and open, more indeterminate, modes of writing in the 1930s poets, a similar dualism is to be found in the writings of the New Writers' Press poets – in the difference, say, between the pathos of Smith's symbolism and the projective quality of Squires's phenomenological verse. Discriminating between the achievements of the 1930s poets, in short, helps to contextualise more rewardingly the equally varied poetics of their neo-modernist 'successors'. A final advantage in looking anew at the relationship between the 1930s modernists and the neo-modernists is that it provides a backdrop against which to place the recent work of Joyce and that of several younger Irish poets, Randolph Healy, Billy Mills, Maurice Scully and Catherine Walsh, whose work is valuably read as a neo-avant-garde tendency in contemporary Irish poetry; that is, it is a poetry that performs, for the 1980s and 1990s, the role of problematising the category of the aesthetic that was played earlier in the century by the historical avant-garde outside Ireland.

Regardless of the impact of literary modernism on Irish poetry, the noisy declamations of the historical avant-garde, of Futurism, Dada, Surrealism et al., do not find a corresponding voice in Irish poetry in the decades leading up to the Emergency, the latter in any case muffling to a great extent the intermittent conversations with artistic experiments in Europe undertaken by various journals, such as *The Dublin Magazine*, in the pre-war period. The cultural isolationism of the Republic of Ireland during the 1940s and 1950s was challenged by *The Bell* and, from 1949 to 1951, *Envoy* (which included contributions from Nathalie Sarraute and Gertrude Stein). But the energies of *The Bell* were channelled chiefly into combating constricting definitions of Irishness; while *Envoy* was too short-lived to have more than a passing effect on Irish poetry. For Irish poets in the late 1960s and early 1970s drawn towards what we might now term 'linguistically innovative writing', the dissolution of Irish poetic modernism and the lack of an avant-garde moment in Irish writing were compounded by Kavanagh's high reputation at this date, which inevitably marginalised those 1930s poets who wrote under the auspices of literary modernism. One could add to this that Clarke's localist poetics – ironically so close to those of Williams and MacDiarmid[1] – seemed antithetical to the 'internationalism' of modernism as it was then largely conceived.

Still, one must be careful not to view these years in monochrome. During the crucial years in which Ireland began to feel the social and cultural 'expansionism' consequent upon the economic modernisation inaugurated by Seán Lemass, the editors of a number of groundbreaking journals proved receptive to diverse forms of poetry: Michael Smith's and Trevor Joyce's *The Lace Curtain* we have already considered; but James Liddy's *Arena*, Hayden Murphy's *Broadsheet*, and the *University Review* under the far-sighted editorship of Lorna Reynolds, all provided fora for a wide range of writing, from the lyric mode to concrete poetry. Yet such sporadic enterprises hardly constitute a sustained attempt to think through the bequest of high modernism and the avant-garde for Irish poetry. Most of these outlets dried up; moreover, interest in Irish poetry in Britain and the United States soon found a compelling scenario in the North. The critical feeding-frenzy that surrounded the Northern renaissance in Irish poetry during the 1970s and 1980s helped create a dominant image of the characteristic Irish poem: a Movement lyric fractured by the impact of political violence. In the main, contemporary Irish poetry, in the North and the South, has done little to problematise this lyric form, although its content tends to be less volatile. In this respect, the bulk of recent Irish poetry stands towards the poetry of Heaney, Derek Mahon and others much as the poets of the British 'New Gen' stand towards their Movement predecessors – as their sometimes unruly, sometimes docile, progeny.

In the work of the Irish neo-avant-garde the closed lyric, that which Olson disparagingly dubbed '*the private-soul-at-any-public-wall*',[2] has come to seem increasingly antiquated in a global culture dominated by the mass media and communications technology. The 'roughened' texture of these poets' writings, its self-reflexive attitude to its status as a medium of information, 'functions', as Marjorie Perloff says of North American Language poetry, 'to mime the coming to awareness of the mind in the face of the endless information glut that surrounds us'.[3] Such is the role of the neo-avant-garde: to inherit the oppositional nature of the historical avant-garde by creating a poetry both at home in an era of information technology yet resistant to the deformations of sound-bite consumerism.

In a talk at the First Cork Conference on New and Experimental Poetry, in 1997, Trevor Joyce spoke of a 'poetry of expression' – exemplified for him by Mahon's and Eavan Boland's work – that in seeking to articulate others' suffering, betrays it by 'arrogat[ing] the experience of others as one's own'. Such writing is complicit with other media in its belief that language is a neutral purveyor of meaning when, in fact, it displays a rhetorical 'mastery' of 'the resources of language' related to the manipulation of images 'through advertising (where language is most fully mastered and utterly submissive)'. Such a use of language is, at bottom, related to technocratic reason, humanity's domination of 'the resources of the natural world'. In contesting this view of language, Joyce spoke of a poetry 'responsive to language' in less manipulative ways, a poetry 'willing through its own dialogue with language to participate in the world', as exemplified by the chance procedures deployed by John Cage.[4] Joyce's recent poetry, while continuing to mine familiar preoccupations, is close to the work of younger experimental Irish poets in its dialogic forms, its attempt to produce a poetry alive to the way language operates in contemporary society. His 1998 sequence, *Syzygy*, develops further the structural possibilities of 'Chimaera', in *stone floods*, its complex structure of two interlaced parts recalling, even as it excels, the earlier poem's utilisation of the Japanese *renga* form. In *Syzygy*, the 'systematic ambiguity' definitive of the *renga* derives, not from a literary precedent, but from the method of composition described in Joyce's annotations to the sequence. In brief, the 'palindromic net', as Joyce felicitously terms it,[5] is achieved by means of a base text, now fossilised in the second part of the sequence, that dictates the opening and closing segments of each of the twelve units or 'cells' of Part I. Once those cells are complete, their material, mediated through the controlling procedures, determines the remainder of Part II. This approach, of course, is not unique to Joyce:

Cage's famous mesostic texts, his 'writing through' of others' works, are generated in a not unrelated fashion to *Syzygy*. In Irish writing, however, the only comparable text I know of is Randolph Healy's *Flame*, also generated from chance procedures and equally preoccupied with the relationship between order and discontinuity.[6] The partially prescribed nature of the sequence is at one with Joyce's continuing fixation, from *Pentahedron* to *stone floods*, with bounds, order and, latterly, with their breakdown and transgression. For, as Joyce's notes confess, the symmetry of the sequence is not absolute, there is a tiny flaw in the crystalline structure; and it is precisely this alloy that brings the formal qualities of *Syzygy* into alignment with its thematic concern: the relationship between conceptual order and the particularity of the phenomenal world. In a manner reminiscent of Adorno, the text views the former as necessary and inescapable, but stifling and ineluctably involved with other, harsher kinds of domination:

> when the thieving
> that was well advanced faltered
> the imperial presence surveyed
> the ordered territories
> and declared in measured words
> nothing there is savage any more
> intelligence and griefs are tamed
> rage is reduced in parks
> only perhaps along the furthest bounds
> may be some dirt a little ghost
> and these are even as we speak contained
> in three quart jugs[7]

With strikingly evocative concision, Joyce brings together in these lines colonial subjugation of land (in China and Ireland) through force and cartography, a suppressive coercion that is closely bound up with human discourse, the 'measured words' 'we speak.' Such subjection involves rejection of the 'dirt' or debris that refuses to conform to the purifying new order. As Joyce's notes acknowledge, this dimension of the poem draws on the ideas of Mary Douglas, whose *Purity and Danger* atomises the need purity has to reduce that which it spurns to the non-threatening condition of rubbish, whether that be conceptual or human detritus.

Along related lines, a chief concern of the poem is the manner in which lived experiential time is abstracted to clock time, the latter marshalling the former into 'garrisons brief zones / of time and influence':

> until the fixed mesh abstracts
> unerringly each hour
> with all its clamouring brood
> jerking routinely to the tune[8]

Yet the 'clamouring' of reality resists the taxonomic mesh due to its messy particularity, just as one's lifeworld defies total systematisation. Joyce conveys the resistance of dirt, in Douglas's extended sense, to purification through densely punning lines, the ambiguities of which themselves emphasise the fluidity of a supposedly classified, demarcated and regimented world:

> noise of concerns sequestered
> ultimately will get out
> states sundered bleed
> surely each to each
> by breaking bounds ghosts
> traffic through the empty squares[9]

Indeed, the very title word of Joyce's text is ambivalent, trafficking between two senses. Among its meanings, syzygy, in astronomy, can signify either the conjunction or opposition of two heavenly bodies. The strength of this remarkable poem lies in its syzygetic nature: its close correlation of form to a content preoccupied with the opposition that matter, of various kinds, puts up to structuration. (That the word, in prosody, further denotes the admixture of two feet in one metre is also of relevance to the intertwined patterning of the poem's two parts.) In these respects, while *Syzygy* clearly grows out of *stone floods*, it breaks new ground in the compelling intricacy and moving urgency of its formalism.

Randolph Healy's poetry, like Joyce's, explores epistemological concerns through formal means, investigating the ways in which inchoate experience is ordered by various conceptual schemes. His poetry's 'starting point', as he put it in an early essay, is the very inability of logic to verify its own truth-claims, as 'one would need infinitely many axioms for a system to always be able to determine whether a given statement may be regarded as true or false in that system'. This allows a rethinking of logic 'as a game [that] is open, not dogmatic', which provides provisional rather than absolute notations, thus enabling a poetry that creates 'A dialogue with experience . . . moving back and forth from statement to experience without stop'.[10] In his introduction to *25 Poems* Healy states that such a 'dialogue' proceeds in part by means of found material, the appropriation and redeployment of source texts, 'So that meaning, far from being something static, locked within a particular set of words, becomes mobile and culturally dependent'.[11] The resulting poems in the collection simultaneously register the 'mobility' of information in an age of electronic media and impede its easy consumption through their defamiliarisation of the original sources' 'meaning'. 'Gardiner Street', for example, cites a description of the eating-habits of a hunting wasp, 'dithering' the edges of the quotation so that it follows on immediately

from the preceding lines' account of 'a front-page photo of a brand new /
luminary, spokesman of heroes!'

> ready to fry his dearest for the principle
> which leads him head and neck through the dead,
> rooting luxuriously in their entrails,
> the vivacious animal always going forward,
> who will not budge as long as the feast lasts.[12]

In this instance, the technique serves to emit a satirical charge in a fairly
straightforward fashion. In subsequent work, Healy explores in a far
more complex fashion the power of discursive systems, using formal
strategies that reveal the limits of those conceptual schemes that assert
their normative status. *Arbor Vitae* examines various discourses or
'language games', its 'starting point', deafness and sign language, opening
out into a contestation of the logocentric 'doctrine' 'That true language is
lingual': '*Guth, / /* where *Voice* becomes *God, /* as the suffixed zero-
grade of the same root.'[13] The poem challenges any belief that 'Total
Communication' is possible, owing to the alternative 'ways of world-
making', in Nelson Goodman's phrase, that different sign systems grant
their users.[14] The poem's exploration of 'post-lingual, / pre-lingual, / /
non-lingual' cultures, ranging from signing to Neolithic cave-paintings,
contains, in its own form, a resistance to orality: acrostics in the text
introduce a semantic element indiscernible in a spoken performance.[15]
The poem is a fine example of the kind of constructivist writing Joyce
opposes to the 'poetry of expression'. Its artifice does justice to those
whose conceptual schemes are marginalised as either primitive or
somehow non-normative *not* through empathetic understanding but by
recognising their otherness:

> *their* world a document
> laid out all around you,
> key text centred, bold, underlined,
> illegible, and surrounded by small print,
> growing smaller and smaller . . .[16]

Healy's attention to language's 'dialogue' with the world eschews linguistic
mastery of nature, human nature included. In the words of 'Spirals Dance':

> Tuesday.
> Are my thoughts my own?
> Neither the world nor its representative replies.
> Simple, complex, directed, chaotic?
> No answer.
> Whatever passes for pattern can be accommodated
> as part of a larger random sequence
> or result of any of an arbitrary set of laws.[17]

This concentration on the competing claims of various discourses is, as Robert Archambeau suggests, equally an interrogation 'of what it means to live in a world so information saturated that to attempt to comprehend it is analogous to trying "to send the Complete Shakespeare / by Morse while never getting further than dot".'[18] Healy's dialogic forms refuse any privileged position *vis-à-vis* the world, whether logical or lyrical, but rather open the space for a critique of both scientific and poetic claims to provide a unique and foundational insight into the human subject's place within nature and society.

Like Healy's, Billy Mills's poetry is provisional, open-ended; its engagement with the extra-linguistic world is reminiscent of Zukofsky and the Objectivists in granting the poem a density comparable to other objects in the material world. To this extent, Mills's is not a representational poetic, but neither is it geared towards the construction of the autotelic artwork. In a relatively early essay, Mills rejected 'a focus' on 'the concept of the poem as a closed system, with a logic of its own, reflecting the subjective emotions of the author', in favour of 'a poetry without metaphor, wherein the language will focus on the thing in its own terms, reflecting the objective movement of the author through the external world'.[19] The 'closed' New Critical poem, the 'verbal icon', is passed over in favour of a mode of writing that will reflect the poet's place within a world of objects in which the poem should be seen as another 'thing'. To this end, Mills's expression is chiselled, pared-down. In *Tiny Pieces* this leads to a finely-honed minimalism reminiscent of George Oppen's *Discrete Series*: in both texts the reader is asked to attend to individual words with the attention we would usually reserve for the line or stanza. Such an approach to the word is also, Mills's sequence suggests, an approach to the relationship between word and thing:

> first
> the world
>
> next
> the word
>
> imperfect
> charting[20]

The poem's opening six words contain a revealing ambiguity: on the one hand, the world pre-exists the poem, the latter thus condemned to an 'imperfect / charting' of its pre-text; on the other, however, the world and the word are 'next' to one another in the sense that neither has ontological priority. The former is obviously the more compelling reading, but the latter should be borne in mind: in refusing any quasi-idealist

valorisation of the poetic word, Mills foregrounds his poems' objective
texture, as is evident in the care with which his poems are typographically
arranged on the page.

In *The Properties of Stone*, for instance, the geological preoccupations
are equally aesthetic ones, the rock-forms and crystals examined in the
'Lapidary' section of the book having a textual quality, as in 'Aragonite':

> orthorhombic
>
> white, grey,
> green or
> violet
>
> vitreous . . .
>
> expanding
>
> such forms
> are imaginable
>
> (this little book)[21]

Mills's poetic 'charting' is yet another example of a poetry that breaks
with the monologic expressivity of the lyric, a rupture apparent in the
poet's penchant for collage: the splicing together of voices establishing
another foray into the imperfect mapping of his interactions with his
environment. In 'the stony field' the authorial voice is intercut by
quotations from Charles Darwin, both speakers engrossed with small-
scale phenomena – the poet with his texts, the scientist with worms:

> the slow accretion
> of detail
>
>   things made over
> reused, renewed
> so that nothing is wasted
>
> thus we will sometimes
> say:
>
>   lets cook
> some extra potatoes
>
> and fry them
>   in the morning
> for breakfast

> *As I was led to keep in my study during many months worms in pots filled
> with earth, I became interested in them, and wished to learn how far they
> acted consciously, and how much mental power they displayed.*[22]

The poet's reuse of previously existing materials is, of course, manifested in the text's marshalling of Darwin's words, which are 'renewed' in their fresh context. Darwin's reflections become a commentary on Mills's intertextual poetic, in which the mobilising of other texts becomes analogous to the worm's digestive process: '*the whole country had passed many times through, and will again pass many times through, the intestinal canals of worms*'. In this fashion, Mills pits his work against the kind of hand-me-down romanticism that sees value only in poetic 'originality'. By way of contrast, his poetry's 'slow accretion of detail' is indicative of a quality Mills identifies in the writings of Maurice Scully – a tentatively processual dimension to the poetic act: 'the poet is no longer concerned to produce the kind of artefact which conforms to a particular socio-cultural definition of what a "poem" is; rather he is exploring the process by which poetry might map a complex world.'[23]

The New Futurism of Maurice Scully's explosive poetic collages – and I am thinking specifically of the recently completed but only partially published *LIVELIHOOD, The Set* (1986–96)[24] – comes close to the incendiary quality of the historical avant-garde. Scully's uneasy though witty manipulations of lyric form in his first collection, *Love Poems and Others* (1981), give way in his subsequent work to an interest in a sequential, cumulative poetry, one that bears the mark of his interest in Zukofsky's '*A*'. In between *Love Poems* and his second book, *5 Freedoms of Movement* (1987), Scully published a short article, 'As I Like It', in which he advocated a poetry that 'moves with the shape of the world':

> I like poems that do not have designs on me, that are not closed systems, undoubting their own importance in a simple world. The world is extremely complex and the most complex poem the mind can conceive and execute is extremely simple in the world. A poem is beautiful to the degree it records an apt humility in face of the complexity it sees but fails to transmit, doubting its presumption to exist in the light of that.[25]

The article appeared in *The Beau*, a sort of *Lace Curtain* for the early 1980s, which Scully edited between 1981 and its demise in 1983, and which provided a forum for a number of writers – including Healy and Mills – disenchanted with what they saw as 'mainstream' Irish poetry. The issue in which Scully's piece appeared included an extract from Eugene Watters's *The Week-End of Dermot and Grace*, a long narrative poem first published in 1964, the richly interwoven motifs, stunning combination of registers, and interlaced sound-patterns of which prefigure aspects of Scully's own work after *Love Poems and Others*.

There is, however, a crucial difference between Watters's poem and Scully's developing poetic. Watters's allusions in *The Week-End of Dermot and Grace* have a strong flavour of Eliot's practice in *The Waste Land*: in

both poems mythical/legendary material (in Watters's case, the tale of the
pursuit of Diarmaid and Gráinne, from the Fionn cycle) underpins a
surface text preoccupied with the malaise of modernity, in Watters, that
of the atomic age. In this respect, Watters's poem, like Eliot's, has both
'designs' upon its reader and a symbolic closure alien to Scully's mature
work. The openness and 'humility' of Scully's work, confronted by a
world the details of which it seeks to trace 'but cannot transmit', is
apparent in the first section of the *Postlude* to LIVELIHOOD, *The Set*,
a text which in an earlier version bore the title 'History':

> Or the wearing repetition of
> children – towards you/or
> for a long time
>
> the
> crushing
> vividness.[26]

The alternatives posed imply the monotony and the overwhelming
facticity of lived experience. Both are said to lead to a 'fevered delusion',
a failure to comprehend and communicate one's own most intimate
history. The poem does not find an answer to this plight; instead, it
admits to the tentative hold the poem has on that which it represents:

> And then
> she suggested
> this way.
>
> We won't do that
> again she said
> one-two
>
> wobbling finely – the mirror
> tilted – so that
> that
>
> something lodges
> obdurately (in
> the net)
>
> tilted – cool in
> here – in
> history.
>
> Or.

> *But how can you write about emotion*
> *when you forget everything*
> *the next day.*[27]

The images of the mirror and the net suggest the writerly desire to reflect or capture something of one's existential being. But for Scully, as for Healy and Mills, the world eludes the glass or meshes of the text. Rather than attempting to hold a mirror up to nature, the poem suggests tilting it, thus allowing for the inescapably perspectival nature of poetic representation – not a poem that includes history, as Pound said apropos *The Cantos*, but one which modestly confesses to the partiality of the 'something' that finds its way into 'in[to] / the net'. Hence the truncated nature of the final conjunction, 'Or', which, counterpointed by the concluding italicised passage, indicates the occlusions of memory, and their inevitable, though not necessarily deleterious, effects on the text's realisation of its autobiographical pre-text.

Scully's last sentence brings to mind Lyn Hejinian's *Writing Is an Aid to Memory*, in which the poetic transcription of experience is both a recognition of the loss between the event and its recording and an awareness of the gain that the text, as a supplement to the original experience, provides. Hejinian writes of her 'conscious[ness] of the disquieting runs of life slipping by, that the message remains undelivered, opposed to me. Memory cannot, though the future return, and proffer raw confusions.' Yet 'Memory is the girth, or again': 'ellipsis makes its promise leaving us to get out / dreams think of how we thought.'[28] These reflections also have an affinity with the poetry of Catherine Walsh, the autobiographical substratum of which is refracted through a disjointed, elliptical surface. In *Making Tents* Walsh includes her own variant on the Irish *dinnseanchas*, in which, as Mills has noted, Walsh lists the names of fields on a farm familiar to her as a child:

> Dan's yard
> The mill field
> The bog
> The big field
> The L field
> The murdering field
> The relics
> The grove
> The lower garden
> The river
> The field at the school
> The 2 acres
> Martin's
> Jordans'
> Dan's field
>
> – if what comes back is cautious
> or incomplete
> harsh words can be counted upon – [29]

The bald cataloguing of place-names stands in sharp contrast to Heaney's use of the same Irish form in a number of poems in *Wintering Out*, such as 'Anahorish', a poem which also returns to a childhood locale by means of its linguistic topography:

> My 'place of clear water',
> the first hill in the world
> where springs washed into
> the shiny grass
>
> and darkened cobbles
> in the bed of the lane.
> *Anahorish*, soft gradient
> of consonant, vowel-meadow[30]

Heaney's poem is governed by the fanciful conceit that in the aural properties of the signifier, 'Anahorish', one can sense and re-experience the geographical reality of the signified locale. It is a conceit the strain of which can be detected in the way in which it self-deconstructs, owing to the poem's contradictory reliance on typographical imagery ('soft gradient / of consonant, vowel-meadow') to sustain its phonocentric premises. Walsh's place-names are signs that denote places which, one presumes, are as redolent to her as Anahorish is to Heaney. Both Walsh and Heaney are aware that the place-names, as signifiers, 'stand-in' for their referents; as such, they signify through the absence of the place, any sense of which is consequently mediated through language and through a memory dependent upon language. Where her text differs from his is in not attempting to dissolve language's mediation of reality through positing a 'sense of place' (to quote the title of an early essay by Heaney) somehow inherent in the very phonemes of the place-names themselves.[31] Hence Walsh's Hejinian-like observation that 'what comes back' in memory may be 'incomplete' – and this not in spite of but because 'harsh words can be counted upon'. The passage from *Making Tents* ends by ruefully noting: 'more or less / everything / still / in the same place', a phrase in which the 'more or less' points to precisely the supplementary nature of writing as an aid to memory.

Walsh's work subsequent to *Making Tents* shatters practical language in its rejection of a transparent or normative discourse. Heaney's early poetry, with its lush onomatopoeia, is one of the more powerful attempts in recent poetry to sustain the belief that language can hook up to reality in any straightforward fashion. If so, the internal collapse of a poem like 'Anahorish' reveals the unsustainability of this conviction. Walsh's disjunctive, disorientating poetry acknowledges language as a medium which constructs our relation to others, to objects, to ourselves. Her poetic subjects are always *Idir Eatortha*, caught 'between two worlds':

a reasonable axis for all
   the I   survival
      necessity of inquiry
         wander and wonder
changing shadows round
   to get lost in

unlimited life   getting caught
   incomprehensible   in the reduction
                    of nothing
measuring time
     between   living things

        tight line

Nearly Nowhere   layers of geological
                    aggregates compacted
                    in the slightest grain

  the word I tried to remember to say to you[32]

The 'reasonable axis' of 'the I' in Walsh's work does not exert linguistic mastery over the world in which it 'wander[s] and wonder[s]'. Life is 'unlimited', at root 'incomprehensible', though there is the unavoidable 'necessity of inquiry'. The typographical layout of *Idir Eatortha* and other recent works including *Pitch* and *City West*, foregrounds her preoccupation with indeterminacy, their spatial distribution on the page allowing the reader to construct a number of sequential or temporal readings. For instance, is 'unlimited life' simply 'incomprehensible', or only so when 'caught / in the reduction'? In the latter case, experience *becomes* obscure when 'inquiry' seeks to discern a meaningful structure in its 'layers of geological / aggregates', when wandering shades into the inevitable wondering. In an interview with Peterjon Skelt, Walsh emphasised the conflictual nature of communication: 'Why do I write? How can anybody write? I mean this is the basic contradiction. But . . . it parallels the very fact that we try to communicate with each other. The kind of misunderstandings that crop up are as much a part of our lives and are as important as the understandings.'[33] Like Healy's, though drawing upon different techniques, her work foregrounds the vicissitudes of communication in an age which has devoted more energy to its dissemination that any before. In 'Pitch' she comments:

     stratification
     of experience
     no narrative
     easy in the mind

     where are we   out there
     on there   in side of what
     knows?[34]

The 'violence' that Walsh's disorientating forms commit on ordinary speech – to appropriate the words of Roman Jakobson – mimics even as its subtly interrogates the superabundance of discourse, the welter of language that contributes to the opacity of the contemporary world. Walsh's interest in the communicative possibilities of poetry, her preoccupation with information, its materiality, its transmission and reception, grounds her work as much as that of Healy or Scully within late twentieth-century Ireland.

This last point introduces the question of to what degree the poetry discussed above resembles that of American Language poetry. There *are* points of contact between the two poetries, but these should not obscure crucial differences. Language poetry is a broad church, but it can be roughly characterised as foregrounding, in a fashion which recalls the historical avant-garde – particularly Futurism – language as an artificial medium, poetry as artifice. This, at least, is Marjorie Perloff's understanding of the work of a number of figures central to Language writing, including Bruce Andrews, Charles Bernstein, Lyn Hejinian and Ron Silliman. For Perloff the work of these writers, and others, constitutes a genuinely oppositional aesthetic; one which contests 'the dominant paradigms of representation' in contemporary society, those which govern manipulative, 'instrumental discourses' such as advertising and the media, not by railing against the deforming effects of such discourses on human nature (Joyce's 'poetry of expression'), but by disrupting the communicative model on which such discourses subsist. She continues: 'The poetic function, in this scheme of things, subordinates the informational axis (language used as a pure instrument of efficient communication) to what we might call the axis of redundancy, "meaning" now being created by all those elements of reference that go beyond the quantifiable communication of data from A to B.'[35] Informing Language poetry's antipathy towards the 'informational axis' is the belief that the reduction of language to a referential tool is an inevitable outgrowth of capitalism, a corollary of which is that realism is a literary form whose potential for critique was stunted from its inception. As Ron Silliman argues:

> Where the bourgeois is the rising class, the expressive, gestural, labor-product nature of consciousness tends to be repressed. The objects of consciousness are reduced to commodities and take on the character of a fetish. Things which appear to move 'freely', absent all gesture, are the elements of a world of description. The commodity fetish in language becomes one of description, of the referential, and has a second higher-order fetish of narration. . . . The rise of capitalism sets the preconditions for the rise of the novel, the invention of the optical illusion of realism, the final breakdown of gestural poetic forms.[36]

In short, to contest capitalism requires a poetry that contests referentiality. One over-hasty response, Bruce Andrews contends, is 'a poetics of sub-version': a kind of poetical 'Jacobinism' in which reference is destroyed, 'obliterated, diminished, forgotten'. The problem with this approach, Andrews maintains, is that the 'commodification of language . . . has actually carried quite far the erosion of the system of differences on which signification depends'; and thus, 'to call for a heightening of these deterritorializing tendencies may risk a more <u>homogenizing</u> meaning-lessness . . . – an "easy rider" on the flood tide of Capital'.[37] A more advantageous approach to the homogenised world of capital is to make the informational axis of language play second fiddle to that which Perloff calls the 'axis of redundancy': to '<u>charge</u> material with possibilities of meaning', in Andrews's words, 'not by demolishing relations but creating them, no holds barred, among units of language'.[38] The resulting text will be, in Charles Bernstein's formulation, 'antiabsorptive', its opaque-ness rebuffing easy assimilation by the reader. By refusing to yield a straightforward referential meaning the poem resists commodification; and in so doing may actually, as Bernstein claims in his verse-essay, 'Arifice of Absorption',

> get the reader
> absorbed into a more ideologized
> or politicized space; if not to say,
> less programatically,
> one that really *can* engross: not
> ersatz but, at last, the real
> goods.[39]

There is much in Language poetics that seems applicable to the work of Healy, Scully and Walsh, if less so to Joyce and Mills. The former's writings also proliferate reference rather than demolishing it, creating an 'antiabsorptive' patina to the poetry that '*can* engross' the reader through its exhilarating challenge to ingrained preconceptions regarding poetry. They are, nonetheless, reluctant to view their work as an Irish offshoot of Language writing, though Scully has testified to the invigorating effects of encountering Silliman's anthology, *In the American Tree*, and Bernstein's volume of essays, *Content's Dream*. The intensely politicised nature of much Language poetry, at least as it is formulated in its accompanying poetics, is largely absent from the work of the writers I have considered, which is of course not to say that their poetry is not engaged in social and political issues. One further, and crucial, point of divergence can be glimpsed in the persistence of 'the I' in Walsh's poetry (work which would seem, on the face of it, particularly close to Language writing), despite her work's 'stratification / of experience' – the recognition that there is 'no narrative / easy in the mind'. In this respect, one can see continuities between Walsh's sequences and those of Geoffrey Squires, for whom language is always secondary to consciousness. The afterimage of the individual ego, the exoskeleton of the lyric I, is faintly perceptible in the poetry of the Irish neo-avant-garde. This may be accounted for, at least to a degree, as evidence of the strong pull of modern Irish poetry, which, in contrast to much twentieth-century North American poetry, has largely retained the lyric subject.

Nevertheless, the poetry of Joyce, Healy, Mills, Scully and Walsh bears comparison with Language poetry through their shared challenge to claims that the avant-garde has died in postmodernity, its demise brought about by the supposed collapse of boundaries between pop and high art, and the canonisation of works, like Marcel Duchamp's, once viewed as aesthetically offensive. One of the most persuasive exponents of this view is Peter Bürger, who claims that the neo-avant-garde differs from earlier movements such as Dada and Surrealism in that it lacks the 'shock value' of the historical avant-garde, the likes of Andy Warhol little more than a damp squib after Duchamp, as the innovations and aspirations of the avant-garde are inevitably diluted beyond recovery in their repetition and in their absorption by the academy. The failure of the avant-garde's attempt to reinvest art in the praxis of life means that 'the neo-avant-garde institutionalizes the *avant-garde as art* and thus negates genuinely avant-gardiste intentions'.[40] Given its artefacts' current price-tags, it seems unarguable that the historical avant-garde failed in its effort to smash the category of the aesthetic. Yet the neo-avant-garde may not be doomed, as Bürger would appear to suggest, to replay that failure, only this time as farce. Hal Foster has powerfully contested Bürger's dismissal of the neo-avant-garde as disabled by its belatedness, arguing that the very notion of the avant-garde disturbs the linear and causal historiography on which Bürger relies:

> the avant-garde work is never historically effective or fully significant in its initial moments. It cannot be because it is traumatic – a hole in the symbolic order of its time that is not prepared for it, that cannot receive it, at least not immediately, at least not without structural change. . . . [T]he neo-avant-garde acts on the historical avant-garde as it is acted on by it; it is less *neo* than *nachträglich*; and the avant-garde project in general develops in deferred action.[41]

The relevance of Foster's revision of Bürger is perhaps not readily apparent in the Irish context, as the Irish neo-avant-garde, it can be objected, has no immediate or national historical precursor upon which it can act. This much may be conceded, but the poets with whom I am concerned do not position themselves solely in relation to Irish literary history (indeed, it is arguable that it is only certain literary historians who imagine Irish poets wear national blinkers), and thus engage with avant-garde writing produced elsewhere. That said, it is interesting that none of these poets has sought to disassociate his or her work from the label 'Irish': on the contrary, their work frequently foregrounds, through subject matter and language, its Irishness (Scully's deployment of Irish-language phrases in several works, Mills's insistence upon the importance of Gaelic nature poetry to his work, and Walsh's use of the *dinnseanchas*, being merely three obvious instances of this). In its *liminality*, I would suggest, lies the pertinence of Foster's remarks to their work: the 'trauma' of this poetry is that, on the one hand, it cannot be domesticated as an Irish adjunct to a global (read: North American) neo-avant-garde; on the other, it obdurately refuses to conform to the dominant procedures of much contemporary Irish poetry. It creates a 'hole', as Foster has it, in both homogenising narratives of a putatively global postmodernism and reductively national literary histories. Its 'deferred action' forces its readers to rethink, to recode, what an Irish poetic modernism might mean in the late twentieth century. There have been a few programmatic reconstructions of the recent literary past made by some of these poets – as in Joyce's involvement with *The Lace Curtain*, and, to a lesser extent, Scully's and others' contributions to *The Beau*. But more notable, I think, is the way in which their recent poetic practice makes us re-imagine Irish poetry *in its possibilities*. In Foster's words, 'the avant-garde did return, and it continues to return, but *it returns from the future*: such is its paradoxical temporality'.[42]

The neo-avant-garde's importance, I would contend, lies in its reconfiguration of the artwork as something other than a Dadaist dis-mantling of existing asethetic criteria, a rethinking as made by Bernstein's notion of an 'artifice of absorption'. In considering the relevance of such an artefact for readers of Irish poetry at the beginning of the twenty-first century, one can take a lead from Mills's speculation that because Ireland, with the exception of Belfast, 'missed out on the process known as the Industrial Revolution', its modernism is of a different cast from that of other First World countries.[43] Mills is arguing against the commonplace association of modernity (and hence modernism) with the alienation attendant on rapid industrialisation. But his comment can be read more profitably in the context of that which Luke Gibbons sees as the 'regressive modernization' of Ireland, in which industrialisation has occured largely in areas such as communications and information technology, 'a form of advanced industrial development which, unlike the initial Industrial Revolution, has no commitment to social, political or cultural modernization'. The promotional literature of the Industrial

Development Authority which Gibbon analyses yokes ersatz images of the past, glossy photographs of Newgrange and the rural West, to statements of untarnished technological potential ('We're the Young Europeans'), one of his examples furnishing the wisdom: 'Missing the Industrial Revolution was the best thing that ever happened to the Irish.'[44] Gibbons's point is that the phenomenon which passes as the 'Celtic Tiger' is a peculiarly hybrid creature, a cross-breeding of Celticism and rapacious micro-electronics. The Irish neo-avant-garde poets may be seen to court accusations of wilful periphalism in their admittedly overstated attacks on the hidebound traditionalism of modern Irish poetry, as they choose to depict it. Nevertheless, in extending the formal bounds of the contemporary Irish poem in 'antiabsorptive' directions, their poetry pays witness to the divergent, and often contradictory, discourses of contemporary Ireland: the anachronistic rural idyll marketed by Bord Fáilte; the forward-looking nation at the heart of Europe promoted by governmental and corporate interests. If it is possible to see in the poetry promoted by New Writers' Press in the 1970s both the impress and a critique of the Lemassian modernisation of Ireland, then the poetry of Healy, Mills, Scully and Walsh registers, even as it contests, the contours of Ireland at the *fin de siècle*.

NOTES

1 'A BROKEN LINE': IRISH POETIC MODERNISMS

1 The allusion here is to the Russian Formalists' conception of literary history as essentially antagonistic; see Boris Eichenbaum, 'The Theory of the "Formal Method"' in Lee T. Lemon and Marion J. Reis (eds), *Russian Formalist Criticism: Four Essays* (Lincoln: U of Nebraska P, 1965), p. 135.

2 Robert F. Garratt, *Modern Irish Poetry: Tradition and Continuity from Yeats to Heaney* (Berkeley: U of California P, 1986), pp. 94, 96.

3 See Marjorie Perloff, *Radical Artifice: Writing Poetry in the Age of Media* (Chicago: U of Chicago P, 1991), p. 243; and Peter Nicholls, *Modernisms: A Literary Guide* (London: Macmillan, 1995). Richard Kearney relies on a similar, if more subtly developed, distinction to Garratt's in his analyses of Irish literature, film and ideology in *Transitions: Narratives in Modern Irish Culture* (Dublin: Wolfhound, 1988).

4 Joseph Frank's theory of the spatial, as opposed to the temporal, form of the modernist artefact is extremely close to the New Critical conception of the autotelic artwork. See Joseph Frank, *The Widening Gyre: Crisis and Mastery in Modern Literature* (Urbana: Indiana UP, 1963); and, on the links between Frank and the New Critics, see Michael Davidson, 'Ekphrasis and the Postmodern Painter Poem', *Journal of Aesthetics and Art Criticism*, 42 (1983), 69–79.

5 John Wilson Foster, *Colonial Consequences: Essays in Irish Literature and Culture* (Dublin: Lilliput, 1991), pp. 55, 46. On the nationalism of modernism prior to the First World War, see Marjorie Perloff, *The Futurist Moment: Avant-Garde, Avant Guerre, and the Language of Rupture* (Chicago: U of Chicago P, 1986).

6 Terry Eagleton, *Heathcliff and the Great Hunger: Studies in Irish Culture* (London: Verso, 1995), p. 284.

7 Eagleton, *Heathcliff and the Great Hunger*, p. 300.

8 See T. S. Eliot, 'Tradition and the Individual Talent' (1919) in his *Selected Essays*, 3rd ed. (London: Faber, 1951), p. 15. J. C. C. Mays goes so far as to say that 'Ireland anticipated the Modern Movement among English-speaking nations, one consequence of which was that Modernism was a thing of the past in Ireland before it can be said to have begun in America or England.' Mays attributes the early emergence of modernism in Ireland to Irish writers'

'turn from specifically English traditions to European models that appeared to promise a critique and an alternative' (J. C. C. Mays, introduction, *Poems and Exiles*, by James Joyce [Harmondsworth: Penguin, 1992], pp. xl–xli).

9 Terence Brown, 'Ireland, Modernism and the 1930s' in Patricia Coughlan and Alex Davis (eds), *Modernism and Ireland: The Poetry of the 1930s* (Cork: Cork UP, 1995), p. 32.

10 AE, *Collected Poems* (London: Macmillan, 1913), p. 219. On Russell's place within the literary revival, see Phillip L. Marcus, *Yeats and the Beginning of the Irish Renaissance*, 2nd ed. (Syracuse: Syracuse UP, 1987), pp. 181–95.

11 W. J. McCormack, *From Burke to Beckett: Ascendancy, Tradition and Betrayal in Literary History* (Cork: Cork UP, 1994), p. 252.

12 Linda Dowling, *Language and Decadence in the Victorian Fin de Siècle* (Princeton: Princeton UP, 1986), p. 247.

13 W. B. Yeats, *Letters to the New Island*, eds George Bornstein and Hugh Witemeyer (New York: Macmillan, 1989), p. 60.

14 Dowling, *Language and Decadence*, p. 258. See Yeats, 'What is Popular Poetry': 'There is only one kind of good poetry, for the poetry of the coteries, which presupposes the written tradition, does not differ in kind from the true poetry of the people, which presupposes the unwritten tradition. Both are alike strange and obscure, and unreal to all who have not understanding, and both, instead of that manifest logic, that clear rhetoric of the "popular poetry", glimmer with thoughts and images whose "ancestors were stout and wise", "anigh to Paradise" "ere yet men knew the gift of corn"' (W. B. Yeats, *Essays and Introductions* [London: Macmillan, 1961], p. 8). On the founding of the Rhymers' Club, see Norman Alford, *The Rhymers' Club: Poets of the Tragic Generation* (London: Macmillan, 1994), pp. 1–11. Yeats 1891 piece for the Boston *Pilot*, 'The Celt in Ireland', makes a link between the author's quest for 'stories of the fairies and the phantoms' in rural Ireland and the 'doctrines' expressed in 'Pater's jewelled paragraphs – the Platonic theory of spiritual beings having their abode in all things without and within us' (Yeats, *Letters to the New Island*, p. 53).

15 See Ian Fletcher, 'Explorations and Recoveries – II: Symons, Yeats and the Demonic Dance', *London Magazine*, 6 (1960), 46–7.

16 W. B. Yeats, *Autobiographies*, eds William H. O'Donnell and Douglas N. Archibald (New York: Scribner, 1999), p. 240.

17 Seamus Deane, headnote to 'Poetry 1890–1930' in Seamus Deane (ed.), *The Field Day Anthology of Irish Writing* (3 vols, Derry: Field Day Publications, 1991), vol. 2, p. 720.

18 See 'Parnell' and 'In England' in Lionel Johnson, *Poems* (London: Elkin Mathews, 1895), pp. 31–7.

19 On this dimension to the 1890s, see Elaine Showalter, *Sexual Anarchy: Gender and Culture at the Fin de Siècle* (London: Bloomsbury, 1991).

20 Dowling, *Language and Decadence*, p. 195.

21 Johnson, *Poems*, p. 30.

22 Ezra Pound, *The Cantos of Ezra Pound*, 13 imp. (New York: New Directions, 1995), p. 815.

23 See Ezra Pound, *Literary Essays of Ezra Pound*, ed. T. S. Eliot (London: Faber, 1954), pp. 361–70.

24 Oscar Wilde, *The Complete Works of Oscar Wilde*, 3rd ed. (Glasgow: HarperCollins, 1994), p. 17.

25 William Blake, *The Complete Poems*, ed. W. H. Stevenson (London: Longman, 1971), pp. 840–1.

26 W. B. Yeats, *The Variorum Edition of the Poems of W. B. Yeats*, eds Peter Allt and Russell K. Alspach, 3rd imp. (New York: Macmillan, 1966), p. 64.

27 Yeats's relationship to the *symbolistes*, which is as much a matter of related concerns as a conscious 'influence', is discussed in Frank Kermode, *Romantic Image* (London: Routledge & Kegan Paul, 1957). Edward Engleberg provides a valuable summary of the kinds of symbolism in Yeats's work in the course of an excellent overview of arguments for and against reading Yeats as a modernist in his *The Vast Design: Patterns in W. B. Yeats's Aesthetic*, 2nd ed. (Washington, D. C.: Catholic U of America P, 1988), pp. 211–60. Stan Smith's contention that Yeats's modernism should be be dated from 1910, from the poems collected in *The Green Helmet*, 'which mark the major breakthrough in his style, heralding a new, tough, argumentative dialogism . . . rather than retreating to the twilight's glimmer' does not address the modernism of his earlier Symbolist poetry (Stan Smith, *The Origins of Modernism: Eliot, Pound, Yeats and the Rhetorics of Renewal* [Hemel Hempstead: Harvester Wheatsheaf, 1994], p. 208). Smith correctly contests the common assumption that Pound's relationship with Yeats resulted in the latter 'becoming' a modernist in the poems collected in *Responsibilities* (1914). However his conception of modernism would appear to lack the dialogism he ascribes to Yeats after 1910: a more capacious conception would see *The Green Helmet* as signalling a change in a poetic already coloured by modernism in its Symbolist form.

28 Nicholls, *Modernisms*, p. 10.

29 Raymond Williams, *The Politics of Modernism: Against the New Conformists*, ed. Tony Pinkney (London: Verso, 1989), p. 71.

30 See Edward Larrissy, *Yeats the Poet: The Measures of Difference* (Hemel Hempstead: Harvester, 1994), pp. 72–83. Larrissy explores at length the ambivalence of Yeats's nationalism as it is articulated through the symbolism of *The Wind Among the Reeds*.

31 Yeats, *Poems*, p. 415.

32 Yeats, *Poems*, p. 424.

33 Yeats, *Poems*, p. 632.

34 Eagleton, *Heathcliff and the Great Hunger*, p. 305.

35 Yeats, *Autobiographies*, p. 361.

36 R. F. Foster, *Paddy & Mr Punch: Connections in Irish and English History* (London: Allen Lane, 1993), pp. 279, 229.

37 Austin Clarke, *Reviews and Essays of Austin Clarke*, ed. Gregory A. Schirmer (Gerrards Cross: Colin Smythe, 1995), p. 69.

38 Clarke, *Reviews and Essays*, pp. 199, 92.

39 Peter Bürger, *Theory of the Avant-Garde*, trans. Michael Shaw (Minneapolis: U of Minnesota P, 1984), pp. 26–7.

40 Bürger's thesis has not gone uncriticised for its narrow conception of modernism: see Charles Bernstein, *A Poetics* (Cambridge, Mass: Harvard UP, 1992), pp. 101–5; Christopher Butler, *Early Modernism: Literature, Music and Painting in Europe 1900–1916* (Oxford: Oxford UP, 1994), pp. 268–9; Hal Foster, *The Return of the Real: The Avant-Garde at the End of the Century* (Cambridge, Mass: MIT, 1996), pp. 8–20; and Perloff, *Radical Artifice*, pp. 5–9. I have deployed Bürger's account of high modernism, and

his crucial distinction between high modernism and the avant-garde, in the following two chapters. My own reservations on the validity of Bürger's refelections on contemporary neo-avant-gardism are made in the coda.

41 Yeats, *Poems*, p. 608.
42 For an informative and concise discussion of the revival's and Irish Ireland's visions of Irishness, see Neil Corcoran, *After Yeats and Joyce: Reading Modern Irish Literature* (Oxford: Oxford UP, 1997), pp. 57–65.
43 Yeats, *Poems*, pp. 601–2.
44 Yeats, *Poems*, p. 630.
45 Paul de Man, *The Rhetoric of Romanticism* (New York: Columbia UP, 1984), pp. 165, 168, 177; David Lloyd, *Anomalous States: Irish Writing and the Post-Colonial Moment* (Dublin: Lilliput, 1993), pp. 59–87.
46 Yeats, *Poems*, pp. 491–2.
47 Lloyd, *Anomalous States*, p. 68.
48 Lloyd, *Anomalous States*, p. 71.
49 Rainer Emig, *Modernism in Poetry: Motivations, Structures and Limits* (London: Longman, 1995), pp. 50, 40.
50 Yeats, *Poems*, pp. 68–9.
51 Patrick Kavanagh, 'Yeats' in *The Complete Poems*, ed. Peter Kavanagh (Newbridge: Goldsmith, 1984), p. 349.
52 On this regional inversion of European literary chronology, see Foster, *Colonial Consequences*, pp. 56–7; and Brown, 'Ireland, Modernism and the 1930s', pp. 37–9.
53 Clarke, *Reviews and Essays*, pp. 166, 175. Reviewing MacGreevy's *Poems* (1934) for *The Observer*, Clarke sourly commented that 'the Modernist revolt has at last reached the Irish Free State' (quoted in Susan Schreibman, introduction, *Collected Poems*, by Thomas MacGreevy [Dublin: Anna Livia], p. xxxii).
54 Dillon Johnston, *Irish Poetry after Joyce*, 2nd ed. (Syracuse: Syracuse UP, 1997), p. 8.
55 Terence Brown, *Ireland: A Social and Cultural History 1922–1985* (London: Fontana, 1985), pp. 73, 168.
56 S. B. Kennedy, *Irish Art and Modernism 1880–1950* (Belfast: Institute of Irish Studies, 1991), p. 205; and see also Bruce Arnold, *Mainie Jellett and the Modern Movement in Ireland* (New Haven: Yale UP, 1991).
57 Harry White, *The Keeper's Recital: Music and Cultural History 1770–1970* (Cork: Cork UP, 1998), p. 159. See also White's discussion of the crucial role played by Séan Ó Riada later in the century in 'silenc[ing] the claim of original art music as a tenable voice in the Irish cultural matrix . . . [by] advanc[ing] the claim not of original composition but of the ethnic repertory itself' (White, *The Keeper's Recital*, p. 149).
58 Mervyn Wall, 'Michael Smith asks Mervyn Wall some Questions about the Thirties', *The Lace Curtain*, 4 (1971), 80, 81, 83. Wall claims that, in contrast to the '1916 poets', Yeats's influence on his generation was negligible: 'I do not think that Devlin and Coffey were influenced by Yeats at all. Their early interest was in the Surrealists, and they read a great deal of contemporary French poetry' (Wall, 'Some Questions', p. 82).
59 Samuel Beckett, *Disjecta: Miscellaneous Writings and a Dramatic Fragment*, ed. Ruby Cohn (London: John Calder, 1983), p. 86.
60 Beckett, *Disjecta*, pp. 70, 75.

61 Edna Longley, *The Living Stream: Literature and Revisionism in Ireland* (Newcastle: Bloodaxe, 1994), p. 203. A notable exception is Coffey's *Third Person* (1938)

62 Patricia Coughlan, '"The Poetry is Another Pair of Sleeves": Beckett, Ireland and Modernist Lyric Poetry' in Patricia Coughlan and Alex Davis (eds), *Modernism and Ireland: The Poetry of the 1930s* (Cork: Cork UP, 1995), p. 179.

63 Pound, *Literary Essays*, p. 396.

64 Beckett, *Disjecta*, p. 70.

65 See also Beckett's 1934 review of Pound's *Make it New*, 'Ex Cathezra', in which Beckett's interest in Occitan literature chimes with Pound's (Beckett, *Disjecta*, pp. 77–9). John Pilling argues with reference to 'The Yoke of Liberty', an uncollected early poem published in Samuel Putnam et al. (eds), *The European Caravan* (1931), that 'Along with other poems of the period, it suggests [Beckett] had more to learn from Pound than Eliot'. Eliot is still relevant to Beckett's poetry: as Pilling says of 'Sanies II', 'The Eliotic reminiscence, reminding us how near *Ash Wednesday* is, does so at the cost of reminding us also how much more successful Eliot's organization of material is' (John Pilling, *Samuel Beckett* [London: Routledge & Kegan Paul, 1976], pp. 160, 167). The importance of the troubadours to Devlin's poetry is discussed in chapter 4.

66 Beckett, *Disjecta*, p. 76.

67 See chapter 5.

68 Denis Devlin, letter to Thomas MacGreevy, 31 August 1934, Thomas MacGreevy Papers, Trinity College, Dublin, MS 8112/5. Devlin's hostility towards Higgins is the counterpart of Beckett's vilification of Clarke in 'Recent Irish Poetry' and in the satirical portrait of Austin Ticklepenny in *Murphy*. Both Devlin and Beckett had little interest in Higgins's and Clarke's experiments in the kind of 'Irish Mode' of poetry which, in his *Literature in Ireland* (1916), Thomas MacDonagh had argued offered an alternative to the 'Celtic Note' of the revival. Given Devlin's and Beckett's disparagement of such a poetic mode as antiquated and stale, it is worth recalling that MacDonagh had believed that an English-language poetry inflected by 'Gaelic versification' contained an 'element of disturbance, of revolution' faintly analogous to that of the Futurist avant-garde (Thomas MacDonagh, *Literature in Ireland: Studies Irish and Anglo-Irish* [Dublin: Relay, 1996], p. 5). That Devlin's opinions on the 'Irish Mode', as well as his view of Yeats, mellowed over the years is clear from the brief introduction to his 1953 selection of Irish poetry in *New World Writing*. There, Beckett's 'antiquarians' and 'others' make a reappearance, albeit in a more neutral purview that that of 'Recent Irish Poetry'. Irish poetry, writes Devlin, 'could perhaps be said to fall into two categories: One has developed the themes of the Celtic revival, while at the same time exploring the medieval rather than the pagan Irish literature and experimenting in the transfer of the intricate assonantal and stanza schemes of Gaelic poetry into English; the other has been more or less gladly turned towards the prevailing metropolitan poetries' (Denis Devlin, 'Ten Irish Poets' in *New World Writing* [New York: New American Library of World Literature, 1953], p. 258).

69 Brian Coffey, 'A Note on Rat Island', *University Review* (Dublin), 3.8 (1966), 25–6.

70 Yeats, *Poems*, p. 603.

71 Brian Coffey, *Poems and Versions 1929–1990* (Dublin: Dedalus, 1991), p. 70.
72 See Jack Morgan, '"Missouri Sequence": Brain Coffey's St Louis Years, 1947–1952', *Éire-Ireland*, 28.4 (1993), 100–14.
73 Robert F. Garratt's misreading of *Crón Tráth na nDéithe* as overly indebted to the allusive 'techniques' of *Ulysses* is another example of his reductive reading of Irish poetic modernism. Garratt cites, as evidence of MacGreevy's anxiety over his poem's dependence upon Joyce, MacGreevy's own note to the poem, in which the poet 'acknowledge[s] the debt . . . to Mr Joyce and one or two writers in English who have successfully adapted the techniques of *Ulysses* to their own literary purposes' (quoted in Garratt, *Modern Irish Poetry*, p. 96; and see MacGreevy, *Collected Poems*, p. 57). However, it is arguable that, regardless of MacGreevy's knowledge of, and admiration for, Joyce, *Crón Tráth na nDéithe* is most rewardingly read in the light of Eliot's interpretation of Joyce's strategy in *Ulysses* – the famous 'mythical method' Eliot defined as 'simply a way of controlling, of ordering, of giving a shape and a significance to the immense panorama of futility and anarchy which is contemporary history' ('"Ulysses", Order, and Myth' in *Selected Prose of T. S. Eliot*, ed. Frank Kermode [London: Faber, 1975], p. 177). Eliot's words, of course, are more applicable to his own practice in *The Waste Land* than to Joyce's novel; and it is to Eliot's poem, and the aloofness from reality that MacGreevy felt characterised its 'method', that MacGreevy's own long poem is best read as a response. See my discussion of the poem later in this chapter.
74 MacGreevy Papers, MS 8110/41.
75 Brian Coffey, letter to Thomas MacGreevy, 27 October 1936, MacGreevy Papers, MS 8110/23/2.
76 Coffey, *Poems and Versions*, p. 72.
77 Laura (Riding) Jackson, *A Selection of the Poems of Laura Riding*, ed. Robert Nye (Manchester: Carcanet, 1994), p. 146.
78 Coffey, *Poems and Versions*, p. 73.
79 Coffey, *Poems and Versions*, p. 86.
80 Coffey, *Poems and Versions*, p. 77.
81 Coffey, *Poems and Versions*, p. 70.
82 Coffey, *Poems and Versions*, p. 72.
83 Beckett, *Disjecta*, p. 74.
84 MacGreevy, *Collected Poems*, p. 1.
85 Lee Jenkins, 'Thomas McGreevy and the Pressure of Reality', *The Wallace Stevens Journal*, 18.2 (1994), 149–50.
86 Thomas McGreevy, *Richard Aldington: An Englishman*, (London: Chatto & Windus, 1931), pp. 31–2.
87 McGreevy, *Richard Aldington*, p. 31.
88 Coffey, *Poems and Versions*, p. 81. See also Coffey's comments on the 'humanity' of poetry and the dangers of Mallarmé's poetic in 'Brian Coffey, An Interview by Parkman Howe', *Éire-Ireland*, 13.1 (1978), 113–23.
89 Fredric Jameson, *The Ideologies of Theory: Essays 1971–1986* (2 vols, London: Routledge, 1988), vol. 2, p. 131.
90 McGreevy, *Richard Aldington*, p. 31. See also Thomas McGreevy, *T. S. Eliot: A Study* (London: Chatto & Windus, 1931).
91 MacGreevy, *Collected Poems*, p. 14.
92 MacGreevy, *Collected Poems*, p. 110.

93 The debate over onomatopoeia has tended to concur that the meaning of the utterance is as important to its effect as is the sound – such at least is the conclusion reached by such influential commentators as John Crowe Ransom and William Empson. Saussure famously held that the relationship between sound and sense in onomatopoeic words is as arbitrary as it is for any other sign. For a scrupulous interrogation of this whole issue see Peter Makin, *Basil Bunting: The Shaping of His Verse* (Oxford: Oxford UP, 1992), pp. 239–65 and 337–41.

94 Charles Altieri, 'The Poem as Act: A Way to Reconcile Presentational and Mimetic Theories of Literature', *Iowa Review*, 6 (1975), 111.

95 MacGreevy, *Collected Poems*, pp. 15–16.

96 Hans Arp et al., 'Poetry is Vertical', *transition*, 21 (1932), 148–9.

97 Beckett, *Disjecta*, p. 74.

98 On this dimension to Beckett's work see Theodor W. Adorno, 'Trying to Understand *Endgame*' in his *Notes to Literature*, trans. Sherry Weber Nicholsen (2 vols, New York: Columbia UP, 1991), vol. 1, pp. 241–75; and his *Aesthetic Theory*, eds Gretel Adorno and Rolf Tiedemann, trans. Robert Hullot-Kentor (Minneapolis: U of Minnesota P, 1997), *passim*.

99 Samuel Beckett, *Collected Poems 1930–1978* (London: John Calder, 1984), pp. 21–2. For details of the Occitan verse-forms in *Echo's Bones*, see Lawrence Harvey, *Samuel Beckett: Poet and Critic* (Princeton: Princeton UP, 1970), pp. 78–98.

100 Beckett, *Collected Poems*, p. 16.

2 COMMUNICATIONS FROM THE EIFFEL TOWER: *INTERCESSIONS*

1 Devlin's contributions to this collective enterprise, which includes translations by Beckett, are versions of 'Nudité de la vérité', 'Celle de toujours, toute', 'Les Amoureuses', 'Les Semblables' and 'Une pour toutes'. See *TE* 163–85 for these and other, previously unpublished, translations of Éluard. For a detailed account of the poet-publisher George Reavey and his Europa Press see Thomas Dillon Redshaw, '"Unificator": George Reavey and the Europa Poets of the 1930s' in Patricia Coughlan and Alex Davis (eds), *Modernism and Ireland: The Poetry of the 1930s* (Cork: Cork UP, 1995), pp. 249–75.

2 *Contemporary Poetry and Prose*, 4–5 (1936), 82–5. The poems are: 'Plutôt la vie', 'L'Aigrette', 'Allotropie' and 'Le Sphinx vertébral'; see *TE* 186–95.

3 Mervyn Wall, 'Michael Smith asks Mervyn Wall some Questions about the Thirties', *The Lace Curtain*, 4 (1971), 82.

4 Brian Coffey, 'About the Poetry of Denis Devlin', *Poetry Ireland*, 2 (1962), 84.

5 Brian Coffey, 'Of Denis Devlin: Vestiges, Sentences, Presages', *University Review* (Dublin), 2.11 (1963), 12. Elsewhere Coffey comments: 'Pure automatism of writing [Devlin believed] would not terminate in poems' (Coffey, 'About the Poetry', p. 83).

6 On Coffey's neo-scholasticism and its relevance to an understanding of his poetry, see my '"Poetry is Ontology": Brian Coffey's Poetics' in Patricia Coughlan and Alex Davis (eds), *Modernism and Ireland: The Poetry of the 1930s* (Cork: Cork UP, 1995), pp. 150–72.

7 André Breton, *Manifestoes of Surrealism*, trans. Richard Seaver and Helen R. Lane (Ann Arbor: U of Michigan P, 1969), p. 6.

8 Raymond Williams, *The Politics of Modernism: Against the New Conformists*, ed. Tony Pinkney (London: Verso, 1989), p. 73.

9 Breton, *Manifestoes*, p. 14.

10 On the strained relationship between Surrealism and orthodox communism, see Anna Balakian, *Surrealism: The Road to the Absolute*, 3rd ed. (Chicago: U of Chicago P, 1986), pp. 226–30. See also the lectures and reflections on this topic in Breton, *Manifestoes*, pp. 205–78.

11 Peter Bürger, *Theory of the Avant-Garde*, trans. Michael Shaw (Minneapolis: U of Minneapolis P, 1984), pp. 12–13.

12 Bürger, *Theory of the Avant-Garde*, p. 27.

13 Coffey, 'About the Poetry', p. 82.

14 Robert Hughes, *The Shock of the New: Art and the Century of Change*, 2nd ed. (London: Thames & Hudson, 1991), p. 9.

15 Blaise Cendrars, *Complete Poems*, trans. Ron Padgett (Berkeley: U of California P, 1992), pp. 56–7.

16 Blaise Cendrars, *Selected Writings of Blaise Cendrars*, trans. Walter Albert (New York: New Directions, 1962), p. 238.

17 Marjorie Perloff, *The Futurist Moment: Avant-Garde, Avant Guerre, and the Language of Rupture* (Chicago: U of Chicago P, 1986), p. 205. Perloff, it should be noted, reads Cendrars within the context of Futurism, despite the poet's refusal (largely nationalist in origin) to admit to Marinetti's influence on his work.

18 F. T. Marinetti, 'Destruction of Syntax – Imagination without Strings – Words-in-Freedom' in Umbro Apollonio (ed.), *Futurist Manifestos* (London: Thames & Hudson, 1973), p. 105.

19 '*Autumn, 1930*: Denis went on [a National University of Ireland] Travelling Studentship to Munich. . . . [He] enjoyed what he called the put-together-ness of Munich, its guide-book-like assortment of architectures, the element of all mankind realised in the students from many lands there assembled (and how grown up these people seemed after innocent student Dublin). Also he encountered anti-semitism in practice and he never forgot the experience' (Coffey, 'Of Denis Devlin', p. 5).

20 Samuel Beckett, *Disjecta: Miscellaneous Writings and a Dramatic Fragment*, ed. Roby Cohn (London: John Calder, 1983), p. 93. My thanks to Anne Fogarty for discussing the poem's *bisticcio* with me.

21 Coffey, 'About the Poetry', p. 82. In Breton's words: 'It is, as it were, from the fortuitous juxtaposition of the two terms that a particular light has sprung, *the light of the image*, to which we are infinitely sensitive. The value of the image depends upon the beauty of the spark obtained; it is, consequently, a function of the difference of potential between the two conductors' (Breton, *Manifestoes*, p. 37).

22 Coffey, 'About the Poetry', p. 82.

23 Redshaw, 'George Reavey and the Europa Poets', p. 257.

24 See Randall Jarrell, 'The Poet and His Public', *Partisan Review*, 13.4 (1946), 492–3.

25 Brian Coffey, 'For the Record' in *Advent VI* (Southampton: Advent Books, 1976), p. 21.

26 Stephen Spender, 'Some American and British Poets', *Life and Letters*, 17 (1937), 144.

27 'You Don't Know a Good Thing When You See It' appeared in *transition*, 25 (1936), 9, and was collected, under the new title 'Celibate Recusant' in *Lough Derg and Other Poems*. I discuss the relationship between Devlin's poetry and the aesthetics of *transition* in the next chapter.

28 Spender, 'Some American and British Poets', p. 144. Spender's comments, needless to say, are very much of their time; compare, for instance, the rather different view of the literary merits of British working-class writing in William Empson's opening remarks to *Some Versions of Pastoral*: 'It is hard for an Englishman to talk definitely about proletarian art, because in England it has never been a genre with settled principles, and such as there is of it, that I have seen, is bad' (William Empson, *Some Versions of Pastoral* [London: Chatto & Windus, 1974], p. 3). Empson's 1974 Preface reminds us that *Some Versions* was first published in 1935, 'and the first sentence of it will seem a bit raw unless one knows that'.

29 W. H. Auden, 'In Memory of W. B. Yeats' in *Collected Poems*, ed. Edward Mendelson, 2nd ed. (London: Faber, 1991), p. 248.

30 Peter McDonald, 'Believing in the Thirties' in Keith Williams and Steven Matthews (eds), *Rewriting the Thirties: Modernism and After* (London: Longman, 1997), p. 72. Spender's retreat from the position outlined in his 1937 review, and other writings of that date and earlier, also came in 1939, in his pamphlet *The New Realism*.

31 See Jonathan Petropoulos, *Art as Politics in the Third Reich* (Chapel Hill: U of North Carolina P, 1996), pp. 51–74.

32 Redshaw, 'George Reavey and the Europa Poets', p. 257. Vivienne Koch, reviewing *Lough Derg and Other Poems* (in which 'Bacchanal' was reprinted), astutely observed that the poem is 'as "red" a poem of social revolt as any written by an English or American poet of the thirties. But the differential inevitably enters, the lie is given to the dream, with a subtle reserve, a willing suspension of belief, quite foreign to the mood of easy optimism animating the British "social" poets in that "social" decade' (Vivienne Koch, 'Poetry Chronicle', *The Sewanee Review*, 54 [1946], 701). Beckett also found *Intercessions* 'Extraaudenary' (Beckett, *Disjecta*, p. 94).

33 Devlin sent MacGreevy 'Bacchanal' and other poems on 22 January 1937. In a subsequent letter, he responds to MacGreevy's warnings: 'I should never respect myself if I did not publish it. I'm not risking my job lightly especially as I have other responsibilities besides myself, but I must publish it. It should not be forgiven me because it is a poem of course but it is part of my "transcendental actuality" (Do you like that?)' (Denis Devlin, letter to Thomas MacGreevy, 15 February 1937, Thomas MacGreevy Papers, Trinity College, Dublin, MS 8112/12).

34 Walter Benjamin, *Selected Writings*, eds Michael W. Jennings, Howard Eiland and Gary Smith, trans. Rodney Livingstone et al. (3 vols, Cambridge, Mass.: Harvard UP, 1999), vol. 2, p. 215.

35 'Language Event One' in Jerome Rothenberg and Pierre Joris (eds), *Poems for the Millennium: The University of California Book of Modern and Postmodern Poetry* (2 vols, Berkeley: U of California P, 1995), vol. 1, p. 472.

36 Bürger, *Theory of the Avant-Garde*, p. 49.

37 Coffey, About the Poetry', p. 83. Gerald Dawe, in the course of briefly comparing Devlin with David Gascoyne, properly sees Devlin's avant-gardisms as 'playful', an 'experimentation with surrealism' as opposed to an

ideological commitment to its tenets. (Gerald Dawe, 'The European Modernists: MacGreevy, Devlin and Coffey' in Theo Dorgan [ed.], *Irish Poetry Since Kavanagh* [Dublin: Four Courts, 1996], p. 37).

38 The origins of 'Bacchanal' are discussed, and the text of 'News of Revolution' reprinted, in Coffey, 'For the Record', pp. 21–4.

39 Tristan Tzara, *Seven Dada Manifestos and Lampisteries*, trans. Barbara Wright (London: John Calder, 1977), p. 5.

40 Terry Eagleton, *Heathcliff and the Great Hunger: Studies in Irish Culture* (London: Verso, 1995), p. 299.

41 Nathaniel Hawthorne, *The American Notebooks*, ed. Claude M. Simpson (Ohio State UP, 1932), pp. 248–9.

42 Leo Marx, *The Machine in the Garden: Technology and the Pastoral Ideal in America* (Oxford: Oxford UP, 1964), pp. 19, 29.

43 J. J. Lee, *Ireland 1912–1985: Politics and Society* (Cambridge: Cambridge UP, 1989), p. 639.

44 W. B. Yeats, *The Variorum Edition of the Poems of W. B. Yeats*, eds Peter Allt and Russell K. Alspach, 3rd imp. (New York: Macmillan, 1966), p. 611.

45 For a detailed discussion of modernism's, and in particular Pound's, response to the commodification of lyric poetry, see Frank Lentricchia, *Modernist Quartet* (Cambridge: Cambridge UP, 1994), pp. 47–76.

46 Tzara, *Seven Dada Manifestos*, p. 5.

47 Wallace Stevens, *Opus Posthumous*, ed. Milton J. Bates, 2nd ed. (New York: Alfred A. Knopf, 1989), pp. 75, 76.

48 Stevens, *Opus Posthumous*, p. 80.

49 Theodor W. Adorno, *Notes to Literature*, trans. Shierry Weber Nicholson (2 vols, New York: Columbia UP, 1992), vol. 2, p. 93.

50 Alan Filreis, *Modernism from Left to Right: Wallace Stevens, the Thirties, and Literary Radicalism* (Cambridge: Cambridge, UP, 1994), p. 143.

51 In a 1989 interview, Burnshaw was asked: 'Did you see yourself, then, as one of the few literary radicals attempting to bring together the advances of modernism and the new politics?' To which he replied: 'I didn't consider free verse such a revolutionary thing. I wrote a review and published it in 1925 in *The Forum* on E. E. Cummings. Was I pro-modern? Yes! I thought it was marvelous. I though Cummings was great. My book on André Spire is still being used. . . . So you see my orientation was clear; I had no problem with modernism; this was part of the given for me' (Alan Filreis and Harvey Teres, 'An Interview with Stanley Burnshaw', *The Wallace Stevens Journal*, 13.2 [1989], 115). Filreis supports Burnshaw's self-appraisal, viewing him as a radical who, because of his interest in formal experimentation, disparaged the left's predominant emphasis on the content of art (see Filreis, *Modernism from Left to Right*, p. 6).

52 Denis Devlin, 'Statement of an Irishman', Brian Coffey Papers, University of Delaware Library, Newark, Del. The poem is dated 'Paris, 1933'. For Kinsella's views on the bifucated nature of the Irish poet's cultural inheritance, see his *The Dual Tradition: An Essay on Poetry and Politics in Ireland* (Manchester: Carcanet, 1995).

53 For Devlin's and Montgomery's translations of Nerval, Rimbaud, Baudelaire, Mallarmé and Apollinaire into Irish, see *CP* 123–7.

54 Anon, rev. of *Intercessions*, *Times Literary Supplement*, 23 Oct. 1937, 786.

55 Beckett, *Disjecta*, pp. 91, 92.

56 Thomas McGreevy, 'New Dublin Poetry', *Poetry Ireland*, 2.10 (1937), 81–2.
57 Roland Barthes, *The Pleasure of the Text*, trans. Richard Miller (Oxford: Basil Blackwell, 1990), p. 8.
58 Samuel Beckett, *Collected Poems 1930–1978* (London: John Calder, 1984), p. 9.
59 See Lawrence Harvey, *Samuel Beckett: Poet and Critic* (Princeton: Princeton UP, 1970), pp. 112–16.
60 The reference to the myth of Attis and Cybele implies a partial indebtedness to Eliot's *The Waste Land*. For a contemporaneous redeployment of the vegetation myths central to that work, compare Basil Bunting's 1931 poem, *Attis: Or, Something Missing* in *The Complete Poems*, ed. Richard Caddel (Oxford: Oxford UP, 1994), pp. 12–17. Bunting's ironic reworking of Cattulus's version of the myth is closer in spirit to Beckett's manipulation of Ovidian material in *Echo's Bones* than to Devlin's earnest allusion.
61 Anne Fogarty, 'Gender, Irish Modernism and the Poetry of Denis Devlin' in Patricia Coughlan and Alex Davis (eds), *Modernism and Ireland: The Poetry of the 1930s* (Cork: Cork UP, 1995), p. 222.
62 Fogarty, 'Gender, Irish Modernism and the Poetry of Denis Devlin', p. 223.
63 Beckett, *Disjecta*, p. 172.
64 Daniel Murphy, *Imagination and Religion in Anglo-Irish Literature 1930–1980* (Dublin: Irish Academic P, 1987), pp. 90, 88.
65 On the links between idealism and philosophy after 'the linguistic turn', see Richard Rorty, *Consequences of Pragmatism* (Minneapolis: U of Minnesota P, 1982), pp. 139–59.
66 See Coffey, 'About the Poetry', p. 84. See Horace, *Ars Poetica* ll. 333–4: 'aut prodesse uolunt aut delectare poetae / aut simil et iucunda et idonea dicere uitae' (Horace, *Epistles Book II and Epistle to the Pisones ['Ars Poetica']*, ed. Niall Rudd [Cambridge: Cambridge UP, 1989], p. 69). My thanks to Carmel McCallum-Barry for identifying the passage in question.
67 George Every, rev. of *Intercessions*, *The Criterion*, 17 (1938), 338, 333.
68 Michael H. Levenson, *A Genealogy of Modernism: A Study of English Literary Doctrine 1908–1922* (Cambridge: Cambridge UP, 1984), p. 219. On Hulme's importance as a precursor for the 'classicist' modernism championed by Eliot and others in the pages of *The Criterion*, see Levenson, *A Genealogy of Modernism*, p. 38.
69 T. E. Hulme, *The Collected Writings of T. E. Hulme*, ed. Karen Csengeri (Oxford: Oxford UP, 1994), pp. 62–3.
70 Coffey, 'About the Poetry', p. 85.

3 'WITH MULLIONED EUROPE SHATTERED': *LOUGH DERG AND OTHER POEMS*

1 See Denis Devlin, 'Lough Derg', *The Southern Review*, 7.4 (1942), 856–9. Warren recalled meeting Devlin in the summer of 1944, at a dinner party given by Katherine Anne Porter in Georgetown, Washington (Robert Penn Warren, 'Denis Devlin: A Recollection', *Éire-Ireland: Weekly Bulletin of the Department of External Affairs*, 493 [1960], 6.) Warren says that it was Tate who encouraged Devlin to submit 'Lough Derg' to *The Southern Review*. For more details, see William G. Downey, 'Thinking of Denis Devlin', *Éire-Ireland*, 14.1 (1979), 107; and Joan Givner, *Katherine Anne Porter: A Life*, 2nd ed. (Athens: U of Georgia P, 1991), p. 334.

2 John Fekete, *The Critical Twilight: Explorations in the Ideology of Anglo-American Literary Theory from Eliot to McLuhan* (London: Routledge & Kegan Paul, 1977), p. 45. The antecedents of the New Criticism are explored at length by Fekete. Its origins lay in the Fugitives, a group of Southern intellectuals whose ideas, expressed in the pages of *The Fugitive* (1922–25), were opposed to the scientism they felt was coming to dominate human behaviour. Art, for Ransom in this period, 'is always the exhibit of Opposition and at the same time Reconciliation between the Conceptual or Formal and the Individual or Concrete' (quoted in Fekete, *The Critical Twilight*, p. 57). That is, art recaptures the immediacy of sensuous experience without totally rejecting the conceptualisation associated with scientific reason. In the face of increased infiltration of the South by Northern interests and policies, the Fugitive movement's aesthetic concerns took on a more worldly dimension, looking to an idealised Southern past for spiritual succour and a way of life inimical to that of the North. Thus arose the Agrarian movement, conservative, religious, ruralist, anti-scientist and anti-capitalist, in which art becomes a privileged means of access to the particularity of the natural world. This is, of course, an impossible nostalgia for a precapitalist mode of being-in-the-world, and prompts Fekete to counter: 'What could have been a genuine critique of capitalism, indicating a rational distribution and liberating redevelopment of priorities, thus becomes again an obfuscating critique of "industrialism" from a basis in natural anthropology' (Fekete, *The Critical Twilight*, p. 71). And he further notes, of the essays collected in *The World's Body*: 'It is with an aesthetic . . . that is effectively the counterpart of that alienated modern poetry that seeks to escape from an unbearable historical reality and to reach the world of objects in themselves without social mediation, that Ransom tries to attain to substantial concreteness' (Fekete, *The Critical Twilight*, p. 75) or to an apprehension of the world's body. The theoretical vacuity and practical inconceivability of Agrarianism led to its demise by the end of the 1930s. Its ideas, stripped of their socio-political dimensions, fed, via Ransom, into the academy and specifically into the humanities.

3 Fekete, *The Critical Twilight*, p. 91.

4 Allen Tate and Robert Penn Warren, preface, *Selected Poems*, by Denis Devlin (New York: Holt, Rinehart & Winston, 1963), pp. 13, 14. In Warren's view, 'The Passion of Christ' 'crowned' Devlin's later work (Warren, 'Denis Devlin', p. 6).

5 Marjorie Perloff, *The Poetics of Indeterminacy: Rimbaud to Cage* (Evanston: Northwestern UP, 1983), p. vii. Perloff has refined her argument through a series of subsequent books, including *The Dance of the Intellect: Studies in the Poetry of the Pound Tradition* (Cambridge: Cambridge UP, 1985); and *Poetic License: Essays on Modernist and Postmodernist Lyric* (Evanston: Northwestern UP, 1990).

6 Denis Devlin, 'Twenty-Four Poets', *The Sewanee Review*, 53.3 (1945), 465.

7 See Ashbery's poem with this title in his *Houseboat Days* (New York: Viking, 1977), pp. 2–3.

8 Perloff, *The Poetics of Indeterminacy*, p. 13.

9 Situated in south-east Donegal, the lake-island of Lough Derg has for centuries been an important site of pilgrimage. Saint Patrick, according to legend, fasted there and was vouchsafed a vision of the next world. Ernest Renan,

among others, believed Dante's *Divina Commedia* was informed by the visionary experiences of pilgrims at Lough Derg, a belief to which the tenth stanza of Devlin's poem alludes. There have been several modern literary treatments of Lough Derg by writers as diverse as William Carleton ('The Lough Derg Pilgrim'), Patrick Kavanagh (*Lough Derg*) and Seamus Heaney (*Station Island*).

10 'The only way of expressing emotion in the form of art is by finding an "objective correlative"; in other words, a set of objects, a situation, a chain of events which shall be the formula of that *particular* emotion; such that when the external facts, which must terminate in sensory experience, are given, the emotion is immediately evoked' (T. S. Eliot, *Selected Essays*, 3rd ed. [London: Faber, 1951], p. 145).

11 T. S. Eliot, *The Complete Poems and Plays of T. S. Eliot* (London: Faber, 1969), p. 52.

12 Wallace Stevens, *The Collected Poems of Wallace Stevens* (New York: Alfred A. Knopf, 1954), pp. 68, 69. Stevens, incidentally, owned a copy of Devlin's *Lough Derg and Other Poems* – the gift of Tate, perhaps? See Robert Moynihan, 'Checklist: Second Purchase, Wallace Stevens Collection, Huntington Library', *The Wallace Stevens Journal*, 20.1 (1996), p. 85.

13 Hart Crane, *Complete Poems*, ed. Brom Weber (Newcastle: Bloodaxe, 1984), p. 173 (Crane's ellipsis). The similarity to Crane was not lost on one of the reviewers of *Lough Derg and Other Poems*. Selden Rodman wrote that 'his obscurities, like Hart Crane's, are acceptable: the senses are electrified even when the idea evades the mind' (Selden Rodman, 'Daemonic Poet', *The New Republic*, 29 July 1946, 106). There is a brief comparison of the two poets in M. L. Rosenthal, *The New Poets: American and British Poetry Since World War II* (New York: Oxford UP, 1967), p. 273. Devlin's papers in the National Library of Ireland, Dublin, contain a number of unpublished, early poems addressed to Crane.

14 Perloff, *The Poetics of Indeterminacy*, p. 20.

15 See Dillon Johnston, *Irish Poetry after Joyce*, 2nd ed. (Syracuse: Syracuse UP, 1997), pp. 168–74; Robert Welch, 'Language as Pilgrimage: Lough Derg Poems of Patrick Kavanagh and Denis Devlin', *Irish University Review*, 13.1 (1983), 62; and Robert Welch, '"My Present Unresolved": Denis Devlin and Montaigne' in Barbara Hayley and Christopher Murray (eds), *Ireland and France, A Bountiful Friendship: Literature, History and Ideas* (Gerrards Cross: Colin Smythe, 1992), pp. 138–41. See also Welch's less rewarding description of Devlin's style cited in the following note.

16 Charles Olson, *Collected Prose*, eds Donald Allen and Benjamin Friedlander (Berkeley: U of California P, 1997), pp. 244, 239. In the light of Olson's association of projective verse with Keats's concept of Negative Capability, I find the ascription to Devlin's poetry of the latter quality by Robert Welch unconvincing. Welch's reading identifies in Devlin 'a humility before the object' that the procedures of Devlin's love poetry – which I discuss in the second section of the present chapter – hardly supports (Robert Welch, 'Devlin's Rhythm' in *Advent VI* [Southampton: Advent Books, 1976], p. 14).

17 See Denis Devlin, 'Ank'hor Vat', *University of Kansas City Review*, 10.2 (1943), 117.

18 Charles Olson, *The Collected Poems of Charles Olson, Excluding 'The Maximus Poems'*, ed. George F. Butterick (Berkeley: U of California P, 1987), p. 86.

19 Sherman Paul, *Olson's Push: Origin, Black Mountain and Recent American Poetry* (Baton Rouge: Louisiana State UP, 1978), p. 14. Fernand remains unidentified, though Paul notes his resemblance to Malraux. Another Frenchman, Saint-John Perse, may account for Devlin's spelling of the Cambodian temple. As Mays observes, 'Perse served and travelled in the region at the beginning of his diplomatic and literary career' (*CP* 344).

20 Eliot, *Complete Poems and Plays*, p. 175.

21 Olson, *Collected Prose*, p. 205.

22 Ezra Pound, *The Cantos of Ezra Pound*, 13 imp. (New York: New Directions, 1995), p. 91.

23 Crane, *Complete Poems*, p. 48.

24 Crane, *Complete Poems*, p. 52.

25 The desire, on Crane's part, to transcend materiality can be related to his interest in Ouspensky's speculations in *Tertium Organum* on the idea of the fourth dimension as a possible liberation of human consciousness from the constraining shackles of three-dimensional space. As R. W. Butterfield observes: 'The intention of ['For the Marriage of Faustus and Helen'] is misunderstood and its tone distorted, if it is interpreted in terms of Laforguean irony rather than Ouspenskian ebullient optimism' (R.W. Butterfield, *The Broken Arc: A Study of Hart Crane* [Edinburgh: Oliver & Boyd, 1969], p. 55). Among Devlin's papers in the National Library of Ireland is a list of the contents of his library in Rome as of 1959, which shows that he owned a copy of Ouspensky's *The Psychology of Man's Possible Evolution*.

26 Crane, *Complete Poems*, p. 49.

27 Theodor W. Adorno, *Aesthetic Theory*, eds Gretel Adorno and Rolf Tiedemann, trans. Robert Hullot-Kentor (Minneapolis: U of Minnesota P, 1997), p. 227.

28 Randall Jarrell, 'The Poet and His Public', *Partisan Review*, 13.4 (1946), 492.

29 Roman Jakobson, *Language in Literature*, eds Krystyna Pomorska and Stephen Rudy (Cambridge, Mass.: Harvard UP, 1987), p. 70.

30 See Victor Erlich, *Russian Formalism: History – Doctrine*, 3rd ed. (New Haven: Yale UP, 1981), pp. 63–9.

31 On the 'auto-referentiality' of Jakobson's poetic function, see Fredric Jameson, *The Prison-House of Language: A Critical Account of Structuralism and Formalism* (Princeton: Princeton UP, 1972), p. 203; and on Saussure's 'closed nature of language' as 'a central issue and the most important problem of modernism', see Rainer Emig, *Modernism in Poetry: Motivations, Structures and Limits* (London: Longman, 1995), p. 11.

32 See Douglas McMillan, *transition: The History of a Literary Era 1927–1938* (London: Calder and Boyars, 1975), pp. 125–47.

33 Paul Giles, *Hart Crane: The Contexts of the Bridge* (Cambridge: Cambridge UP, 1986), p. 139.

34 See Denis Devlin, 'You Don't Know a Good Thing When You See It', *transition*, 25 (1936), 9.

35 Hans Arp et al., 'Poetry is Vertical', *transition*, 21 (1932), 149.

36 McMillan, *transition*, p. 67. Devlin's library as of 1959 contained a copy of Buber's *I and Thou*.

37 See McMillan, *transition*, pp. 67–8. By 1936 the Vertigralism of *transition* was less impassioned than in previous issues; nevertheless, it remained a key concept in the magazine.

38 Reviewing *Lough Derg and Other Poems*, Valentin Iremonger sourly noted that 'many of Mr Devlin's poems have a *transition* taste: literary, bookish' (Valentin Iremonger, 'Less Than Passion', *The Bell*, 13.2 [1946], 166).

39 On Devlin's Jansenism see Welsh, 'Language as Pilgrimage', p. 61 and Stan Smith, '"Precarious Guest": The Poetry of Denis Devlin' in Patricia Coughlan and Alex Davis (eds), *Modernism and Ireland: The Poetry of the 1930s* (Cork: Cork UP, 1995), pp. 235–9. Smith usefully directs his readers to Lucien Goldmann's classic study of Jansenism, *The Hidden God*, trans. Philip Thody (London: Routledge & Kegan Paul, 1964).

40 Quoted in Goldmann, *The Hidden God*, p. 35.

41 The beginnings of 'The Statue and the Perturbed Burghers', 'After Five O'Clock', 'The Blind Leading the Blind', 'Celibate Recusant' and 'Summer Jujube' lie in the 'Adventure' project.

42 Smith, 'Precarious Guest', p. 239.

43 The speaker's error is clearer in the version of 'Jansenist Jouney' published in *Urbana*, 4.2 (1944), 72–3: 'The pure diamond / Is locked inside; safe and fast. / . . . / I opened mine: Nothing but a ball of gold.'

44 Stevens, *Collected Poems*, pp. 249–50.

45 'Obstacle Basilisk' also ends its quest-romance on a bathetic note. The quester, at sundown, attains 'the city gates / Defended by a groom and three sick colts.' The 'mean groom' is hardly a worthy opponent, and, as if to underscore this fact, the horseman's mount 'backs away and defecates, / Transformed into a whippet, off he bolts' (*CP* 188).

46 Andrew Marvell, *The Complete Poems*, ed. Elizabeth Story Donno (Harmondsworth: Penguin, 1972), p. 56.

47 Vivienne Koch, 'Poetry Chronicle', *The Sewanee Review*, 54 (1946), 700.

48 Denis Devlin, 'Encounter', *Urbana*, 4.2 (1944), 72.

49 Wallace Stevens, *Opus Posthumous*, ed. Milton J. Bates, 2nd ed. (New York: Alfred A. Knopf, 1989), p. 88.

50 Stevens, *Opus Posthumous*, p. 76.

51 Stan Smith, 'Frightened Antinomies: Love and Death in the Poetry of Denis Devlin' in *Advent VI* (Southampton: Advent Books), p. 27.

52 See Peter Bürger, *Theory of the Avant-Garde*, trans. Michael Shaw (Minneapolis: U of Minnesota P, 1984), pp. 47–8.

53 W. B. Yeats, *The Variorum Edition of the Poems of W. B. Yeats*, eds Peter Allt and Russell K. Alspach, 3rd imp. (New York: Macmillan, 1966), pp. 638–9.

54 Two reviewers of *Lough Derg and Other Poems*, Babette Deutsche and Pearse Hutchinson, noted this dimension to the volume. Deutsch comments: 'there is a kind of homelessness about his poetry. . . . [T]he place where things happen to Denis Devlin is his own mind' (Babette Deutsch, 'A Learned Craftsman of Verse', *New York Herald Tribune Weekly Book Review*, 28 July 1946, 8); while Hutchinson writes that '[Devlin has] a slight addiction to the type of "private mythology" that enjoyed a certain sporadic vogue between the wars' (Pearse Hutchinson, *The Irish Bookman*, 1.6 [1947], 23).

55 See Denis Devlin, 'From Government Buildings', *Briarcliff Quarterly*, 2.7 (1945), 65–6.

56 Samuel Beckett, *Collected Poems 1930–1978* (London: John Calder, 1984), p. 32.

57 Jean-Paul Sartre, *The Psychology of Imagination* (London: Methuen, 1972), p. 13.

58 Johnston, *Irish Poetry after Joyce*, p. 173.
59 Denis Devlin, 'Farewell to Her', Denis Devlin Papers, National Library of Ireland. Johnston's reading is also marred by the misprint of 'split' for 'spilt' in the penultimate line of 'Farewell and Good' as printed in *CP* (Coffey) 85, the text from which he cites. Thus, what Johnston views as *antistasis* ('The rhetorical term for the repetition of a word in a different or contrary sense' [Johnston, *Irish Poetry after Joyce*, p. 173]) is, in fact, absent from the poem. Rather, the shift from 'split' to 'spilt' is indicative of the very fluidity of Devlin's verse which Johnston's overall analysis anatomises so adroitly.
60 Denis Devlin Reading Poems with Comment to the Writer's Club of the Library of Congress in the Coolidge Auditorium, audiotape, rec. 3 Jan. 1946. Library of Congress, Archive of Recorded Poetry and Literature.
61 Smith, 'Precarious Guest', p. 238 (my italics).
62 John Keats, 'To Benjamin Bailey', 22 Nov. 1817, *Letters of John Keats*, ed. Robert Gittings (Oxford: Oxford UP, 1970), p. 37. Keats of course is referring to Milton's version of the biblical account; see *Paradise Lost*, VIII. 452–90.
63 Sartre, *The Psychology of Imagination*, p. 141.
64 Anne Fogarty, 'Gender, Irish Modernism and the Poetry of Denis Devlin' in Patricia Coughlan and Alex Davis (eds), *Modernism and Ireland: The Poetry of the 1930s* (Cork: Cork UP, 1995), pp. 225, 226.
65 Lorna Reynolds, 'Denis Devlin: An Approach to the Palimpsest of his Poetry' in *Advent VI* (Southampton: Advent Books, 1976), p. 5.
66 Koch, 'Poetry Chronicle', p. 704.
67 Susanne Kappeler, *The Pornography of Representation* (Cambridge: Polity, 1986), pp. 57, 102.
68 Naomi Schor, 'The Portrait of a Gentleman: Representing Men in (French) Women's Writing' in R. Howard Bloch and Frances Ferguson (eds), *Misogyny, Misandry, and Misanthropy* (Berkeley: U of California P, 1989), p. 126.
69 Helena Mitchie, *The Flesh Made Word: Female Figures and Women's Bodies* (New York: Oxford UP, 1989), p. 139.
70 Elizabeth Butler Cullingford, *Gender and History in Yeats's Love Poetry* (Cambridge: Cambridge UP, 1993), p. 204.
71 Cullingford, *Gender and History in Yeats*, p. 260.

4 'HEART-AFFAIRS DIPLOMAT': LATER POEMS

1 Brian Coffey states that the poem 'preoccupied Devlin from very early in the thirties until its publication in 1950 – following which event, Devlin continued to work over the text until his death in 1959' (Brian Coffey, 'Denis Devlin: Poet of Distance' in Andrew Carpenter [ed.], *Place, Personality and the Irish Writer* [Gerrards Cross: Colin Smythe, 1977], p. 152.) The manuscripts and typescripts associated with this project, plus other material relevant to the genesis and development of *The Heavenly Foreigner*, are reproduced in *HF* 39–67. The text of *HF* is that of the revised version of the poem, completed before Devlin's death, and which is reproduced in *CP*. Readers of *CP* may wish to note the error on *CP* 261, where '*mad, unphonetic works*' should read '*mad, unphonetic worms*' (corrected on an erratum slip in *HF*).
2 Compare Maurice Scève, *The 'Délie' of Maurice Scève*, ed. I. D. McFarlane (Cambridge: Cambridge UP, 1966), p. 320. My thanks to Dick Collins both

for assistance with Scève's text and for sharing with me his wide knowledge of Occitan literature, Devlin's relationship to which I discuss below.

3 Odette de Mourgues, *Metaphysical, Baroque and Précieux Poetry* (Oxford: Oxford UP, 1953), p. 22.

4 For Devlin's translations of Du Bellay, see *TE* 22–34 and 316. The poems Devlin chose to translate post-date Du Bellay's Petrarchist sonnet-sequence, *L'Olive*, all being drawn from the *Antiquitez de Rome* and *Les Regrets*, both of which reject Petrarchist conventions. (I say more in the third section of this chapter about Du Bellay's representation of Rome in relation to Devlin's experience as a diplomat in the city.) From Ronsard, Devlin rendered into English 'Quand vous serez bien vieille', from the Petrarchist *Sonnets pour Hélène* (see *TE* 35), familiar to readers of Irish poetry as the base-text for Yeats's 'When You are Old'. On Devlin's knowledge of Petrach himself, see *CP* (Coffey) xix.

5 As Basil Payne noted, 'the poem is almost entirely a sustained sequence of *becoming* rather than *being*' (Basil Payne, rev. of *The Heavenly Foreigner*, ed. Brian Coffey, *Studies*, 57 [1968], 105).

6 Dillon Johnston comments: 'These important lines from the poem's opening section ["Time virtual is what keeps me in time: / Leave me in abeyance"] terminate in an anacoluthon; we either have to reconstruct the subject for *leave* to be the compound "Time virtual and Time", meaning his conception of time's boundaries, the enclosing "miniscus of discontent", and his actual experience, I suppose, or accept the verb as imperative: meaning we must not try to extract him from his condition' (Dillon Johnston, *Irish Poetry after Joyce*, 2nd ed. [Syracuse: Syracuse UP, 1997], p. 180). Johnston's astute interpretation of *The Heavenly Foreigner* should be read in full.

7 On the personal background to the poem, see also Brian Coffey, 'Of Denis Devlin: Vestiges, Sentences, Presages', *University Review* (Dublin), 2.11 (1963), 5. The importance of *Délie* to Devlin during the slow gestation of *The Heavenly Foreigner* may also be registered in the plan to an unwritten poem, 'An Invented City', the five parts of which envisage a structure bearing some comparison to that of Scève's *canzonerie*: 'The Meeting, Tryst, Parting, Absence, Reunited without corporal consubstantiation'. In a note on the back of the sheet bearing this plan Devlin refers to the woman in the projected sequence as 'D' (*HF* 39–40). It is also possible that 'Alembic' in *Intercessions*, draws upon *Délie, dizain* 206, which uses the same alchemical image as Devlin's poem (see Scève, *Délie*, p. 232 and the emblem on p. 231).

8 Doranne Fenoaltea, *'Si haulte Architecture': The Design of Scève's 'Délie'* (Lexington: French Forum, 1982), pp. 21–2.

9 Scève, *Délie*, p. 11.

10 McFarlane points out the appeal of Scève for the reader familiar with Baudelaire, Mallarmé and Valéry (Scève, *Délie*, p. 4), while Fenoaltea claims that, 'In reading the *Délie*, modern readers are naturally attracted to the expressions of alienation, suffering, deprivation, and lack of integration which many of the dizains trace so carefully and express so movingly. We respond to the knotty and difficult syntax, which reflects the intensity of the lover's suffering and the entrapment of the human condition. We also respond to the rare moments of joy, of complete awareness, which stand out like brilliant and translucent jewels against the darker fabric of the text, and to the rich and evocative expression of man's relation to nature' (Fenoaltea, *'Si haulte Architecture'*, p. 187).

11 Dorothy Gabe Coleman, *Maurice Scève, Poet of Love: Tradition and Originality* (Cambridge: Cambridge UP, 1975), p. 118.

12 T. S. Eliot, *The Complete Poems and Plays of T. S. Eliot* (London: Faber, 1969), p. 73. Eliot's allusion in these lines to Luke 24.13–16 suggests that his 'third' is also a Heavenly Foreigner.

13 See *CP* (Coffey) xix; and Coffey's introduction to *HF*, which further links Devlin's reading in the troubadours to his warmth for Scève: 'One can understand that a poet responsive to songs of the courts of love might feel deeply, through resonance, the pull towards Scève's world' (*HF* 9). Niall Sheridan's introduction to a selection of Devlin's poems in *Poetry Ireland* draws a parallel between *The Heavenly Foreigner* and 'the Catharist songs of the Troubadours' in their treatment of sexual and sacred love (Niall Sheridan, introduction, *Poetry Ireland*, 10 [1950], 3).

14 Ezra Pound, *Literary Essays of Ezra Pound*, ed. T. S. Eliot (London: Faber, 1954), p. 101.

15 Rouben C. Cholakian, *The Troubadour Lyric: A Psychocritical Reading* (Manchester: Manchester UP, 1990), p. 1.

16 Cholakian, *The Troubadour Lyric*, pp. 2, 8–9.

17 Marina Warner, *Alone of All Her Sex: The Myth and the Cult of the Virgin Mary* (New York: Random House, 1976), pp. 135, 137. See also Moshe Lazar's detailed account of this change in Occitan poetry: 'With the growing influence of Bernard de Clairvaux's allegorical interpretation of the biblical *Song of Songs* toward the end of the twelfth century, and particularly after the crusade against the Albigensians (the heretic Cathars), which prompted the demise of the secular culture of the south, there begins a process of psychological inhibition and repression in the domain of love songs, a trend towards spiritualisation and allegorization that would eventually lead to the *Roman de la Rose*, to the *dolce stil nuovo* of a Guido Guinizelli or Cavalcanti, and to the *Vita Nuova* of Dante. During this process, some aspects of the courtly vocabulary will also be transferred to the love hymns addressed to Mary, "*our* Lady" replacing now "*my* lady" and "*midons*" of the troubadours. During the thirteenth century, in a changing cultural context, poets now invest their talent in "divine love" songs. *True love* and *good love*, fair body and sweet face, kisses and embraces, desire and joy, garden of delights and dying from passionate love, are so many expressions recuperated from the troubadours' vocabulary by the devotional hymns to Mary, including *fine amour* and *fin amant*, but totally emptied of their profane erotic and sexual connotations' (Moshe Lazar, '*Fin'amor*' in F. R. P. Akehurst and Judith M. Davis [eds], *A Handbook of the Troubadours* [Berkeley: U of California P, 1995], p. 92).

18 See *Antony and Cleopatra* II. ii. 196–226.

19 Though not always – see 'Schwabing': 'Rodents in the corn like the black gas in the heart of the sun. / The chase and the loving under the damp ditch; / Her blond laughter now indecent, her sexual / Ascetic face with the bones loosened' (*CP* 263). Frank L. Kersnowski claims that Devlin's 'ambivalence about the feminine' stems from, firstly, the Church and, secondly, 'the example of Eliot', though he goes on to argue that *The Heavenly Foreigner* shows the extent to which Devlin has moved from 'Eliotesque repugnance' to a view of woman as the 'source . . . of ecstatic understanding' (Frank L. Kersnowski, 'The Fabulous Reality of Denis Devlin', *The Sewanee Review*, 81 [1973], 116, 121).

20 Cholakian, *The Troubadour Lyric*, p. 179. Warner comments: 'At one level, the argument that Mary and the saints intercede with God rather than wield power in their own right is necessitated by monotheism. The jurisdiction of the One True God cannot be encroached upon by other powers. But at another level the doctrine of Mary's intercession coheres with other characteristics that establish her as the ideal *woman* – with her submission and her purity and her gentleness' (Warner, *Alone of All Her Sex*, p. 288).

21 Eliot, *Complete Poems and Plays*, p. 173. Daniel Murphy relates Devlin's contention in *The Heavenly Foreigner* that 'The momentary perfection of human love is illusory and transient, yet it symbolises a spiritual stillness which is neither' to Eliot's 'still point' (Daniel Murphy, *Imagination and Religion in Anglo-Irish Literature 1930–1980* [Dublin: Irish Academic P, 1987], pp. 80, 82).

22 Jean-Paul Sartre, *The Psychology of Imagination* (London: Methuen, 1972), p. 142.

23 Stan Smith, '"Precarious Guest": The Poetry of Denis Devlin' in Patricia Coughlan and Alex Davis (eds), *Modernism and Ireland: The Poetry of the 1930s* (Cork: Cork UP, 1995), p. 240.

24 See also a related prose passage by Devlin: 'There it is, in the end I have lost her. She is a human being of the female sex, one thing to her doctor, another to her parents, to third-parties charming and volatile, tiresome and hysterical, or in my impressions as they leap hither and thither like an aimless mad monkey while I am being concerned with the signing of an attendance-book or the intercalation of a career between parent and grandchild: how she may stand, hypothetical-eyed and metaphor-breasted; then I am convinced that she is my vision, that I have made her more that the others who have only suffered her view. One among women? Why can I particularise myself with that phrase which means exactly, one among hundreds of millions of cogenerate similars. This is where, O bed-reality, tigersmooth-armed! I am at a loss, for I do not possess this one similar' (*HF* 45).

25 Seamus Deane, *A Short History of Irish Literature* (London: Hutchinson, 1986), p. 232.

26 Sartre, *The Psychology of Imagination*, p. 224.

27 See Lorna Reynolds, 'Denis Devlin: An Approach to the Palimpsest of His Poetry' in *Advent VI* (Southampton: Advent Books, 1976), p. 3; and William G. Downey, Jr, 'Appréciation: Thinking of Denis Devlin', *Éire-Ireland*, 14.1 (1979), 103.

28 Robert Welch, '"My Present Unresolved": Denis Devlin and Montaigne' in Barbara Hayley and Christopher Murray (eds), *Ireland and France, A Bountiful Friendship: Literature, History and Ideas* (Gerrards Cross: Colin Smythe, 1992), p. 141.

29 Murphy, *Imagination and Religion*, p. 86. A similarly sanguine Devlin emerges in the course of Declan Kiberd's argument that, in contrast to Beckett, Devlin's 'sexual partners . . . know a moment of healing oneness', and that this Devlin 'elevated into an aesthetic principle which annihilated the distance between subject and object, achieving that very fusion which Beckett had pronounced impossible in his early book on Proust' (Declan Kiberd, *Inventing Ireland: The Literature of the Modern Nation* [London: Jonathan Cape, 1995], p. 463).

30 Allen Tate, *Essays of Four Decades* (Chicago: Swallow, 1968), pp. 67–8; quoted in Murphy, *Imagination and Religion*, p. 87.

31 Tate, *Essays of Four Decades*, pp. 63, 64.
32 Murphy, *Imagination and Religion*, p. 87.
33 Johnston, *Irish Poetry after Joyce*, p. 175.
34 Eliot, *Complete Poems and Plays*, p. 193.
35 *The Divine Comedy of Dante Alighieri*, trans. John D. Sinclair (3 vols, New York: Oxford UP, 1939), vol. 1, *Inferno*, p. 53. Dante, in his turn, is alluding to the sixth book of the *Aeneid*, in which Aeneas, descending to the underworld, sees the dead crowding the banks of Acheron: 'As numerous were they as the leaves of the forest which fall at the first chill of autumn and float down' (Virgil, *The Aeneid*, trans. W. F. Jackson Knight, 2nd ed. [Harmondsworth: Penguin, 1958], p. 156). That Aeneas is the son of Venus, the presiding deity of the opening of 'The Colours of Love', may throw some light on the identity of the 'hero' who appears in the poem's middle sections. Coffey attests to Devlin's knowledge of Dante; see *CP* (Coffey) xix.
36 Harold Bloom, *The Breaking of the Vessels* (Chicago: U of Chicago P, 1982), p. 75. Bloom's argument here builds on his discussion of 'Milton and His Precursors', in which Bloom analyses Milton's transumption of Homer, Virgil and Dante in *Paradise Lost*; see Harold Bloom, *A Map of Misreading* (Oxford: Oxford UP, 1975), pp. 125–43.
37 Bloom, *The Breaking of the Vessels*, p. 89.
38 Wallace Stevens, *The Collected Poems of Wallace Stevens* (New York: Alfred A. Knopf, 1954), p. 130.
39 Quoted in Lyndall Gordon, *Eliot's Early Years* (Oxford: Oxford UP, 1977), p. 60.
40 Though anything but uxorious, the poem is dedicated, not to the woman of 'that young year' who is the poem's pretext, but '*To my wife Caren*' (Marie Caren Radon, whom Devlin married in 1946).
41 Johnston, *Irish Poetry after Joyce*, p. 176.
42 Tim Armstrong, 'Muting the Klaxon: Poetry, History and Irish Modernism' in Patricia Coughlan and Alex Davis (eds), *Modernism and Ireland: The Poetry of the 1930s* (Cork: Cork UP, 1995), p. 63. The static quality of the sequence may have some relation to it being inspired by Dürer's collection of woodcuts, the *Kleine Passion* (1511); see Mays's note in *CP* 355.
43 Radcliffe Squires, *Allen Tate: A Literary Biography* (New York: Pegasus, 1971), p. 151.
44 Allen Tate, *Collected Poems 1919–1976* (New York: Farrar, Straus & Giroux, 1977), p. 120.
45 W. B. Yeats, *The Variorum Edition of the Poems of W. B. Yeats*, eds Peter Allt and Russell K. Alspach, 3rd imp. (New York: Macmillan, 1966), p. 483.
46 Yeats, *Poems*, p. 479.
47 Smith, 'Precarious Guest', p. 237.
48 Tate, *Essays of Four Decades*, p. 67.
49 Smith, 'Precarious Guest', p. 237.
50 Tate, *Essays of Four Decades*, p. 215.
51 Tate, *Essays of Four Decades*, pp. 18, 19.
52 Seamus Deane, 'Irish Poetry and Irish Nationalism' in Douglas Dunn (ed.), *Two Decades of Irish Writing: A Critical Survey* (Cheadle Hume: Carcanet, 1975), p. 10.
53 Deane, 'Irish Poetry and Irish Nationalism', p. 11.
54 Deane, 'Irish Poetry and Irish Nationalism', p. 10. The most extensive commentary on Kavanagh's realism and his 'parish myth' is to be found in

Antoinette Quinn, *Patrick Kavanagh: Born-Again Romantic* (Dublin: Gill & Macmillan, 1991), esp. pp. 195–253. On Kavanagh's 'de-nationalisation' of Irish poetry, see Quinn's introduction to Patrick Kavanagh, *Selected Poems*, ed. Antoinette Quinn (Harmondsworth: Penguin, 1996).

55 Deane, 'Irish Poetry and Irish Nationalism', p. 11.
56 Austin Clarke, *Reviews and Essays of Austin Clarke*, ed. Gregory A. Schirmer (Gerrards Cross: Colin Smythe, 1995), p. 166.
57 P. S. O'Hegarty, 'Personal Recollections of Michael Collins', *Sunday Independent*, 26 August 1945, 14. I wish to thank Mary FitzGerald, formerly of the Fitzgerald Museum, Cork, for bringing this article to my attention.
58 Coffey, 'Denis Devlin: Poet of Distance', pp. 140–1. Coffey adds: 'Deane has got it wrong: people like me who were boys in 1920 and 1921 recall mainly a great heroic presence or remember to have heard someone say of Collins: "He is a statesman" – and that is a word we do not often use today' (Coffey, 'Denis Devlin: Poet of Distance', p. 140). Devlin's father, Liam, owned a public house in Parnell Square, which Collins used as lodging house and meeting place; for further details see Tim Pat Coogan, *Michael Collins: A Biography* (London: Hutchinson, 1990), p. 134.
59 Coffey, 'Denis Devlin: Poet of Distance', p. 141.
60 Jacques Maritain, *Art and Scholasticism and Other Essays*, trans. J. F. Scanlan (London: Sheed & Ward, 1930), pp. 93, 94.
61 Coffey, 'Denis Devlin: Poet of Distance', pp. 142, 149, 151.
62 Terence Brown, headnote to 'The Counter-revival 1930–65: Poetry' in Seamus Deane (ed.), *The Field Day Anthology of Irish Writing* (3 vols, Derry: Field Day, 1991), vol. 3, p. 132.
63 Mays is citing Coffey's 'Of Denis Devlin', p. 17.
64 T. S. Eliot, *Selected Essays*, 3rd ed. (London: Faber, 1951), pp. 17, 21.
65 Denis Devlin Papers, National Library of Ireland, Dublin. Another draft, titled 'Memorial to the Death of Michael Collins', describes Collins's assassin as 'some criminal, some fool, some clown', and, oddly, as 'a friend'; the published poem, in contrast, refers to 'the angel / Whose hurt and misty rifle shot him down'.
66 M. L. Rosenthal, *The New Poets: American and British Poetry Since World War II* (New York: Oxford UP, 1967), p. 273.
67 Vincent B. Leitch, *American Literary Criticism: From the Thirties to the Eighties* (New York: Columbia UP, 1988), p. 30.
68 Tate, *Essays of Four Decades*, p. 378; quoted in Leitch, *American Literary Criticism*, p. 34.
69 Tate, *Collected Poems*, p. 104.
70 Squires, *Allen Tate*, p. 158.
71 Tate, *Collected Poems*, p. 20.
72 Of further relevance in this context is Tate's 'To the Romantic Traditionists' (1935), the titular figures of which offer a double-edged understanding of history: an 'Immaculate race!', the 'final knowledge' they offer is of dubious use to humanity being 'set / In a cold frieze' (Tate, *Collected Poems*, p. 81). Robert S. Dupree provides the following commentary on Tate's poem: 'The worship of the past creates golden utopias that never existed; the worship of the future creates utopias that will never come into existence. Both attitudes are built upon a lie that emerges from a diseased imagination. When grasped analogically, these images of the past or future can contribute to an understanding

of human history and destiny. Viewed as true pictures of the human order, complete in every detail, they are worse than misleading; for their shadowy darkness, like the images of Plato's cave, is perversely taken to be light' (Robert S. Dupree, *Allen Tate and the Augustinian Imagination: A Study of the Poetry* [Baton Rouge: Louisiana State UP, 1983], p. 9). Devlin's elegy can be read as an interrogation of the 'romantic traditionism' that fails to realise that Collins, in death, can be read only as an 'analogue' of the literal man.

73 John Burt, *Robert Penn Warren and American Idealism* (New Haven: Yale UP, 1988), p. 84. The effect of Warren's poem cannot be reproduced in brief quotation. The full text can be found in Robert Penn Warren, *Selected Poems: New and Old 1923–1966* (New York: Random House, 1966), pp. 223–39.

74 See Richard Gray, *American Poetry of the Twentieth Century* (London: Longman, 1990), pp. 119–20. Warren's own ambiguous elegies, one might note, follow a similarly convoluted course to *The Ballad*.

75 Denis Devlin, letter to Thomas MacGreevy, 5 and 22 October 1935, Thomas MacGreevy Papers, Trinity College, Dublin, 8112/7.

76 Michael Kennedy, *Ireland and the League of Nations 1919–1946: International Relations, Diplomacy and Politics* (Dublin: Irish Academic P, 1996), p. 252. My account of Ireland's relationship with the League is indebted to Kennedy's book. I am very grateful to Dr Kennedy for further information regarding Devlin's diplomatic career.

77 Silone returned the tribute in a reminiscence of Devlin contributed to *Éire-Ireland: Weekly Bulletin of the Department of External Affairs,* 493 (1960), 4.

78 Mervyn Wall, 'Denis Devlin Remembered' in *Advent VI* (Southampton: Advent Books, 1976), p. 20.

79 Yeats, *Poems*, p. 640.

80 The translations from Du Bellay may date from Devlin's sojourn in Washington: the manuscript in which they are to be found bears a deleted dedication to Robert Penn Warren and his wife, Eleanor Clark. However, Rome seems a more likely context in which Devlin would have turned his attention to *Les Antiquitez de Rome*, as Roger Little observes (*TE* 316). It is worth noting the irony, whether conscious or not, that Mussolini's most infamous poet-apologist, Ezra Pound, also translated the present sonnet, many years before his notorious radio broadcasts from Mussolini's capital. See 'Rome' in Ezra Pound, *Personae: The Shorter Poems*, eds Lea Baechler and A. Walton Litz (New York: New Directions, 1990), p. 39. (Pound's translation was first published in his *Canzoni* [1911].)

81 Devlin's translations of Perse's 'Pluies', 'Neiges' and 'Poème à l'Étrangère' were first published, respectively, as 'Rains', *The Sewanee Review,* 52.4 (1944), 483–92; 'Snows', *The Sewanee Review,* 53.2 (1945), 186–97; and 'Poem to a Foreign Lady', *Briarcliff Quarterly,* 2.8 (1946), 217–21. The latter two translations were accompanied by Perse's originals. Devlin's rendering of Perse's entire tetralogy, with Devlin's version of 'Exil' added to the existing translations, was published as *Exile and Other Poems* (New York: Pantheon, 1946). Devlin's reflections on the enterprise can be found in his 'St John Perse in Washington', *Cahiers de la Pléiade,* 10 (1960), 86–9. For more details, see *TE* 322–4.

82 Roger Little, introduction to *Exil*, by Saint-John Perse, ed. Roger Little (London: Athlone, 1973), p. 7. My summary of Perse's life in the 1930s draws upon Little's account in his introduction.

83 'Broad similarities cover the same indissoluble blend of religious and nationalist feeling, the same consciousness of being at the edge of European culture, the same traumatic and shabby beginnings as a modern state. . . . The racial distinction between Turcoman and Turk which the title presumes, with all its cultural and social pretensions, is as closely approximate to the ever-subtle distinction between Gael and Irishman as one might ever get. Attempts at bourgeois-democratic reform in Ireland may not have been as dramatic as under Attaturk, but the drift of Irish society since independence has been consciously towards something similar, against similar obstacles. . . . These could indeed be the memoirs of a TD' (James Mays, 'A Poem by Denis Devlin, with some Questions and Conclusions' in *Advent VI* [Southampton: Advent Books, 1976], p.11).

84 Steven Winspur, countering the early critical reduction of *Exil* to its biographical context, argues that the 'exile that Leger lived out from 1940 onwards is merely a historical version of a deeper sense of absence' (Steven Winspur, *Saint-John Perse and the Imaginary Reader* [Genève: Librairie Droz S A, 1988], p. 76). Little comments: 'each poem in the tetralogy depends for the inspiration of its image-structure on the particular chance of immediate circumstances and yet far transcends them, expressing not only the pain of exile as a geographical removal from one's homeland but also the sense of exile as an integral part of man's spiritual nature' (Perse, *Exil*, p. 8). Commenting on Devlin's translations from Perse, Little argues that 'its central theme, 'l'éternité de l'exil dans la condition humaine', would have appealed to the translator's own deep sense of alienation' (Roger Little, 'Saint-John Perse and Denis Devlin: A *Compagnonnage*', *Irish University Review*, 8.2 [1978], 193).

85 Smith, 'Precarious Guest', pp. 240–1.

86 Winspur, *Saint-John Perse and the Imaginary Reader*, p. 67.

87 Winspur, *Saint-John Perse and the Imaginary Reader*, p. 76.

88 Eliot, *Complete Poems and Plays*, p. 68.

89 Mays, 'A Poem by Denis Devlin', pp. 12, 13.

5 DEVLIN, 'THE THIRTIES GENERATION' AND NEW WRITERS

1 Further information regarding New Writers' Press can be found in Trevor Joyce, 'New Writers' Press: The History of a Project' in Patricia Coughlan and Alex Davis (eds), *Modernism and Ireland: The Poetry of the 1930s* (Cork: Cork UP, 1995), pp. 276–306. Joyce's essay includes a useful bibliography of NWP's publications up to 1995.

2 Michael Smith and Trevor Joyce, editorial, *The Lace Curtain*, 1 (1969), n. pag. *The Lace Curtain* ran to six issues, from Autumn 1969 to Autumn 1978.

3 Michael Smith and Trevor Joyce, editorial, *The Lace Curtain*, 2 (1970), 2.

4 Michael Smith, 'Irish Poetry and Penguin Verse', editorial, *The Lace Curtain*, 3 (1970), 5, 7, 9.

5 Smith, 'Irish Poetry and Penguin Verse', p. 5.

6 Michael Smith, editorial, *The Lace Curtain*, 4 (1971), 3.

7 Michael Smith, 'Irish Poetry Since Yeats: Notes Towards a Corrected History', *Denver Quarterly*, 5 (1971), 8, 10.

8 Brian Coffey, 'Joyce! "What Now?"', *Irish University Review*, 12.1 (1982), 30.

9 'Brian Coffey, An Interview by Parkman Howe', *Éire-Ireland*, 13.1 (1978), 122.

10 My summary of Ireland in the 1960s in this paragraph draws upon Dermot Keogh, *Twentieth-Century Ireland: Nation and State* (Dublin: Gill & Macmillan, 1994), pp. 243–94.

11 Steven Matthews, *Irish Poetry: Politics, History, Negotiation; The Evolving Debate, 1969 to the Present* (London: Macmillan, 1997), p. 96. Matthews's detailed reading of Kinsella in the light of Adorno's *Aesthetic Theory* accords with my sketchier remarks.

12 Thomas Kinsella, *Nightwalker and Other Poems* (Dublin: Dolmen, 1968), p. 59.

13 Kinsella, *Nightwalker*, p. 64.

14 Thomas Kinsella, *The Dual Tradition: An Essay on Poetry and Politics in Ireland* (Manchester: Carcanet, 1995), p. 103.

15 Kinsella, *The Dual Tradition*, pp. 102–3.

16 Kinsella, *The Dual Tradition*, pp. 104, 105.

17 Michael Smith, 'The Contemporary Situation in Irish Poetry' in Douglas Dunn (ed.), *Two Decades of Irish Writing: A Critical Survey* (Cheadle Hume: Carcanet, 1975), p. 155.

18 Michael Smith, *With the Woodnymphs* (Dublin: New Writers' Press, 1968), p. 5.

19 Smith, 'The Contemporary Situation in Irish Poetry', p. 156.

20 Smith, *With the Woodnymphs*, p. 14.

21 Smith, 'Irish Poetry Since Yeats', pp. 18, 19.

22 Michael Smith, *Stopping To Take Notes* (Dublin: New Writers' Press, 1979), p. 28.

23 Patrick Kavanagh, *The Complete Poems*, ed. Peter Kavanagh (Newbridge: Goldsmith, 1984), p. 100.

24 See Antoinette Quinn, *Patrick Kavanagh: Born-Again Romantic* (Dublin: Gill & Macmillan, 1991), p. 157.

25 Smith, *Stopping To Take Notes*, p. 29.

26 Smith, *With the Woodnymphs*, p. 25.

27 W. B. Yeats, *Uncollected Prose by W. B. Yeats: First Reviews and Articles 1886–1896*, ed. John P. Frayne (London: Macmillan, 1970), p. 153.

28 Michael Smith, letter to the author, 1 July 1997.

29 Smith, *Stopping To Take Notes*, p. 27.

30 Michael Smith, *Lost Genealogies & Other Poems* (Dublin: New Writers' Press, 1993), p. 45.

31 Samuel Beckett, 'Recent Irish Poetry', *The Lace Curtain*, 4 (1971), 58.

32 Smith, *Lost Genealogies*, p. 20.

33 See *Dublin: The People's City: The Photographs of Nevill Johnson 1952–53* (Dublin: Academy P, 1981).

34 See Smith, 'The Contemporary Situation in Irish Poetry', p. 161.

35 Paul Klee, *On Modern Art*, trans. Paul Findlay (London: Faber, 1948), p. 13. The blurb to *Sole Glum Trek* (Dublin: New Writers' Press, 1967) states that Joyce 'agrees with Klee that the artist does not reflect beauty but creates it. Poetry creative in that sense is not symbolist but realistic. Its reality is the same reality as that of the scientist, even if it is not yet accessible to scientific methods. For those who find such inaccessibility intolerable many of the poems in this book will mean nothing.'

36 Michael Smith [and Trevor Joyce], 'Considering a Poetic', *The Lace Curtain*, 3 (1970), 48.

37 Smith [and Joyce], 'Considering a Poetic', p. 49.

38 Smith [and Joyce], 'Considering a Poetic', p. 50.

39 Klee, *On Modern Art*, p. 15.

40 Trevor Joyce, *Pentahedron* (Dublin: New Writers' Press, 1972), p. 12.

41 Joyce, *Pentahedron*, p. 25.

42 See Joseph Frank, *The Widening Gyre: Crisis and Mastery in Modern Literature* (Urbana: Indiana UP, 1963).

43 Joyce, *Pentahedron*, p. 51.

44 Joyce, *Pentahedron*, p. 52.

45 Poem XXI and the first four stanzas of poem XXII in Trevor Joyce, *The Poems of Sweeny Peregrine: A Working of the Corrupt Irish Text*, ed. Michael Smith (Dublin: New Writers' Press, 1976), n. pag., appear, in earlier versions, in Joyce, *Sole Glum Trek*, pp. 25, 13, as 'Farannan' and 'Sweeny's Dilemma', respectively.

46 Seamus Heaney, introduction, *Sweeney Astray* (London: Faber, 1984), n. pag. Sweeny has appealed to many modern Irish writers as a figure somehow emblematic of the artistic condition. For a discussion of his presence in the work of writers as diverse as Austin Clarke and Brian Keenan, see Neil Corcoran, *After Yeats and Joyce: Reading Modern Irish Literature* (Oxford: Oxford UP, 1997), pp. 19–25. Corcoran, incidentally, does not mention *Sweeny Peregrine* in this context.

47 Phillip L. Marcus, *Yeats and the Beginning of the Irish Renaissance*, 2nd ed. (Syracuse: Syracuse UP, 1987), p. 240.

48 Seamus Heaney, *Station Island* (London: Faber, 1984), p. 114.

49 Seamus Heaney, *The Government of the Tongue: The 1986 T. S. Eliot Memorial Lectures and Other Critical Writings* (London: Faber, 1988), p. xviii.

50 Heaney, *The Government of the Tongue*, p. 93.

51 See David Lloyd, *Nationalism and Minor Literature: James Clarence Mangan and the Emergence of Irish Cultural Nationalism* (Berkeley: U of California P, 1987). Lloyd produces a very different Mangan from Yeats's: a 1980s post-colonial Mangan, rather than, as in Yeats, a *fin de siècle* Decadent. J. C. C. Mays says of the Poundian aspects of *Sweeny Peregrine*: '[Joyce's] version of Sweeney was something new in Irish letters; the version was his in the sense that Pound appropriated Confucius' (J. C. C. Mays, 'Flourishing and Foul: Ideology, Six Poets and the Irish Building Industry', *Irish Review*, 8 [1990], 10). The blurb to *Sweeny Peregrine* claims that 'The model for this exciting and pioneering version is not Synge or Hyde, but the Pound of *Cathay* and the *Seafarer*.'

52 Stan Smith, *The Origins of Modernism: Eliot, Pound, Yeats and the Rhetorics of Renewal* (Hemel Hempstead: Harvester, 1994), p. 7.

53 The impossible chronology (impossible, that is, to a realist narrative) is clearer in Heaney's version of this incident: 'And now, Sweeney, said Alan [the Man of the Wood], tell me what your own fate will be. Sweeney told him what this story goes on to tell and they parted. The Briton set out for the waterfall and when he reached it he was drowned in it' (Heaney, *Sweeney Astray*, p. 58).

54 Frank Lentricchia, *After the New Criticism* (London: Athlone, 1980), p. 56.

55 Trevor Joyce, 'Mirror: Of Galzier Velasquez', *The Lace Curtain*, 6 (Autumn, 1978), 9.

56 Trevor Joyce, personal interview, 22 July 1997.

57 Samuel Beckett, *Collected Poems 1930–1978* (London: John Calder, 1984), p. 59; see Lawrence Harvey, *Samuel Beckett: Poet and Critic* (Princeton: Princeton UP, 1970), pp. 227–8.

58 Trevor Joyce, *stone floods* (Dublin: New Writers' Press, 1995), p. 7.
59 Joyce, *stone floods*, p. 11.
60 Joyce, *stone floods*, p. 51.
61 William Empson, *Seven Types of Ambiguity*, 3rd. ed. (London: Chatto & Windus, 1953), p. 50.
62 Joyce, *stone floods*, p. 26.
63 Under the title 'Landscapes'; see *Irish University Review*, 13.1 (1983), 38–42.
64 Geoffrey Squires, *Drowned Stones* (Dublin: New Writers' Press, 1975), p. 14.
65 Squires, *Drowned Stones*, p. 12.
66 William Carlos Williams, *Paterson*, ed. Christopher MacGowan (New York: New Directions, 1992), p. 3. Squires may be also alluding to Williams's poem in dividing *Drowned Stones* into six sections; Williams left his epic unfinished, but a projected *Paterson VI* exists in rudimentary form.
67 Squires, *Drowned Stones*, p. 36.
68 Squires, *Drowned Stones*, p. 48.
69 Squires, *Drowned Stones*, p. 23.
70 Geoffrey Squires, personal interview, 26 March 1997.
71 Charles Olson, *Collected Prose*, eds Donald Allen and Benjamin Friedlander (Berkeley: U of California P, 1997), pp. 240, 243.
72 Olson, *Collected Prose*, pp. 244, 247.
73 Squires, *Drowned Stones*, p. 9.
74 Squires, *Drowned Stones*, p. 64.
75 Squires, *Drowned Stones*, p. 65.
76 Geoffrey Squires, *Figures* (Belfast: Ulsterman Publications, 1978), p. 8.
77 Squires, *Figures*, p. 18.
78 Olson, *Collected Prose*, p. 239.
79 Charles Olson, *The Collected Poems of Charles Olson, Excluding 'The Maximus Poems'*, ed. George F. Butterick (Berkeley: U of California P, 1987), p. 93.
80 Squires, *Figures*, p. 22.
81 John Montague, *Collected Poems* (Oldcastle: Gallery, 1995), p. 5.
82 Robert F. Garratt, *Modern Irish Poetry: Tradition and Continuity from Yeats to Heaney* (Berkeley: U of California P, 1986), p. 223.
83 Montague, *Collected Poems*, p. 32.
84 Montague, *Collected Poems*, p. 33.
85 This was the subtitle to this section of *The Rough Field* prior to *Collected Poems*. Among other minor revisions, the latter volume also, lamentably, omits the woodcuts that punctuate the poem in earlier editions.
86 Marjorie Perloff, *The Futurist Moment: Avant-Garde, Avant Guerre, and the Language of Rupture* (Chicago: U of Chicago P, 1986), p. 76.
87 Dillon Johnston, *Irish Poetry after Joyce*, 2nd. ed. (Syracuse: Syracuse UP, 1997), p. 193.
88 John Montague, personal interview, 27 Oct. 1996.
89 Montague, *Collected Poems*, p. 37.
90 John Montague, *The Figure in the Cave and Other Essays*, ed. Antoinette Quinn (Dublin: Lilliput, 1989), pp. 212, 213.
91 Montague, *The Figure in the Cave*, p. 214.
92 Montague, *The Figure in the Cave*, pp. 218, 219.
93 Geoffrey Squires, *Landscapes & Silences: A Sequence* (Dublin: New Writers' Press, 1996), p. 15.

94 Geoffrey Squires, letter to Trevor Joyce, 30 April 1997. In this letter Squires makes the distinction between centripetal and centrifugal poetry referred to above.

95 Geoffrey Squires, *XXI Poems* (London: Menard, 1980), p. 9.

96 Geoffrey Squires, *A Long Poem in Three Sections* (London: Levraut de Poche, 1997), n. pag.

97 Maurice Merleau-Ponty, *The Primacy of Perception and Other Essays on Phenomenological Psychology, the Philosophy of Art, History and Politics*, ed. James M. Edie (Evanston: Northwestern UP, 1964), p. 163.

98 Olson, *Collected Prose*, p. 161.

99 Squires, *Landscapes & Silences*, p. 33.

100 Squires, *Landscapes & Silences*, p. 20.

101 Geoffrey Squires, *Poem for Two Voices, hardPressed Poetry: the Journal*, 1 (1998), 29.

102 Squires, *Poem for Two Voices*, p. 34.

103 Squires, *Landscapes & Silences*, p. 36.

104 Squires, *Poem for Two Voices*, pp. 29, 30.

105 Gary Snyder, *The Real Work: Interviews and Talks 1964–1979*, ed. Wm. Scott McLean (New York: New Directions, 1980), p. 5.

Coda 'NO NARRATIVE EASY IN THE MIND': THE IRISH NEO-AVANT-GARDE

1 On this aspect of Clarke, see Patrick Crotty (ed.), *Modern Irish Poetry: An Anthology* (Belfast: Blackstaff, 1995), p. 13.

2 Charles Olson, *Collected Prose*, eds Donald Allen and Benjamin Friedlander (Berkeley: U of California P, 1997), p. 239.

3 Marjorie Perloff, *Radical Artifice: Writing Poetry in the Age of Media* (Chicago: U of Chicago P, 1991), p. 205.

4 Trevor Joyce, 'The Point of Innovation in Poetry' in Harry Gilonis (ed.), *For the Birds: Proceedings of the First Cork Conference on New and Experimental Irish Poetry* (Sutton: Mainstream Poetry/Dublin: hardPressed Poetry, 1998), pp. 19, 25, 26.

5 Trevor Joyce, *Syzygy* (Bray: Wild Honey, 1998), p. 14.

6 See Randolph Healy, *Flame* (Bray: Wild Honey, 1997).

7 Joyce, *Syzygy*, p. 7.

8 Joyce, *Syzygy*, p. 5.

9 Joyce, *Syzygy*, p. 6.

10 Randolph Healy, 'Logic as a Starting Point for Poetry', *The Beau*, 3 (1983/84), 11.

11 Randolph Healy, introduction, *25 Poems* (Dublin: Beau, 1983), p. 3.

12 Healy, *25 Poems*, p. 16. Dithering is a technique in computer graphics for increasing the perceived range of colours in an image at the cost of spatial resolution. Adjacent pixels are assigned differing colour values. When viewed from a distance, these colours seem to blend into a single intermediate colour. Metaphorically understood, dithering is to the poetry of Healy (and Joyce) what collage was to many high modernists.

13 Randolph Healy, *Arbor Vitae* (Bray: Wild Honey, 1997), pp. 4, 15.

14 See Nelson Goodman, *Ways of Worldmaking* (Indianapolis: Hackett, 1978).

15 Healy, *Arbor Vitae*, p. 14.

16 Healy, *Arbor Vitae*, p. 14 (Healy's ellipsis).

17 Randolph Healy, *Rana Rana!* (Bray: Wild Honey, 1997), p. 28.

18 Robert Archambeau, *Another Ireland: An Essay* (Bray: Wild Honey, 1997), p. 10. Archambeau is quoting Healy's 'Envelopes' in *Rana Rana!*, p. 21.

19 Billy Mills, 'A Brief Note on Three Gripes', *The Beau*, 3 (1983/84), 12.

20 Billy Mills, *Tiny Pieces* (Bray: Wild Honey, 1998), p. 7.

21 Billy Mills, *The Properties of Stone* (London: Writers Forum, 1996), p. 4.

22 Billy Mills, *Five Easy Pieces* (Plymouth: Shearsman, 1997), n. pag.

23 Billy Mills, 'Other Places: 4 Irish Poets' in Harry Gilonis (ed.), *For the Birds: Proceedings of the First Cork Conference on New and Experimental Irish Poetry* (Sutton: Mainstream Poetry/Dublin: hardPressed Poetry, 1998), p. 27.

24 The parts of this poem currently available are: *The Basic Colours: A Watchman's Log* (Durham: Pig Press, 1994); *Priority* (London: Writers Forum, 1994); *Prelude* (Bray: Wild Honey, 1997); *Interlude* (Bray: Wild Honey, 1997); *Postlude* (Bray: Wild Honey, 1997); and *Steps* (London: Reality Street, 1998).

25 Maurice Scully, 'As I like It', *The Beau*, 3 (1983/84), 10.

26 Scully, *Postlude*, p. 6; the earlier version can be found in *The Basic Colours*.

27 Scully, *Postlude*, pp. 7–8.

28 Lyn Hejinian, *Writing Is an Aid to Memory*, 2nd ed. (Los Angeles: Sun & Moon, 1996) n. pag., preface and section 2.

29 Catherine Walsh, *Idir Eatortha and Making Tents* (London: Invisible Books, 1996), p. 76. *Making Tents* was first published in 1987. On the biographical background to the poem, see Mills, 'Other Places', p. 34.

30 Seamus Heaney, *Wintering Out* (London: Faber, 1972), p. 16.

31 See Seamus Heaney, *Preoccupations: Selected Prose 1968–1978* (London: Faber, 1980), pp. 131–49.

32 Walsh, *Idir Eatortha*, p. 47.

33 Catherine Walsh, interview in Peterjon Skelt (ed.), *Prospect into Breath: Interviews with North and South Writers* (Twickenham and Wakefield: North & South, 1991), p. 184.

34 Catherine Walsh, *Pitch* (Durham: Pig Press, 1994), p. 36.

35 Perloff, *Radical Aritifice*, pp. 11, 49, 187. For detailed discussions of Language poetry, see George Hartley, *Textual Politics and the Language Poets* (Bloomington: Indiana UP, 1989); and Linda Reinfeld, *Language Poetry: Writing as Rescue* (Baton Rouge: Lousiana UP, 1992) .

36 Ron Silliman, 'Disappearance of the Word, Appearance of the World' in Bruce Andrews and Charles Bernstein (eds), *The L=A=N=G=U=A=G=E Book* (Carbondale and Edwardsville: Southern Illinois UP, 1984), p. 126.

37 Bruce Andrews, *Paradise and Method: Poetics and Praxis* (Evanston: Northwestern UP, 1996), pp. 25, 26.

38 Andrews, *Paradise and Method*, p. 31.

39 Charles Bernstein, *A Poetics* (Cambridge, Mass.: Harvard UP, 1992), pp. 53–4.

40 Peter Bürger, *Theory of the Avant-Garde*, trans. Michael Shaw (Minneapolis: U of Minnesota P, 1984), p. 58.

41 Hal Foster, *The Return of the Real: The Avant-Garde at the End of the Century* (Cambridge, Mass.: MIT, 1996), p. 29.

42 Foster, *The Return of the Real*, p. 29.

43 Billy Mills, letter to the author, 3 June 1997.

44 Luke Gibbons, *Transformations in Irish Culture* (Cork: Cork UP, 1996), pp. 91, 93.

INDEX